AMERICAN EDUCATION

Its Men

Ideas

and

Institutions

Advisory Editor

Lawrence A. Cremin
Frederick A. P. Barnard Professor of Education
Teachers College, Columbia University

Eleazar Wheelock

James Dow McCallum

ARNO PRESS & THE NEW YORK TIMES
New York * *1969*

Reprint edition 1969 by Arno Press, Inc.

*

Library of Congress Catalog Card No. 78-89200

*

Reprinted from a copy in the
Office of Education Library

*

Manufactured in the United States of America

Editorial Note

AMERICAN EDUCATION: *Its Men, Institutions and Ideas* presents selected works of thought and scholarship that have long been out of print or otherwise unavailable. Inevitably, such works will include particular ideas and doctrines that have been outmoded or superseded by more recent research. Nevertheless, all retain their place in the literature, having influenced educational thought and practice in their own time and having provided the basis for subsequent scholarship.

Lawrence A. Cremin
Teachers College

Eleazar Wheelock

ELEAZAR WHEELOCK

Founder of Dartmouth College

BY

JAMES DOW McCALLUM

Manuscript Series, Nº 4

DARTMOUTH COLLEGE PUBLICATIONS

HANOVER · NEW HAMPSHIRE · 1939

PRINTED IN THE UNITED STATES OF AMERICA
BY E. L. HILDRETH & COMPANY, INC., BRATTLEBORO, VERMONT

TABLE OF CONTENTS

PREFACE

ELEAZAR WHEELOCK was a very pious man. That is granted tacitly by all Dartmouth men, and on the many occasions when they sing Richard Hovey's words, vociferously. And his interest in education, in the Bible, and in good cheer is brought to mind by the poet's reference to the paraphernalia which Wheelock allegedly carried from Connecticut to New Hampshire:

> Oh, Eleazar Wheelock was a very pious man:
> He went into the wilderness to teach the Indian,
> With a *gradus ad Parnassum*, a Bible, and a drum,
> And five hundred gallons of New England rum.

It has seemed to me that the time has come, however, for a more exact characterization than the poet permitted himself, rhythmical and humorous as his is. Just how did Wheelock express his piety? What were his aims in education? How did he carry on his duties as pastor, farmer, father, teacher, administrator?

This biography is not the first revelation of Wheelock's career. In 1811 David M'Clure and Elijah Parish published the first biography of him—a work of love, obviously, but unsatisfactory because the reader does not get an all-round view of the subject. It is probably true that today, one hundred and sixty years after Wheelock's death, more details about him are available than these early biographers, one of whom was his favorite student, knew of. In 1891 Frederick Chase's *History of Dartmouth College* gave the first detailed account of Wheelock's development of Moor's Charity School and his founding of Dartmouth; and in 1932 Professor L. B. Richardson wrote a lucid and excellently balanced story of Wheelock as educator. Thanks to Professor Richardson, that work will never need to be done again.

It has been necessary for me to tell once more, but with less detail, the story of the founding of Dartmouth, but my main emphasis has been on the personality, the "mental configuration," of Wheelock, to the end that the questions stated above, and other related ones, may have an answer.

For this purpose the Archives Room of the Baker Library at Dartmouth contains copious material. The number of eighteenth century documents housed there has never been counted; let it suffice to estimate that there are several thousand items in Wheelock's correspondence alone, some items merely brief notes or receipts, others lengthy personal letters, and expositions of his attitude on topics of religion and church government and the management of the charity school and of the college. These I have read carefully, and have quoted some of them in this biography. In addition it has been necessary to read a wealth of books and articles on the history of colonial churches, religious problems, the Six Nations, eighteenth century currency, early education in New England, town histories ———. In the bibliography are listed only those works referred to in the text.

I have made certain changes in transcribing these early letters, namely, in writing out in full the many common abbreviations such as s^d, y^e, y^t, X^{tian}, the ampersands, and in reducing the capitals of substantives to lower case. The letters may now be read easily and as they were intended to be read, without that spurious quaintness which such abbreviations give to old documents, abbreviations which were no more quaint to Wheelock and his contemporaries than A.M. and P.M. are to us. Those who wish to read a letter replete with these time-saving abridgments will perhaps be satisfied with the one given on pages 108–109. On the other hand, I have not tampered with the diction and spelling.

The frontispiece to this biography is a collotype print of the portrait of Eleazar Wheelock painted, at the direction of the trustees of Dartmouth College, by Joseph Steward (Dartmouth, 1780), between 1793 and 1796. The face was painted from memory; for the body the painter used a Connecticut divine ("Parson Weld of Hampton") as the model; and since the whole was executed in his early days, Steward referred to it as one of his "evil deeds." The original hangs in the Faculty Room of Dartmouth College.

It is a pleasure to thank Professor L. B. Richardson for his criticism of the manuscript; his sound judgment and excellent memory have been invaluable. To Miss Mildred Saunders, archivist of the Baker Library, I am grateful for her patience in finding numerous documents and her helpfulness whenever called on.

J. D. McC.

Hanover, New Hampshire, 1939.

ELEAZAR WHEELOCK

CHAPTER I

ANCESTRY

THE history of the Wheelocks in America begins with the arrival in Watertown, Massachusetts, of Ralph Wheelock. According to an old rime[1]

> In sixteen hundred thirty-seven
> It was he hither came,
> When spread there was the leaven
> Of heresy by name.

Ralph Wheelock's ancestors had been persons of some importance in Shropshire and Cheshire counties, England, and particularly in the village of Whelok, Cheshire. During the reign of Henry the Second, for instance, Roger Mainwaring "released to Hugh de Whelok[2] all his claim to the village of Whelok, which he (the said Hugh) held of Richard de Moston his knight, and (also released him) from suit of mill and court of Warmincham." In 1285 Thomas de Whelok bought lands in Blackwood which his father had given to Nicolas de Blackwood. The son of this Thomas (also named Thomas) was one of the lessees of the town of Middlewich, and as purveyor in the hundred of Northwich to Edward the Second was required to bring "to Chester within a certain day, all the corn and bacon charged upon the said hundred, or 4 s. for every bacon." In the fifteenth year of Edward the Second, Thomas de Whelok and Julian his wife obtained by fine from Ralph de Hassale, chaplain, the manor of Whelok for life, the remainder to pass to Thomas, his son, and wife Alice, and their heirs forever. During the eleventh year of Richard the Second, a Thomas de

---

1 Stiles, *Diary*, II, 535.
2 Ormerod, the historian of Cheshire, from whose account (III, 119–120) I take the information on the ancestry of Ralph Wheelock, spells the family name variously: Whelok, Qwelok, Quelok, Whelock; the last he uses most frequently. Ralph Wheelock's surname is spelled in half a dozen ways in *Dedham Records*.

Whelok had letters of exemption from serving on juries. From the beginning of the fifteenth century, as the result of a successful lawsuit, the Wheloks were underlords of Whelok; in 1439 Richard de Whelok having died without issue, Agnes Leversage was declared his cousin and next heir. According to Ormerod, "it may be added that the Wheloks who became thus early extinct in this township, were probably survived by lines of yeomanry of the name, settled in Bechton and Hassall, where the parent-house, or it is certain, its heirs, the Leversages, formerly held lands."

Ralph Wheelock (the great-grandfather of the founder of Dartmouth College) was born in Shropshire in 1600. Twenty-six years later he received his bachelor's degree from Cambridge (Clare Hall), and in 1631, his Master's degree. Contemporary with him at Clare Hall was Abraham Wheelock, probably a relative, who was the first professor of Arabic and Anglo-Saxon at Cambridge, the editor of Bede's *Ecclesiastical History,* and librarian of the university. He died in 1653 while engaged in publishing the Gospels in Persian.[1]

In Dedham, Massachusetts, whither Ralph Wheelock removed shortly after his coming to Watertown in 1637, he was soon regarded as a leading citizen, being chosen as one of eight persons "whom we had best hopes for soundness of grace and meete guiftes" to assist in organizing the first church.[2] Later (in 1639) he aided in surveying the town, in auditing the books of the tax-collector, and in determining the highway. According to the valuation placed on his holding in 1648 his property was ranked as thirty-second out of a total of seventy-three parcels. Three years later he was cited as delinquent in furnishing labor for the highway, in company with about half the town. At another time, having failed to be appointed to a church posi-

[1] *Dictionary of National Biography:* article *Wheelocke, Abraham*; Sclater, 30.
[2] *Dedham Records, Church and Cemetery,* 5–6.

tion for which he was one of three candidates, he delivered a speech praising his rival and declaring himself unfit, so that all "were intirely knitt unto him in respect thereof."[1] We find him also as deputy from Dedham to the General Court, as clerk of the writs, as commissioned to "marry people there that are dewly published," and as the first schoolmaster of Dedham.

With the restlessness which characterized many of the early settlers, Ralph Wheelock decided to remove from Dedham to a town as yet not incorporated but which became known as Medfield. Once more he played a leading part in managing town affairs. Perhaps to him should go the credit of drawing up the original articles of agreement, which he signed. He was a member, in 1649, of the first board of selectmen—subsequently he served for four years more as selectman—was five times appointed representative to the General Court, became the first schoolmaster of Medfield in 1655, and five years later, but probably not because of the income from that position, was rated as the ninth wealthiest person in the town: one hundred and ninety pounds is the valuation placed on his property. In the year 1683 he died at Medfield; his wife Rebecca had died three years before. Ralph Wheelock was a man of integrity, well-educated, a mainstay of the towns in which he lived, and because of his early activities in Medfield is referred to as the founder of that town. He was the father of nine children, of whom the last born, Eleazar, carries on the line toward the founder of Dartmouth.

The references to this son, Eleazar, are scant. He was born in Medfield in 1654. Twenty-two years later he is credited in the town records with having killed four wolves. In 1678 he married Elizabeth Fuller, and shortly after his marriage removed to Mendon, Massachusetts. Here he was appointed land surveyor in 1681, is said to have been a captain of cavalry, and was

[1] *Idem*, 16–17.

known as a mighty hunter of wild beasts and of Indians. His name appears on two petitions. In the first (dated 1681) he and other inhabitants of Mendon set forth to the General Court that the ravages of the Indians during King Philip's uprising of 1675–76 had caused heavy losses to the residents of the town which they felt unable to bear unless the absentee proprietors also were required to pay the tax rate. "Wee desire earnestly not to be (and hope we are not) of the number of those who dwell in their ceiled houses and yet say the time is not come that the Lord's house should be built."[1] The request was granted. In the second petition (of 1685) Eleazar is bothered with the same problem which vexed his grandson, eighty-five years later: the sale of intoxicants to Indians. The petitioners beg that the General Court will set restrictions on the sale of liquor to savages and will also prohibit the Indians from entering Mendon. In answer the General Court referred the petitioners to a law already in effect which was intended to solve the problem.[2]

Not much remains to be recorded of him. In the last decade of the century he is listed as a constable, and credited with having slain two wolves.[3] About 1701 he returned to Medfield, served as selectman in 1705 and 1720, and died there in 1731. His second wife, Mary Chenery, survived him a year; at her death her grandson, Eleazar Wheelock, was a senior at Yale.

The scene now shifts to Windham, Connecticut. There we find Deacon Ralph Wheelock, a wealthy farmer (the grandson of the original Ralph), and his wife, formerly Ruth Huntington of Norwich, Connecticut. To them was born on April 22,

---

[1] *Annals of Mendon*, 85.   [2] *Idem*, 101–102.

[3] Those who favor the gentler fauna will be pleased that the hunting prowess of these colonials so reduced the wolves that in Woodstock (Conn.) the last was killed in 1732; in Ashford, 1735; and in Pomfret in 1742, when the redoubtable Israel Putnam, irked because a she-wolf had killed seventy sheep and goats, crawled into her den and shot her. (Larned, *History of Windham County*, I, 360.)

1711 (Old Style), Eleazar, their only male child. Ezra Stiles, president of Yale, remarks caustically that the future president of Dartmouth received from his mother "his ambitious and enterprizing spirit, from his father his piety or rather pious complexion."[1] The evidence on which he founded his conclusion is missing, for the most part. We know that Ralph Wheelock was a deacon of the First Church in Windham, that he served as a representative to the Windham County Consociation, and that he was regarded as a very religious man.

Not a single detail is known of Wheelock's early youth, and any conclusions regarding it can be nothing but speculation, the extent of which will depend on the imagination of the speculator. Our first fact is that Eleazar Wheelock entered Yale in 1729. As an undergraduate he distinguished himself by winning a share in the award of the Dean Berkeley Donation.[2] Additional evidence that he was studious may perhaps be found in the heavy-paced jocularity of a friend who writes urging Wheelock to leave his abstruse studies in mathematics and deign to descend from the Via Lactea to the planet called Terra. From Wheelock, himself, there is a letter written in 1733, his senior year, on the subject of happiness.

Most Dear and Honour'd Parents.
    Tho the great and principal things that we seam to have respect

---

1 Stiles, *Diary*, II, 535.

2 Wheelock shared the award with his future brother-in-law, Benjamin Pomeroy. They were the first recipients. In 1733 Dean Berkeley had deeded a farm of some ninety-six acres, situated in Rhode Island, to Yale College, for five shillings. The income (supposed to be one hundred pounds sterling a year) was to be given to the three students who passed the best examinations in Greek and Latin. The President of Yale and the senior Episcopal minister in Connecticut were to examine candidates for two hours in Greek and for the same length of time in Latin. (*Conn. Hist. Soc. Papers*, I, 147 ff.) Ezra Stiles (*Diary*, II, 534–535) records that Pomeroy told him that he and Wheelock had received only sixteen pounds each. The rent of the farm, Stiles adds, was seventy pounds, but the expenses of assemblying the trustees and transacting the remaining business of the award reduced the available amount to thirty-two pounds.

to in all our actions is hapiness a desire of which is implanted in our natures by their author and which seams to be absolutely necessary for us in order to self preservation yet the life of man, more eminently of some than of others, seams to be little else but a ceres of crosses, perplexities and disapointments, we are almost always flattering ourselves with the prospect of something that we hope to take satisfaction in, which if we han't wholly disapointed of yet we sildom find that satisfaction in fruition which we promised ourselves. Either there are some unhappy attendants of it or we fear some evil will ensue that altho we enjoy some things which are very agreable to us, yet on the other hand the fear of their removal from us or of evils that may interrupt our pleasure in the enjoyment of them seams almost to create an uneasieness equal to the pleasure, that a man can't say of himself for one hour I am happy in the possession of these things. Very good reason I think had the wise man to pronounce vanity of them all for verily all is vanity. And they are mean and inferior pleasures at the best which result from the enjoyment of them, but such is our unhapy state of nature that we do naturally pursue our hapieness in the enjoyment of them, being blind and darkned in our understanding, and ignorant that our true hapieness lies in unseen things, 'till by the mighty power of God we are born after the Spirit. And then we see things in another light, other and more noble objects of our hapieness, and can with our whole souls pronounce a vanity on all things else; now says the soul thus enlightned "I see the vanity of my former imaginations of hapieness here, these were not designd for the peace of my hapieness, no: my hopes of hapieness are placed in things above that are unseen and all the providences of God are to fit and ripen me for that state but I han't time to add on this subject but shall inform you that I am well in health but my sister is not so well as she was when she came from home but I think I have reason to hope that in the room of health God is about to give that which is infinitely better even the discoveries of himself. My father gave some hints from which I thought that he design'd to come up here this winter if providence favours I should be very glad if he would and yet there is no special reason to urge the matter. It is a time of health here. I am

Your Dutifull Son

Eleazar Wheelock

ANCESTRY

P.S. Please to give my service and proper regards to all friends not forgetting neighbour Hiberd and his family, Joseph and Robard and his wife and Joshua Hendee and his &c.

The twenty-two-year-old student was obviously pious, ponderous, and studious. Pious he remained throughout his life. Experience humanized him; he never seems to have been light-hearted, and throughout his many letters has not introduced the slightest evidence of jocularity. The scholarly promise shown in winning the Berkeley award was not fulfilled: the year following his graduation he spent as a student of theology at Yale; thereafter parish work, labors as an evangelist and, later, extensive administrative duties were to keep him from his studies.

CHAPTER II

WHEELOCK'S pastoral career began in Lebanon, Connecticut, and in that part of the town which was then known variously as the Second or North Society, and Lebanon Crank, and which now forms part of the town of Columbia. On February 24, 1735, the inhabitants of the parish, at a meeting lawfully convened, voted to call him as pastor. Two months later (April 29) Wheelock married Mrs. Sarah Maltby, widow of Captain William Maltby of New Haven, and daughter of the Reverend John Davenport of Stamford.[1] Still a month later—Wheelock having accepted the call—the inhabitants met again to arrange terms of settlement and salary; and in June, 1735, the new pastor was installed in the parish of which he was to be the leader for the next thirty-four years.

According to the criticisms of certain historians contemporary with Wheelock, the colony of Connecticut was spiritually dead throughout the first three decades and a half of the eighteenth century, up to approximately the year in which Wheelock took over the pastorate in Lebanon. A listlessness toward religion, it was said, had settled over the inhabitants. The religion of the founders, with its emphasis on conversion profoundly felt and publicly attested, had been replaced by formalism and traditionalism. Worldliness and profane speaking were common. These are some of the criticisms.

How are we to estimate these condemnations? How translate them into the vocabulary of the present day? From our point of view the phraseology of these early historians (and more inti-

---

1 Ormerod mentions (III, 120) that the Davenports were landowners in the town of Whelok, England, during the fifteenth and sixteenth centuries. It is interesting to note that the two families were brought together again by this marriage.

mately, the phraseology of individuals corresponding with their friends) is earmarked as overstatement. The terms of endearment, the pessimistic comments by a writer on his sinful state, the rhapsodies of the saved—just what do they mean today? A "sin" for the eighteenth century may be to us a merely verbal or social flippancy, or a pleasant and quite legal pastime. Thus, shortly after the middle of the century a man was fined, including costs of prosecution, twelve and three pence for "profanely swearing"—he had said "Damn me."[1] "Go to the devil" cost fourteen shillings and one pence. Perhaps the sinister actions implicit in these imperatives were real to our forebears; the processes of *damning* and *going* were probably better understood then than now and accepted as the literal meaning of the culprits. Hence the fines. Or again, three young men and two women were fined for walking the streets on the Lord's Day "upon no religious occasion"; and a young man was fined five shillings for watching, also on the Lord's Day, the ice go down a river.[2] Are these instances of worldliness and profane swearing? When Wheelock in the years to come "carries the Indians twenty times a day to the throne of Grace," does he on his bended knees seek divine aid that number of times for the unregenerate savages, or does he simply remember now and then during the day's routine that the business of educating and converting the Indians is exacting, that he has a charge to fulfill? The heightened expression does not necessarily indicate insincerity; it is more likely the result of the heightened emotionalism to which many in the eighteenth century abandoned themselves.

However, it is clear that to Wheelock and his contemporaries the religion of the founders was being neglected. The blame for the existing apathy is usually placed on the Half-

[1] Caulkins (*History of Norwich, Conn.*), 178. [2] *Idem*, 290.

Way Covenant, which had been approved by the General Court of Connecticut in 1664.[1] As its title suggests, the Covenant was a compromise in determining who should be church members. Before the enactment, mere baptism in infancy did not qualify an adult for membership. By the Covenant infant baptism admitted an adult to membership although not to full church privileges. Personal regeneration, a knowledge that one had been born again, and the ability to testify publicly to that rebirth were no longer required as qualifications. Herein was found by the critics of the age the cause of the prevailing immorality and of the current apathy. That God was incensed seemed clear. The Indians had been sent as a scourge on the colony. Droughts were inflicted. On October 29, 1727, "when the Almighty arose," Connecticut was shaken by a severe earthquake; and in 1734 God showed his displeasure by a second visitation, "that dreadful disease called the throat distemper," which carried off many.

Less than a year before Wheelock's installation signs of what was to become the greatest revival in the history of the colonies were observed in Northampton, Massachusetts. This "first morning peep of mercy" followed the exhortations of Jonathan Edwards, who, like Wheelock, was to be an instructor of Indians (at Stockbridge) and the president of a college (now Princeton). Edwards has told the story in his *Narrative of Surprising Conversions*, one of the saddest and most illuminating documents of the period. From the *Narrative* we learn that a degeneracy had prevailed for some years. The young people frequented taverns or went on "frolicks." Others indulged in night-walking and lewd practices, and many were "indecent in

[1] H. M. Dexter, for example, considered the Covenant "spiritually devitalizing" to the eighteenth century (483). The Covenant may reasonably be held, however, to have been the result of a changed point of view, rather than the cause of it.

their carriage at meeting." But shortly after Edwards became pastor at Northampton a change took place. The immediate cause was the sudden death, by pleurisy, of a young man in the bloom of youth, "together with what was preached publicly on that occasion." Soon after this tragedy a second occurred, the death of a young woman who had been exercised about her soul. Edwards thereupon suggested to the young people that they spend certain evenings in "social religion." By December of 1734 "the Spirit of God began extraordinarily to set in," and five or six were converted. "Other discourse than of the things of religion would scarcely be tolerated in any company," "the world was a thing only by the by," and parishioners were even tempted to neglect worldly affairs too much. By the summer of 1735 the town was full of love, joy, and distress. A melancholia spread among the inhabitants. A poor workman, resident in Northampton, tried to slash his throat, and, as Edwards writes, many had suicide urged on them as though some one had said, "Cut your own throat, now is a good opportunity." The sad joy of the revival was felt even by babes. Phebe Bartlett at the age of four "was greatly affected by the talk of her brother, who had been hopefully converted a little before, at about eleven years of age, and then seriously talked to her about the great things of religion." She was observed to retire to her closet five or six times a day for secret prayer and "was so engaged in it, that nothing would at any time divert her from her stated closet exercises." Her story, as Edwards tells it, is a pitiful commentary on the treatment of the young.

So successful was the revival in Northampton that out of a population of two hundred families, some three hundred souls were saved. And in Lebanon, "where the Reverend Mr. Wheelock, a young gentleman, is lately settled," the fervor was caught and maintained. Soon the rest of New England was feeling the effects of the Great Awakening, partly because of the zeal of resident and traveling native ministers, partly because of the mighty efforts of the English evangelist, George White-field. To such an extent was personal conduct reformed that "it was the opinion of men of discernment and sound judg-ment—that bags of gold and silver, and other precious things, might, with safety, have been laid in the streets, and that no man would have converted them to his own use."[1]

From East Lyme John Lee wrote Wheelock that "two per-sons while preaching were so overcome with a sense of the wrath of God ready to fall on them (as they exprest it) that they died away with fear and sorrow and were with difficulty bro't to again, and when sermon was ended a great number cryed out in such anguish as I never see. It seem'd to me that some of them could not ha' born it many hours, five more per-sons died away with great sorrow and when a little come too made such dreadful outcry as (had it been on any other occa-tion) 'twould have broke the hardest heart.—Almost the whole congregation was drounded in tears and 11 or 12 persons fainted or near fainted so that they were obliged to be removed out of the meeting house." Young people who formerly gath-ered to make merry now met to weep. Wheelock informed the Reverend Stephen Williams that Theodora, Wheelock's oldest child, then four-and-a-half years old, seemed to be converted: "she gives a clear account—and has several times fainted under a sense of the love of God." At Windham, boys were overcome at meetings, "crying out under horror of mind," so that they were brought home only with difficulty. John Maltby, Whee-lock's stepson, gives the following description of conditions at Yale (November 18, 1742):

Honored Father and Mother

 I should have wrote before but have had no opertunity. O my

[1] Trumbull, II, 111.

father and mother my soul is dried up in this wilderness of sin and coruption. O my leaness my leaness it testifies against me. O that the Lord would shine into my soul and set it on fier with His love. If He should do so, He would be to me as the shadow of a great rock in a weary land, then shuld I set under His shadow with great delight and His fruit would be sweet to my taste. O that it were so. The world the flesh and the divil wont have it so by any means. But the Lord will have it so if He pleases tho all hell were ingaged in the war; but O that I had a true sorow for sin, and so brought to submit intierly to the Lords will let it be what it will. This is a land of drouth and famine, where no water is, in short heres a famin for the Word. Heres nothing to feed upon but Jesus Christ. If one lives here and lives in the exercises of the Spirit they must live intierly upon the Lord and what shall I do I am a great way from the Lord. O that I could get neare to Him and tell Him all my wants as my father. If you think it worth your while tell our Christians from me a poor unworthy worm that they know nothing what priviliges they have. They know nothing what it is to go without preaching 2 or 3 months and when they had preaching to be scorn'd vilified for it, both those that preach and those that heare their is very litel religious discarse amoung Christians. Christians are dreadfull dead here. The children of God sink down there seams to be no might no strength in a great many of them. The opposers seem to reign and have the uper hand of the blesed children of God. O that our Christians could intierly prise their advantages, while this litel flock of Christ has no pastor to lead and guide them but are as it were scatered about to and fro and ravening wolfs are thick seeking to distroy them. They have a pastor that can under God lead them and guide them in the way that is good and right. O that our Christians were made in some measure to prise their advantages but they will not till they are made to. O my soul has longed for to with them and have Christian conversation with them but may be it will not be so when I shall see them if the Lord ever permits it to be. O that God would mak me intierly resined to His will in everything. I am now living at Mr. Perpoints for what reason you may easely conclude though the boys attributed it alltogether to carnal reasons my removing. I told them it was truely for the good of my own and their souls that I did move. Att last they said they believed I was mad. I told them I was not mad but could pity them and pray for them as heartily as ever I could in my life and so gave them a word of exortation and prayed with em but did not take my leve of the family that night but the next night I took my leve of them. I desired the leftenant if he had anything against me or knew of anything that I had been wrong in to indevor to make me see but he said he had nothing against me but was intierly easy with I had don and thought it was for the best and so taking my leve of the family disiring their prayers for me departed and came on the day before Thansgiving and have no small thanks to give to the Lord the giver of all mercies. Mr. Beel is not yet com home and things remaine in respect to that just as they were when you was here. I have bought me a basselony hankerchife and 5 oringes which oringes I send to you with this leter concluding they will be acceptabel to you. The hankercheife cost 8 and 6 pence the oringes be 5. I am now in good health blesed be God for it blesed be God he helps me in my learning. I am now in Castatio. Sir if you have got one I should be glad you would send it to me if I stay here as soon as you can. This Honored father and mother with my duty to you and love to sisters and love in special to good Mr. Wright and all Christian freinds desiring earnest prayers to the throne for me a poor unworthy worm and now Honored parents hoping that you will forgive and correct what is wrong in your poor unworthy son desiring your prayers continually for me att the throne grace for needed grace I now subscribe myself

Your most unworthy son and servant

John Maltby

Wheelock was indefatigable during the revival. According to David M'Clure and Elijah Parish, who wrote the first published biography of Wheelock, he preached during the height of the Great Awakening in one year one hundred more sermons than there are days in the year. Pastors and afflicted laymen in neighboring towns urged him to lend the power of his preaching to their churches. Jonathan Edwards asked him to preach at Scantick, the parish of Edwards' father, and to preach "as often as the people will be willing to hear you." This he requested because "you have lately been so remarkably blessed elsewhere," and he desired Wheelock to preach at Northampton, also. Correspondents in prose and verse told Wheelock of their deadness in sin ("Tormenting fear my soul possess'd, Egyptian darkness veil'd my breast"), and of their conversion.

In the fall of 1741 Wheelock journeyed through Rhode Island to Boston. From a journal which he kept during the tour we learn that in some twenty-five days he preached about forty sermons, in addition to attending conferences with groups and giving advice and consolation to individuals. At Voluntown, Connecticut, he noticed "more of the footsteps of Satan than in any place I have yet been in; the zeal of some too furious; they tell of many visions, revelations and strong impressions upon the imagination." On October 23, having got out of bed at three in the morning, he left Voluntown "accompanied by a great number of wounded and comforted." On his way an old man and a woman called him Anti-Christ, and he himself characterized a certain woman as a "bigoted, ignorant Baptist." In Providence he preached to a full assembly, including many scoffers—"one man hired for twenty shillings to come into the meeting-house and fall down, which he did and made great disturbance." So great was the outcry at Taunton that Wheelock was forced to break off his discourse. He was received at Boston by a crowd of welcomers, and as Wheelock notes "rode with Mr. Bromfield in a close chaise, followed to his house after me a great many children to receive a word of exhortation at the gate, which I could not stand long to do, being very wet."

In the following year (1742) Wheelock made a second tour, this time through Connecticut, of which the following letters give a sufficient account:

My Dear and Loving Wife

Yours by Brother D-p-t[1] came. Grateful indeed to hear of my dear absent family and flock, whom may God still preserve and bless. The week before last I preachd 10 sermons. I told you in my last of the power of God at Derby. Last day I preachd 10 times again. My journey was to Guilford where we saw a great shaking among dry bones and hell break lose and in a rage at it. We allso saw a great shaking at Branford and somthing at East Haven. They tell me in the two former places it was greater than ever has been seen before in them. Dear Brother Munson the barer was with me to whom I referr you for a more full and perfect account of matters. He had much of God with him there. I am this day going to preach the round 'tother way as far as Stratfield. Things in this town are much more calm than they were. I mean as to the spirit and temper of people. Mr. Clap[2] with the rest of the church committee are gone to see if they can get Mr. Burr. I have not seen Mr. Noyes since I came to town. I have been proposing terms of reconciliation viz that matters of greviance relating to Mr. N. should be heard by a councill of ministers that live remote viz. Messrs Dickinson, Pemberton, the Boston ministers, Sol. Williams, Mr. Lord &c. I dont think that there is any prospect that Mr. Noyes will submitt to it and unless those grounds of their first separation can be removed I dont think there is any hope of a union. Mr. Clap sticks as fast to Mr. Noyes as his skin to him and loves him as his eyes and counts him a sound orthodox man and indeed I dont at all wonder at it for I beleive they think much alike. Mr. Clap refuses to let me preach in the college or to let the scholarrs come to hear me. O that God would give him another heart. It is not yet certain whether I shall stay one or two Sabbaths more. I would have you get Brother Williams to preach the last if you can and then if I should come home he will be there to assist me. I am exceedingly worn out with constant labour and much watching. I have the young woman now by me, of whom I inform'd you in my last, under deep concern. Dear Brother Peirpoint and sister give love to you and the family and he his love to Brother Josiah Lyman. I have you my dearest and dear family daily in remembrance before God. My heart is with

---

[1] Wheelock's brother-in-law, James Davenport.

[2] Thomas Clap, President of Yale College. See *Dictionary of American Biography:* article *Thomas Clap*, for the later troubles between Clap and Noyes.

you. Give my love to Brother Wright to dear Betty John Sarah Theodora Ruth and take as much as you can reasonably desire yourself from

> Your constant faithfull loving husband
> and companion in tribulation and in the
> Kingdom and patience of Jesus Christ

> Eleazer Wheelock

N.H. June 28, 1742

Brother Deodate (whom I hant yet seen) is a feirce opposer I hear. Friends here are generally well. Give my hearty love to all my dear people as you have opportunity.

> Lebanon Jan. 18, 1741/2

Dearest Brother[1]

I have been expecting a letter from you but have had none. I long to see you more than ever. I love you in the bowells of Christ. I was last week and the week before at Weathersfield and preached many sermons there. Much of the great power of God was seen there the whole town seams to be shaken. Last Monday night the Lord bowed the heavens and came down upon a large assembly in one of the parishes of the town. The whole assembly seam'd alive with distress the groans and outcrys of the wounded were such that my voice could not be heard, and in many other assemblies much of the power of God was seen. Last Thursday night I preach'd to the negros where also I could not go thro' with my sermon their outcry was so great their distress was astonishing their agony groans &c seamd a lively emblem of the damned. Between 30 and 40 I hope were converted while I was in town and many hundreds I beleive were under concern. Dear Brother Lockwood the minister of the town is very much ingaged in these things. There is a great work among the Indians at Mohegan Nihantuck and Stonington many of them converted and the rest mostly under concern. Mr. Davenport under God has been the great instrument of the work among them. The work is yet daily increasing in this government. Opposition grows less and opposers more out of credit. I intended to have

[1] Daniel Rogers, pastor in Littleton.

been at Providence before now but I am constantly full and crouded with busnss and when I shall go I cant tell. Do send me a letter and tell me when you will meet me there and if I can I will come. I long to have you come into these parts. I beleive you might do much service for the Lord here. Take this as token of my love. Do let me hear from you and pray allways for

Your inside Brother &c.

Eleazer Wheelock

P.S. I hear that you are ordain'd an itinerant &c.

Lebanon
May 15, 1743

Reverend and Very Dear Sir[1]

I beleive you think strange that I hant wrote to you for so long a time especially since I did not return by you according to your proposal and my purpose when I left you. I conclude you have before now been acquainted with all the remarkables in my journey and I beleive there was nothing in my conduct you disapprove of unless my preaching at Branford as I did without the consent of their pastor which peice of conduct I beleive you would have justified if you had been there and seen the mans temper and heard the grevious heart affecting complaints that the poor people made of spiritual tyranny and oppression. (Cant there be nothing done for their releiff.) I think the temper of this government is not better than it has been. What will be the issue God knows. It seams to me He designs His children shall see no arm but His own to trust to before He will deliver them and then they will give Him all the glory peace and love. Thro' the goodness of God I yet continue among my dear flock tho' the love of many seams to be waxing cold. Dear Sir I love you and honour you and greatly long to see you. Won't you come down and give us a visit. I and my family that are with me are in usual health. Sarah is att Middletown with a doctor sqwaw to be cured of the king's evil. I saw her there last Friday. They hope she is a little better but yet is very low. I fear she wont continue very long. We all salute you and sister and yours and dear

1 Stephen Williams, pastor in West Woodstock.

earnistly desire your remembrance when near to God. This in hast from

Your poor Brother and humble servant

Eleazar Wheelock

P.S. My wife has had greater refreshments from God of late than she has had for many years.

There were dangers in all this excitement. Passions could not be loosed so completely without a corresponding loosening of the tongue. Traveling preachers freely condemned their audiences; that was part of the glee of the revival, and was not objected to either by layman or cleric. But when the itinerants assumed the right to pass judgment on resident pastors, such criticisms were quite another matter. Gilbert Tennent from New Jersey called the pastors, his hosts, the following names: "hirelings, caterpillars, letter-learned Pharisees, plaistered hypocrites, varlets, the seed of the serpent, dry nurses, dead dogs that cannot bark, daubers with untempered mortar, moral negroes, salt without savour, that stink in the nostrils of God and man, swarms of locusts, dead drones—" to select only a few of the epithets which Charles Chauncy, always an opponent of the revivalists, has listed.[1] To Chauncy the itinerants were "busie-bodies" who took over the labor of other men, boasted of things made ready to their hands, and neglected their own parishes.

Wheelock never demeaned himself by using the gross words ascribed to Tennent, but he too was condemned by Chauncy, and especially for his *enthusiasm,* the eighteenth century equivalent of our *fanaticism.* According to the letters which Chauncy quotes,[2] Wheelock was led astray while an undergraduate at Yale by a Quaker named David Ferris: "Mr. Dav-

[1] In *Seasonable Thoughts on the State of Religion in New England,* 249–250.
[2] *Idem,* 209, 212.

enport, Wheelock, Pomroy, and others, were those who lived with this Ferris most familiarly, and have since divulged his errors, and fill'd places where they have preach'd with the superstitions and groundless opinions, they learned from him, who was their father and dictator as to their belief."

According to another correspondent quoted by Chauncy, "they made a club, and often met together. They did not open their principles to all, but to those whom they imagined they could work upon.—They laid great stress upon impressions and impulses; particularly, upon any sense of Scripture that was suddenly and strongly suggested to their minds.—They were strangely uncharitable; expressing themselves censoriously of most others: they had indeed no opinion of any but themselves on a religious account.—They pleaded for the Spirit's immediate, extraordinary guidance in the manner 'tis now pleaded for; and were in most respects then as they have appeared since."

It is surprising that Wheelock failed to answer this accusation at once. Indeed it was not until October 24, 1759 (sixteen years after the appearance of *Seasonable Thoughts*) that he wrote a denial! And he directed his letter to the Reverend Ebenezer Pemberton rather than to Chauncy because he understood Chauncy to be one who "takes more liberty to insult his inferiors than perhaps the mercury in my own blood will bear while I am so sensible of mean, unmannerly, and unchristian and abusive treatment received from him." The letter follows:

Reverend and Honored Sir

Some years ago (perhaps 10) on a journey and at a tavern, the landlord (who was and had been very violent in his opposition to the religious concern which had then lately been in the land) shewed me a book wrote by Dr. Charles Chauncy of Boston, and pointed me to a place where he pretended to give part of my religious character, particularly at college. I read a few pages and knew not but I had read all that concernd me in the book in which there were, as I remember no less then 12 palpable falshoods, nor was there one word there to my disadvantage that was true. Soon after this I saw Col. Williams who was President when I was member of college and was intimately acquainted with the whole affair which the Dr. pretendes to relate. I told him what I had met with, he told me if I would write against it he would add his attestation thereto. But I supposed my character to be so well known, in this government that there were so many who were knowing to the whole affair—and that the Drs. character among us, excepting with a few Arminians, was such that I did not think that anything he had done or could do of that nature would so prejudice my character or usefulness as to render worth my while to do anything in my own vindication. But tho't it was rather my duty to trample upon it, with many other things of the like nature which I have met with till the time shall come when all things shall be set right. And so I have treated it and have never had any intimation that it has been of any prejudice to me in this government nor indeed anywhere else, till of late I have been advisd by gentlemen of good and publick characters in your government, that my name and religion with it have and do suffer very much, and are in danger of suffering more in succeeding generations by what he has wrote, and that it is expedient and very necessary that something should be done. I am also inform'd that there were other things said of me in that book besides the passage which I read but what they are I cant so much as guess. Nor do I know where to get the book in order to see what they are. I wish some friend would lend me the book and point me to the particular pages which concern me, that I may not have the mortification to read the whole in order to know what he says of me—nor can I particularly remember what I did read, but in general the whole that he says of my acquaintance with my dear Mr. Davenport, more than that I knew him by sight is false. I dont know that I ever spoke a word to him or he to me while we were at college. I am confident I never discoursd 3 minutes with him, nor do I think that there ever was a member of college, while I was there, with whom I had so little acquaintance. Nor had I ever 'till after I had contracted acquaintance with his sister who was afterward my wife. Nor did the

21

sad mistakes which that previous servant of Christ afterwards run into at all origionate from anything he imbibed at college—if I dont mistake he supposd he was converted while he liv'd with his Brother Williams of Long Meadow, about the time he began to preach.

And as to the Doctor representing me as being enthusiastical at college (as he dos if I dont forget) he is very abusive in it. I never held nor pretended to experience that kind of teaching which Calvanistick divines call enthusiasm. The grand points which I was opposd in were the absolute necessity of divine teaching in order to a right and effectual understanding of Divine things, and the absolute necessity of Divine influence and the indwelling of the spirit of Christ in order to a right and acceptable performance of duty to God. That the graces of the spirit may be so sensible and evident, as to be matter of assurance to the subjects of them, that they are passd from death into life. These were the principles cheifly disputed. And to prove that I did not differ from approved divines I usd frequently to quote and appeal to Mr. Flavel part of whose works I had with me. And when the report was spread that I was enthusiastical I made a challenge upon all who had been my opponants to mention one point wherein I had differed in principle from Mr. Hoddard or Mr. Flavel and it was frankly allowed by my most zealous opponants that I was not a greater enthusiast than Mr. Flavel was, and that I had not vented any principles which he did not justify. And I dare now bid the challenge to all the world, let them keep truth on their side and accuse me with holding any principles contrary to the divines, and divines of that sort. My mind was greatly affected with the truth and importance of those things they appeared to me in a stronger light than ever they had done. But I was a child and spake and tho't and understood as a child. Had I been more acquainted with men and things, I had no doubt suppressd that inclination to speak with so much freedom in all companies, which I believe I sometimes imprudently gave vent to, notwithstanding all which I dare make the challenge on all the world; to mention one principle which I vented as my belief contrary to sound Calvinism. Dear Rector Williams to whom I freely unbosomd myself often told me that my principles and my religion would not be opposd at Northampton and many other places where the same are publickly taught and justified. Nor have I ever had occasion to altar my thots since in one material article which was then controverted excepting that when I came to be acquainted with Christians who were new born and educated in places where they were not under oppression and reproach for their religion, but their religion in fashion, and others had been taught and to imitate the same language, I was soon convinced, that forming my sentiments by the little number of my acquaintances who had been refined by trials I had carried my tho'ts of the knowledge which Christians have of one anothers spiritual state too far, tho I never held that they could have a certain knowledge of it.

And as to my honest classmate who, as I remember, the Dr. says was his informer, it is all a chimera—I never had such a classmate as he describes. I've discoursed with Mr. Pomeroy and others and we cant so much as guess who he means, nor can we supposing him to be mistaken in his being classmate, and that he means only contemporary with us at college, so much as guess who the man was because I know of no man to whom that character belongs.

I was upon the same road to N. Haven when that Dr. passed thro' this government (as I understand) to fill his crop with materials for that piece, and I came several times within scent of him (for he left a savor of what he fed upon where he lit) and was at the college at the same time and should have freely given him a full and true account of the whole affair if he had desired to know the truth—and could have proved it to him at that time and place beyond exception. And I suspect he would doubtless have given me the opportunity if the truth had been what he desired—however if I think so hardly of him let others judge who know the circumstances of the case. I am confident I am far from being alone in these tho'ts of him. I should have wrote to the Doctor but I understand he is a gentleman who takes more liberty to insult his inferiors than perhaps the mercury in my own blood will well bear while I am so sensible of mean, unmanly, unchristian and abusive treatment received from him. Tho' as yet I am not sensible of any great impatience under what I have already sufferd from him.

Will you please, Sir, to let the Doctor know that I think that he has made himself a debtor to me and also to Mr. Pomeroy and Mr. Allen by what he has wrote, and more so to the Redeemer and His dear cause, and then if he will risque the consequents of it, he will have none but himself to blame if they prove very bad.

Please also to favor me with your and the Reverend Mr. Foxcrofts advice what is duty and expedient for me to do in the case to retrieve or prevent the injury that has or may accrew to religion by what the Doctor has wrote.

I hope Sir the occasion will excuse the tedious length of this letter. Please to accept most dutiful and affectionate salutation from, and remember in your devoutest hours,

Your unworthy son in the Gospel

Eleazar Wheelock

This letter Wheelock entrusted for delivery to a farmer "who was going with a drove," but by February first of the following year Pemberton had not yet received it. On that date Wheelock wrote an apology to Pemberton: "The letter which concerned Doctor Chauncy was wrote too soon after my hearing of some of his talk in that journey and also the injurious representations he had made of things in that piece as well as the ill improvements made of it. So that altho I dont think I tho't too ill of his conduct in that affair I am tho'tful some expressions therein were too sarcastical and savage. Which I give you full power to alter if you should have occasion to expose it."

Wheelock was not finished with his rebuttal, however. Ten years later, on March 13, 1769 (twenty-six years after the publication of *Seasonable Thoughts*) Wheelock wrote to Chauncy himself. Once more he denied Chauncy's accusations, and since "those books were never vendible, except among Arminians, in the colony of Connecticut," requested a loan of *Seasonable Thoughts* in order that he might refer by page to the offending passages.

While Chauncy's charges lacked full proof,[1] it should be

1 Benjamin Trumbull, II, 202, fn.: "I had an intimate acquaintance with these

noted that Wheelock was in suspected, even convicted, company. He was brother-in-law to James Davenport (whose sister Sarah he had married), and Davenport was the most violent of the revivalists. A graduate of Yale at the age of sixteen, licensed to preach at nineteen, he began his intemperate career by addressing his congregation with a twenty-four-hour exhortation. "He gave an unrestrained liberty," writes Trumbull,[1] "to noise and outcry, both of distress and joy, in time of divine service. He promoted both with all his might, raising his voice to the highest pitch, together with the most violent agitations of the body. With his unnatural and violent agitations of the body, he united a strange singing tone which mightily tended to raise the feelings of weak and undiscerning people, and consequently to heighten the confusion among the passionate of his hearers. This odd, disagreeable tuning of the voice, in exercises of devotion, was caught by the zealous exhorters, and became a characteristic of the separate preachers. The whole sect was distinguished by this sanctimonious tone." Davenport, also, in the fashion of Gilbert Tennent, censured the clergy: one he characterized as a "carnal, old Pharisee,"[2] and of another he said[3] that "thousands are now cursing him in hell for being the instrument of their damnation."

Resident pastors were of course unwilling to hear themselves defamed before their own congregations. Consequently, in their favor the General Court of the colony passed an act[4] de-

gentlemen, and with their people; was brought up under the preaching of Dr. Pomeroy; lived some time in the family of Dr. Wheelock; heard them both preach abundantly; and I never saw or heard of anything, in either of them, which savoured in the least degree of quakerism. They were some of the most distinguishing preachers, in their day, between true and false religion. They were strict in their morals, and extensive in their charity. They ever considered themselves as greatly injured by Dr. Chauncey. He took up reports against his brethren, not at the mouth of two or three witnesses, and without inquiring whether they were friends or enemies."

[1] *Idem*, 126.   [2] *Seasonable Thoughts*, 152.   [3] *Idem*, 157.
[4] *Colonial Records of Connecticut*, VIII, 455–457.

barring any itinerant from preaching without the consent of the resident pastor and of the majority of the parishioners, on pain of being deprived, if an inhabitant of the colony, of his salary; if not an inhabitant, the offending itinerant was to be sent "as a vagrant person by warrant from any one assistant or justice of the peace, from constable to constable, out of the bounds of this Colony." Davenport was arrested under this act. Having heard the evidence, the General Court concluded, May, 1742, that "the said Davenport is under the influences of enthusiastical impressions and impulses, and thereby disturbed in the rational faculties of his mind, and therefore to be pitied and compassionated, and not to be treated as otherwise he might be."[1] By order of the Court he was sent out of the colony to his parish in Southold, Long Island. Unfortunately Davenport had not yet run his course of excesses. Continuing to preach as an unwelcome itinerant, he was again judged insane, this time by a Boston jury. In 1743 he persuaded a group in New London to cast their "wigs, cloaks, and breeches, hoods, gowns, rings, jewels and necklaces" into a bonfire, to which he himself added certain odious books and a pair of plush breeches.[2] In 1744 Wheelock and other friends showed Davenport how unseemly his conduct was, whereupon Davenport wrote a retraction. For the remaining thirteen years of his life he preached in various churches in New York and New Jersey; just before he died, the presbytery of the church at Hopewell, New Jersey, was considering a petition for his dismissal.

Another of Wheelock's brothers-in-law, Benjamin Pomeroy, likewise was arrested because of his breaking the law against itinerants. On the first occasion (he was arrested in company with Davenport) the evidence was judged insufficient, and he was set free.[3] On a second occasion, having preached at Col-

---

1 *Colonial Records of Connecticut*, VIII, 483–484.

2 Chauncy, 220 ff.

3 *Colonial Records of Connecticut*, VIII, 482.

chester, Connecticut, by invitation from the church members but without the permission of the pastor, he was deprived of the legal right to collect his salary,[1] and for seven years was without lawful income from his parish. Once again, in 1744, he was arrested, this time for publicly criticising the law and the authorities, and obliged to pay the costs of prosecution (some thirty-two pounds) and to give bond for fifty pounds.

Even Wheelock's association with the illustrious George Whitefield was a handicap to him, at least from the point of view of the clergy who frowned on itinerants and *enthusiastic* preachers in general. Throughout a period of thirty years the correspondence between Wheelock and Whitefield expresses for the most part confidence and agreement; Wheelock approved of Whitefield's preaching, and in his letters commented favorably on the visiting Englishman's labors. But Whitefield himself was censured by the General Association of Connecticut ministers. In June, 1745, they passed a resolution affirming that "it would by no means be advisable for any one of our ministers to admit him into their pulpits, or for any of our people to attend his administrations."

Because of Wheelock's friendship with Davenport, Pomeroy, Whitefield, and other revivalists, and because too of his own preaching, it is not surprising to learn that the association of ministers at Pomfret sent to him (on August 25, 1745) a memorial in which they besought their brethren to "keep to their notes," and thus avoid the "unguarded expressions of Davenport and of brethren in this county who itinerate." In the same year a correspondent informed Wheelock that, according to what he has heard, Wheelock "yells and pounds the pulpit," that he has been too free in criticising the civil government, and that he is rending churches apart by condemning resident pastors as unconverted. Trumbull states that church

[1] *Idem,* VIII, 566.

members were suspended from communion for attending services conducted by Wheelock and other zealous preachers; and the Reverend Philomen Robbins, he adds, was condemned for his "earnestness in promoting and improving strolling or travelling preachers," among whom was Wheelock.[1]

In a letter (December 27, 1741) to Samuel Whitman, pastor in Farmington, Wheelock defends himself against certain charges:

Reverend and Honored Sir

I received a letter from you dated Octr. 7, 1741, which came to my hand Nov. 17, which I now think it my duty to answer and the great reason why I hant done it before has been a want of leisure. And in the first place I must intreat you to suffer me to write freely to you what appears to me to be true and that you would not be offended with me for it tho I am but a child and I will first answer the particulars which you alledge against me and then observe some things which appear very strange and unscriptural in your conduct.

And first as to your letter you say "In answer to where you say that you did not tell me so (i.e., that I never preachd in any parish where there was a settled minister without his consent &c) but told me that you told Mr. Cotton so that they allow it, but did not by your answer intend to deceive me and lead me to think that you never had. Was not this base and vile dissimulation."

I answer it was no answer at all. I was giving you an account of what passed between Mr. Cotton and I and did design to have gone thro with it and should had not company come in and that sick child in the neighbourhood to which you was calld prevented me nor was there the least intent in my heart to deceive you but come to your house with a full intent to give you a full account of the affair nor do I think you had any reason to think that I aim'd to deceive you.

Again you say "Did you not say also that you did not remember that you had" ever preach'd in any parish without the ministers invitation &c.

Answer: I told you so in the account which I was giving you of

[1] Trumbull, II, 140, 172.

my talk to Mr. Cotton and only as what I had said to him and no otherwise. And what I said more about going with Mr. Meacham to Hartford &c. was in answer to an objection which you cast in by the way relating to your particular affair for you had heard, as I remember, that I did otherwise there, which was not true. This I think is a true representation of the case.

Again you say "And farther in the morning when I read you the resolves of our association and faulted the riding ministers for thrusting themselves into the parishes of others and preachd without their consent did you not tell me that you was not one of them that you had never done it."

Answer: If I did tell you so it was true for I did no more thrust myself into Mr. Cottons parish than you thrust yourself into Coventry last summer when you went thro it from Boston but I beleive those were not the words of my answer but by way of question. When did I ever do it? To which you replyd I dont charge you with it I dont know that ever you did. By the manner of your discourse about ministers thrusting themselves into parishes &c I supposd you did aim to reprove me and tho't that you had heard of my preaching at Mr. Cottons the day before but when you reply that you did not charge me with it &c I supposd then that you had not heard of it and the reason why I did not tell you of it then and at brakefast (when there was a door opned for it) and the only reason, was because I thot it would lead us into discourse that would not tend to fitt us for the publick worship which was speedily to be attended but the contrary.

Again you say "That it was for want of a convenient opportunity by reason of my sudden and unexpected hastning away that you did not tell me of the contradiction at the time of it." Honored Sir don't be offended if I tell you that I cant beleive that to be the reason. Did we not discourse some time of the state of Christians at Hartford after I had done giving you an account of my preaching at the West Division. I stayd with you as long as I thot it convenient to stay in your studdy and wondred that you found no fault with me for what I had done. I came out as deliberately as persons usually do (I beleive). After I came out you went in again with two young women and left me in your room. I went out into the street and discoursed with some wounded persons there and came into the house

to you again and took my leave of you and you came out and stood
by us when we got up on our horses and I beleive it was full an hour
or more after meeting before we went from your house and you had
as fair an opportunity as you could desire, to have told me that you
had something to say to me and if it had been in your heart. And
why Honored Sir did you hate me thus to suffer sin upon me and
how you will excuse yourself from a very gross violation of our
Savior's rule, Matt. 18, 15, 16, I can't tell. It is a rule which I teach
my people to observe as well as any of Christs laws and have dis-
ciplind them for the breach of it and have required and taken a
confession in a case that has not appeard half so bad as the present.
I pray Honored Sir that you would not be offended with me for my
plaines. But what looks most natural and easie for me to beleive is
one of these two things either you had no tho't of a contradiction
when we came out of your studdy which was truly the case with me
I had no thot of contradiction in my talk nor did I suspect anybody
tho't I had been guilty of any or else which is too bad to beleive of
you and which it seams I could not suspect were it not for your after
conduct viz. that you were really glad that I had been thus guilty
that you might have somthing to report to my disadvantage after I
was gone. God and your own conscience know how it was after I
was gone. I wondred that you had found no fault or no more fault
with what I had done the day before and that you appeard so much
more pleasant in your temper and deportment after I had given
you that account than you did before and what was the cause of it I
dont pretend to know but your treatment of me since Honored Sir
has been much more strange for it seams by what I can learn that
you and your son the doctor hant been wanting to spread the scandal far and wide as you could. Did you not report it at N. Haven
and had you not an opportunity there to have discoursd with me if
you had desired it. And from every quarter almost I have heard of
it from you or your son. And did you not when you had wrote the
letter which I have before me give it open to Mr. Pratt after you
had read it to him and order him to read it publickly at the tavern
to a number of people there which he did. That I am credibly informed as was the case and is this right. Dos this become an aged
minister and a father in the church Honored Sir if I have discoverd
an unchristian temper in anything which I have wrote I am sorry

and heartily ask your pardon. I am not now sensible of the least heart rising against you but can (if I know myself) heartily wish and pray for your temporal and eternal wellfare and ask leave Honored Sir to subscribe myself

Your most obedient, humble servant

Eleazar Wheelock

P.S. Sir I am informd that there are other things which you charge me with lying about but you don't mention them in your letter nor do I know particularly what they be and so am not able to answer.

Wheelock's position was not easy to maintain without censure. As an opponent of the Half-Way Covenant, agreeing with many of his day that the Covenant was a too lenient standard of qualification for church membership, he was tempted by the general fashion of the revivalists to indulge in their excesses. As he wrote to Stephen Williams in 1740, "I believe there is vastly less hurt by some degrees of enthusiasm where there is a fervent love to God and souls than there is by that lukewarmness and coldness that has so generally prevailed among ministers. Witness Brother Davenport's extraordinary success since his intemperate zeal also the success of the Tenants and others in the Jersies not to speak of Mr. Whitefield—." And, as has been shown, he was on more than one occasion bracketed with the extremists.

On the other hand, much as he offended some by his *enthusiasm,* he was orthodox and above reasonable censure in regard to church polity. He consistently upheld the Saybrook Platform[1] of 1708, and although he was now and then accused of Separatism, that is, of wishing to reject the Saybrook Platform and to establish the autonomy of the individual church, he was

[1] By the Saybrook Platform district associations of ministers and district consociations of churches were established. These latter become practically ecclesiastical courts to which each church was subject. The individual Congregational churches thus lost their autonomy.

able to boast that during his long pastorate at Lebanon there was never any suspicion, even, of Separatism.

Colonial Connecticut was harsh toward Separatism. By law each parish was required to pay the salary of the lawfully installed minister. If any group wished to dissent to the point of setting up a separate church, it was still not freed from its financial obligations to the original minister. Thus to the irksomeness of the Saybrook Platform was added the burden of contributing to the salary of the lawful pastor as well as to the support of the separate church. In all, some thirty-three Separate churches were organized in Connecticut in the eighteenth century as protests against the Saybrook Platform.

Dissent went to extremes. At Stonington, for instance, the Separates objected to their pastor's using notes while at the same time he prayed for divine assistance in preaching. It might have been more reasonable on their part to have conceded that he knew what he was about. At New Haven a deacon refused to attend the funeral service for his grandson because the father of the child was a Separate, and the timbers of the Separate meeting-house were cut in two by opponents as the frame was about to be raised. At Killingly, as an unintended testimony to the validity of the Saybrook Platform, the Separates appealed to other Separate churches for counsel and assistance when their clerk refused to read the church records!

Wheelock's opposition to the Separates dates from the early years of the revival, and very likely from the beginning of his pastorate. In 1739 he wrote to a correspondent that "the feeble and languishing state of church government requires our utmost care and tenderness," and urged his correspondent to bow to the dictates of the church council. On another occasion he condemned Separates for "pulling off the members (at least some of the fingers and toes) from the body of Christ." Wheelock also rebuked the Separates at Enfield for having caused strife and brought "disgrace upon the glorious work of God. People are afraid to let you come near their children lest you poison their minds with schismatical principles." In 1759 he answered in unequivocal terms an accusation that he had favored Separates. The letter is addressed to Benjamin Lord, pastor in Norwich:

Reverend and Honored Sir

When I received your first and observed several expressions personally pointed (as I tho't) it exercisd my mind much, nor could I after all my study, determine whether to conclude it was a preface to some fault you found with, or blame you was about to lay upon me for something relative to the Separates, or only to improve my mind and tho'ts on that subject. Nothing forbid my coming to the conclusion first mentioned, but your leaving the matter as you did, and my mind necessarily in suspence as to the matter of charge against me, the uneasiness of which I tho't you must have known, and consequently could not think you would treat one so, and therefor I understood you according to the letter, and treated it accordingly. But when I had read a few lines in your last and understood I had mistook your design, and perceived plainly that your jealosie that I was tampering with strengthening and confirming the Separates &c had moved you to write and had also observed the bulk of your letter, I was greived at heart that I should any way occasion you so much trouble and conceived most grateful resentments of your care for me. But on further reading was surprised to find such strong suspicions as you had entertained concerning me, or that you and your honest and judicious people have known no more of my labour in publick and private respecting Separates for 7 years past (and especially considering you think me of so much consequence as to deserve such pains, as you have taken in your letters). Or that neither you nor they have ever heard the Separates or their abettors say as they have often said in your town, that none, even of the open approvers of the late religious operation, have been so severe in treating Separates as I have been. I presume those honest and judicious people were not at meeting when I preachd for you last in which discourses I represented the work of a false

Spirit, or of Satan transforming himself into an Angil of Light, (in discoursing on which I described the principles and practise of Separates so freely that no judicious person could misunderstand me, as a grand and cheif impediment, where it is, to the progress of what is good, and I dare compare notes with every minister in Connecticut and if there be one, according to the opportunity and occasion I have had for it, who has done more in private or preachd more and in fuller and stronger terms than I have for 7 years past, I will own I am wholly mistaken. I have usd the most forcible endeavours within my power to cure Mr. Fuller. Did I not do more than all the world besides to brake him up at Kensington? I presume if Rev. Mr. Burnham could speak from his grave he would do me the justice to testify that I did so. Yea I believe Mr. Fuller himself will own it. And have I not steadily appeard the same from the very first appearance of separation and ministerial exhortation, did I not take a journey to Groton on purpose to stope and diswade Mr. Davenport from his course and was after unwearied pains, under God, the means of convincing him of his error in setting up lay teachers. This you have understood if you have read his printed accounts of it. I spent week after week labouring in publick and private to convince and reclaim Separates, and thro' the blessing of God I trust my labours have not been wholly fruitless—but abundant experience has taught me that 'tis labour in vain unless I can get and keep them in my arms, to deal with them for their bitter and uncharitable spirit with the same spirit is (as I think I once heard you say in some case) to strike a hot iron with a hot one. If I have been so much in favor of Separates, how comes it to pass they have never been able notwithstanding their abundant endeavours so much as to get liberty of a house to preach at in my parish. And yet after all this you say, "I beg of you to take my advice and that is not to tamper with the Separates and virtually strengthen them in that way which you do think is not good had you not better tell them Mr. Fuller and all that it is a bad cause they are in that of error and disorder &c. Sir I cant tell him nor them so if I never go to see them, nor should I think it best to tell them so if it were evident they were in such a temper as incapacitates them to receive conviction. No I had rather spend that visit in friendly conversation on what we are agreed in. Or in paving the way by some preliminaries for an advantagious talk with him or them by and by on the very point. Nor should I think this would be to do evil that good might come, but to imitate the safest pattern even of him who has compassion on the ignorant and them that are out of your ways. I tho't Sir you had known that my steady principles of church government and order are Presbyterian and have been so ever since I have settled on any and I have steadily believed that separations and their apendages and consequents are a rightous rebuke of Heaven, on ministers and peoples that the contrary errors have been so truely sufferd in churches and that we have been so fainthearted respecting endeavours to introduce better principles and a better constitution, without which as I once heard the late Mr. Edwards say I never expect to see the N. England churches in health. How far mental errors are to be treated as moral scandals and what different treatment is due of persons in error, from that to those under moral scandal is another point in which perhaps we may differ more than in the lawfullness of separations &c.

As to my ordaining of Mr. Fuller I dont remember to have heard the thing mentioned but by you.

And now, Sir, if you will bear with me on such an occasion, to say that which looks so much like flattery. I have always esteemd you a godly learned and judicious divine, have lookd upon the separation from you groundless and unreasonable and have ever treated you and that accordingly, and all your jealosies concerning me to the contrary are from unrighteous slander or groundless and uncharitable prejudices—and for time to come I shall alway take it kindly if you will freely and plainly hint to me any suspicion you may entertain different from the foregoing declaration for it is perfectly disagreable to me that those I love and honour, and am conscious to myself miss no opportunity to serve, should all the while think I am seeking to undermine and ruin them.

If there was anything that lookd assuming in my former, please impute it to my misunderstanding of your intention in writing to me and if in this any terms seem too strong, if you review your letter and believe what I have said concerning my principles and practise I dont think you will wonder that I a little wake up in my own vindication, or that you yourself would do less were it your own case. However please to pardon, cover and bury all defects and accept the most solomn profession of duty love and respects from Reverend and Honored Sir

Your unworthy son in the Gospel

Eleazar Wheelock

Benjamin Trumbull records that Wheelock's voice was "smooth and harmonious, the best by far that I ever heard." From the evidence already given it is certain that Wheelock was a moving preacher, frequently sought after by congregations. Other extant data are unsatisfactory as criteria of his preaching. Some notes of sermons from this period remain, written on small sheets of paper in a microscopic hand, abounding in abbreviations, and in large part mere headings. With the aid of these notes Wheelock delivered the sermons which aroused his listeners to a sense of sin and led to many conversions; but the notes are just so much dead matter to one looking at them today, and not a sparkle of the fire which he kindled from them can now be glimpsed.

But although the force of these sermons has been lost, to our observation, that is, it is still possible to learn something of Wheelock the preacher from his published sermons of a later date. Of these the best, the most readable, is the sermon which he preached at the ordination of Charles Jeffry Smith,[1] who was about to depart from Lebanon as a missionary to the Six Nations.

The general plan of this sermon conforms to the accepted

---

[1] *A Sermon Preached before the Second Society in Lebanon, June 30, 1763, at the Ordination of the Rev. Mr. Charles-Jeffry Smith,* Edinburgh, 1767. Other printed sermons by Wheelock are: *The Preaching of Christ an Expression of God's great Love to Sinners, and therefore a sweet Savour to him, though a Savour of Death unto Death to them. Illustrated in a Sermon Preach'd at North Haven, Dec. 25, 1760, At the Ordination of the Reverend Mr. Benjamin Trumble,* Boston, 1761; *Liberty of Conscience or No King But Christ in His Church, A Sermon Preached at Dartmouth Hall, November 30, 1775,* Hartford, no date. (See pp. 201–202 for a consideration of this sermon.)

standard. After a reading of the text (Isaiah II, 2, 3) Wheelock, as one of the "learned clergy," gives an explanation of phrases and references found in it. Then comes the "statement of doctrine": "That the manifestations of Christ among the heathen will powerfully and effectually draw them unto Him," the doctrine being analyzed under various sub-headings lucidly explained. This section in turn is followed by the "improvement," or direct application of the text to the candidate: "When you shall be separated from all earthly friends, and quite out of the reach of all expressions of their care for you, or kindness and love to you, but such as they shall daily make at the throne of grace; you shall not then find yourself alone and comfortless. If you shall be sick among savages, who have neither will, nor skill, to minister suitably for your relief; you may upon this word of promise, safely repose confidence in the great Physician, who will supply, and more than supply, the want of earthly ones.—When your lodging is wet and cold, and you have no covering about you, more than the uninclosed range of the owl, the cormorant, and the bittern, the viper, the wolf, and the bear; you will lye all night in his embraces, and he will give sleep to you, as to his Beloved; and when you awake, you will be still with him, and he will make the curtain of the skies as 'God's house' to you." After this readable passage, with its borrowings from Isaiah, we come to the "address to the people of God," and finally to the "charge" to the candidate. The sermon as a whole has that processional dignity which is suitable for the solemnity of an ordination.

Beyond what has already been given regarding Wheelock as a preacher little is to be said. He had the full equipment of a popular minister: agreeable voice, forceful delivery, and adequate learning. It is no disparagement to append that he added nothing original to the religious thought of his time; his opposition to the Half-Way Covenant and his championing of the Saybrook Platform were approved by many contemporary clergymen. His faults were fashionable in his day: for sweetness and light eighteenth century Connecticut substituted exhortation and censure. He was indefatigable, dogmatically sure of his beliefs, self-sacrificing in his evangelical zeal, and although he personally avoided the worst pulpit eccentricities of the revivalists, he lent his influence in the direction of emotionalism and thus encouraged the very excesses which he later condemned.

CHAPTER III

WHEELOCK AND HIS PARISHIONERS

MEANWHILE Wheelock had his pastoral duties to perform at Lebanon. The history of his association with his parishioners is unfortunately to a large extent a recital of disputes. In this respect he represents many pastors of the eighteenth century in Connecticut. His people took up pen more readily to criticise than to praise him; and he was equally ready to blame and to denounce them.

Trouble began about seven months after Wheelock had accepted the call to Lebanon. In the spring of 1735 the parishioners voted to give Wheelock thirty cords of wood a year, about twenty-five acres of farm land, two hundred pounds in bills of public credit, and a salary of one hundred and forty pounds, old tenor, a year,[1] this salary to be paid in bills of public credit *or* in provisions at certain stated prices: wheat at nine shillings a bushel, rye at seven, Indian corn at five, oats at two

[1] The following data on salaries in Connecticut are given for comparison with Wheelock's:

    (a) 1727, Woodstock, Amos Throop, £300 settlement, a salary of £100 a year, £10 for wood.

    (b) 1729, Canterbury, John Wadsworth, £150 settlement, a salary of £100, and an annual increase after the first three years of £10.

    (c) 1729, Killingly, Marston Cabot, £200 settlement, a salary of £80 increasing £5 a year to a maximum of £100, and wood.

    (d) 1735, Mortlake Society, Ephraim Avery, a salary of £120.

    (e) 1736, Woodstock, Samuel Whittlesey, £400 settlement, a salary of £150.

    (f) 1741, Cornwall, Solomon Parker, a salary of £100 to be increased annually £10 to a maximum of £160, and a tract of land.

    (g) 1743, Ashford, John Bass, £400 settlement, a salary of £200.

    (h) 1747, Plainfield, David Rowland, £700 settlement, a salary of £400, and wood. (The currency was perhaps depreciated.)

    (i) 1749, Farmington, Samuel Newell, a salary of £140, to be increased annually to a maximum in 1758 of £300, and wood.

    (j) 1756, Pomfret, Josiah Whitney, £120 settlement, a salary of £65.

    (k) 1757, Killingly, Noadiah Russel, £165 settlement, a salary of £65, and wood (Stewart, *History of Religious Education in Connecticut;* Larned, *History of Windham County*).

shillings six pence, pork at six cents a pound, and beef at four, "which species are to be the standard by which his sallery is to rise or fall, and to rise or fall proportionably as they in general rise or fall amongst us." The contract, specific as it may seem, was open to misunderstandings which embittered Wheelock's relationship with his parishioners for thirty-four years, and were the cause of much ungraciousness on his part and on theirs.

Difficulties arose shortly concerning the date of payment. Originally March 27 had been designated, but on November 11, 1735, the parish voted to change the date to January 1. This alteration, Wheelock protested, worked to his disadvantage. In a farming community provisions were less abundant as the spring came on and were consequently of greater value. On March 25 provisions would be more costly than on January 1; the parishioners were forcing him to accept provisions on the date less favorable to him. Year after year Wheelock drew up on slips of paper statements of what his salary actually was and what it should be, and time and again vainly petitioned his church to return to the date first set, March 27.

There was a second and more important difficulty. Salary was to be paid *either* in money *or* in provisions. The members of his church, Connecticut farmers, were shrewder than their twenty-four-year-old pastor with their *either, or*. Provisions were less desirable to Wheelock than money, not only because of the trouble involved in selling them but because he, as a farmer himself, stood in need of currency rather than of provisions. Wheelock explained his position on March 22, 1736, as follows:

My Good and Kind People, Friends and Neighbours:
    I never had a tho't that there was such a vote passed in the Society as that my salery should be paid in provisions till about the 4th or 5th of Jan. last but always before then understood that provisions

were only mentioned for a standard by which my salery was to rise and fall. And so I understood the committee which came to treat with me after the Society meeting in which it was voted and so I rote it down from their mouths. Not that I have the least suspicion that they had any design to impose upon me in that matter but suppose that it was a circumstance which they looked upon of but little importance and no way essential which made them not think of being particular in that matter. So that in short I suppose it was an intire mistake but after I understood how it was I was sorry being satisfied that it would labour under many inconveniences with respect to you and me for

1. It opens a door for a continual uneasiness unless there were some judicious men appointed to be judges whether the provisions brought to me be marchantable or not. Some men think that to be merchantable which others do not. I understand that I have already been much blamed by you that I did not take a hogg which was brought and offered when I was not at home and which I never saw and which I am informed was not worth much more than half the market price and I suppose you will easily see that the vote opens a door for such uneasiness unless to prevent them I wrong myself. I dont know that this is the last or only instance that there will ever be of this nature.

2. You may easily see that it wont do in any measure for me to depend upon for my families provision for (1) my families provision all ought to be secured some time before the time of the payment of them comes. (2) It is very uncertain whether there will be enough brought to supply me and if there be much provisions brought then most likely that the species will not be proportioned to sute the occasions of a family. It will be by chance if they be and besides men can generally sute themselves better than others will be likely to sute them. So that you see that I must and yet it will be most imprudent for me not to lay in for my family supplies before time of payment. And then

3. What will be brought in more will be only trouble to me which I am very loth to have. And besides you cant expect I can provide for my family without ingaging money for provisions and I must depend upon the Society for it which I shan't have if provisions are brought instead of it till they are sold which things appear

to lay a foundation for much difficulty as well as uneasiness which it seems may be all prevented by erasing that clause in the vote viz. *or provisions* and putting in the room of it *according to provisions.* Many things more might be added which shew the inconveniency of it but kind sirs I cant but think that if you weigh and well consider what has been urged you will esteem the reasons to be weighty and will see it your way to alter it. I suppose I need not say anything about the confirmation of the land to me. I shall therefore wishing you love and peace and the Presence of God subscribe myself

> Your Souls True and Real Friend and Servant
> for Christ's Sake
>
> E W

On the reverse of this copy Wheelock has written a memorandum:

> This letter was sent into the meeting and was read but they did not see cause to make any alteration of the vote and the principal reason why it was negatived was because they were afraid that there would come a time when there would be no money to pay rates with, as I'm informed.

The Society continued to pay him in provisions; by 1757, twenty-two years after his installation, the parish had paid him in currency only sixty-six pounds and fifteen shillings, lawful money. His brother-in-law, Pomeroy, had received from his parish during the same period slightly more than one hundred and seven pounds.

As though the questions of date of payment (March 27 or January 1) and of kinds of payment (money or provisions) were not sufficient to harass him, another factor was added. Currency itself was not stable, and various terms had to be kept in mind: *proclamation money*, dating from 1704; *bills of old tenor* from 1709 to about 1740, replaced by *bills of new tenor;* and (from about 1754) still another term: *lawful money*. His parishioners when they paid in currency chose to pay Wheelock in *old tenor*, thus depriving him according to his calculation of six shillings in every pound because of the depreciation.

On November 21, 1757, Wheelock wrote a lengthy complaint to his charges. Once more he objected to the change of date, to being paid in provisions, to being obliged to accept depreciated currency. But the parish was unwilling to change its procedure, and on December 14 he addressed the members again, expressing himself as willing to abide by the decision of a committee to be composed of "as crafty and severe men in your dealings as any you have to compute the matter."

A committee of three men of the type which Wheelock had specified was readily formed. It reported that the sum of six pounds and ten shillings should be paid to wipe out all arrears, and that henceforth his salary, exclusive of his wood, should be sixty pounds, ten shillings a year, lawful money. Wheelock was incensed and wrote to a member of the committee, Jonathan Trumbull, that in the opinion of some with whom he had talked the decision "was in itself a right down devilish cheat." So straitened and destitute had his life been, he wrote, that "I have never had the opportunity to study and improve by reading which my father and brethren commonly have. And I have not had fortitude eno' to resist the power of discouragement and many great disadvantages arising from and accompanying it." The reader need not be too concerned however about Wheelock's financial condition; self-pity came easily to him. And the complaint did not help him. The severe and crafty men continued to be severe and crafty, and Wheelock had to abide by their decision. This was not the only instance in which he was overreached in financial matters.

As pastor, Wheelock officiated frequently in the capacity of a judge, and when occasion demanded summoned before him and a church committee the delinquents of the parish. The summonses and testimony here set forth reveal much about the conduct of men and women in the eighteenth century. Some of the charges are grave; others would not be seriously considered today.

To Noah Webster a brother of the North Church in Lebanon

Whereas there has been a report that you are guilty of the breach of a Gospel rule in fighting with William Negus about three weeks or a month ago near the house of Noah Dewey of this parish &c. You are therefore hereby required to be present at my dwelling house tomorrow two hours before sunset to object if you have anything against the evidences that are then to be taken of the abovementioned fact and to say what you have to offer in your own vindication before me and such of the bretheren of the church as I shall desire to be present to advise and assist me in the matter.

Eleazar Wheelock Pastor of the North Parish in Lebanon Novr 21, 1937.

At a meeting of the pastor and church council August 1, 1738:—

Upon a public report that Timothy Hutchinson a brother of the church was guilty of laughing and irreverent deportment in the public worship of God on Lord's Day the 21 of May last, he appeared according to order and pleaded not guilty.

Whereupon sundry evidences testified against him, viz:—

John English testifies and says, that upon the 21 of May last, towards the close of the afternoon sermon, I saw Tim'o Hutchinson laugh or smile and continued in it some time, perhaps 3 or 4 minutes and he looked upon Mr. Wheelock while he laughed, as I thot.

Abigal English testifies and says that upon the 21 of May last, towards the close of the afternoon I saw Timothy Hutchinson smile or laugh and continued in it for some time, his countenance looked more red while he was laughing than usually it does, which I suppose was occasioned by his laughing, then he looked, as I supposed Jedidiah Bill in the face and they both looked with a very guilty countenance upon one another.

Question—Why did you think he looked upon Bill?

Ans.—When they turned their faces and eyes toward one another I thought Hutchinson increased his smiling.

44

Mary Clark testifies and says:—That on the 21 of May last towards the close of the afternoon sermon I saw Timothy Hutchinson with his handkerchief at his face so that it covered most or all of the lower part of it to his eyes, and by the looks of that part of it which I saw I thought he laughed, and so I thought when he put his handkerchief up to his face and while his handkerchief was at his face, he turned his head and upper part of his body and I thought looked upon Martha Root and I supposed it was to make her laugh, and I looked to the front gallery to see if she laughed, but she held her head down that I could not see her face, his looking there was not a trancient glance, but it was of some continuance and by the looks of his eyes and the motion of his eyelids I thought he wanted her to look at him in the face.

Abigal Clark testifies and says:—That on the 21 of May last I saw Timothy Hutchinson in sermon time stand and looked toward the opposite gallery and laughed or smiled some time, and while he was laughing or smiling he put his handkerchief to his face and by all that I could see I thought he laughed after he had his handkerchief to his face.

The above evidences made oath or a solemn declaration to the truth of their testimony on the following words, viz:—

You and each of you do solemnly declare before God, as you expect to give an account to Him at the great day, that the evidence which you have here given in, is the truth, the whole truth and nothing but the truth.

To all of which Timothy Hutchinson testifies and says:

I don't know that I looked upon anybody, but Mr. Wheelock all that sermon time and I had no disposition to laugh till Mr. Wheelock had this expression, viz—That their very horses groaned to be delivered from the service of their fates, and it was a wonder of God's mercy that they did not free themselves of it by throwing their abusive riders swift to hell &c. His speaking of the horses groaning put me in mind of a horse which I formerly used to ride which we called Old Groan when we rode him and the young woman which I carried to frolics laughed about him and I tried to leave off my laughing as soon as possibly I could, and because it was sudden and accidental and not allowed by me, I think I ought not to be obliged to make a public acknowledgment. He further says, I had no disposition to slight or ridicule either the reproof or the reprover but had a more than ordinary desire to hear what there was to be said concerning peoples frolicing and to confirm this, we bring the evidence of Ebenezer Bright, who says that Timothy Hutchinson talked the day before their frolic was and told him that he was at a loss whether it was right or not for young people to frolic.

Two questions seem to arise.

1,—Whether the cause which he assigns can be supposed to be the cause of all that laughing which the evidences testify against him.

2,—What allowance is to be made for human frailty and how much it extenuates his offence, and having weighed and considered the evidences and pleas on both sides, we are of the opinion we ought to give credit to what Brother Hutchinson affirms is the cause of his laughing, but yet think that it is not sufficient to excuse him, but are of the opinion:

1,—That his laughing and continuing in it so long as it appears he did from the various postures that evidences testify him to be in while he laughed a very light and unsuitable temper of mind, especially considering he was nearly concerned in the reproof that was given.

2,—That the whole assembly might justly think that he laughed at the word preached and we think that it lies upon him to remove the scandal.

3rd,—That if he had done what he could to refrain from it he would not have continued so long and have been so open in it, and that his so doing was a breach of Devine Rule and that it is necessary that he publicly make the following declaration of acknowledgment:

I acknowledge I was guilty of irreverently smiling and laughing in the public worship of God on the 21 day of May last, whereby the people of God were justly offended and had reason to think by the time and circumstances of it that I either laughed at the reproofs that were then given or at the reprover, which I declare was not the case, but my laughing was occasioned by the occuring of some thing that were brought to my mind, but yet I do not justify but condemn myself in it and acknowledge it was dishonoring to God and his people, for which I now ask your forgiveness and desire to be more sensible of my sins before God herein.

It is also judged necessary that he be suspended from the communion of the Church in special ordinance till he will publicly make the above written acknowledgment.

> Eleazar Wheelock, Pastor
> with the advice and concurrence
> of the church council.

To Samuel Sprague of Lebanon, North Parish

Whereas you were required by the pastor of this church by a citation dated November 19, 1739, to appear before the pastor and the church council to give in evidence of the truth of what you know relating to Joseph Pinno his being guilty of fornication some time last spring, but you refused and neglected to come and the pastor and church council were informed that you spake contemptuously of the authority of Christ in his church in saying that you did not intend to come and that the pastor had no authority to require you to come and that you would not regard or mind him and the like, which is plainly contrary to the rule of Gods word which requires of you obedience and subjection to the ministers of Christ in such matters Heb. 13, 17. Obey them that have the rule over you and submitt yourselves for they watch for your souls as they that must give account and such disorder and disobedience tend to the destruction and subvertion of all government and order in the church.

You are therefore hereby required to appear before the pastor at his dwelling house in Lebanon North Parish on Wensday the sixth day of February next at one of the clock in the afternoon then and there to hear what evidences shall say against you and to offer what you have to say in your own vindication for not appearing according to order as is mentioned above.

> Eleazar Wheelock, Pastor

Dated at Lebanon N. Parish, Jan. 28, 1739/40

Mr. James Wright a Brother of the Church of Christ in Lebanon North Parish

You are desired to read the above written citation to the above named Samuel Sprague and also to cite Nathaniel Loomis and Mary his wife and Thomas White to appear at the time above mentioned to give evidence in the case.

Eleazar Wheelock, Pastor

Revent Sor:

This coms to inform you that Mr. Right left the sitation which you gave to him which me to red to Mr. Sprague and i red it in his hearin and he desired to see it and i gave it to him to look over and he seamed to be angerey that you sent for him so sodenlly and toale me that i should not have it and i yous all the argement that could but he will not let me have it. So no more. i remaine youe frind and servent

Nathaniel Loomys

Mr. Sprague: I received a line or two from you just now in which you complain of hard treatment in that you are required to appear without more time to prepare for trial. You say you are sure it is neither law nor reason. I answer.

1. You have been told of the affair long ago and if you had had any good excuse for your not appearing before according to order you have doubtless prepard it before now.

2. As to its being neither law nor reason the civil law gives no time at all in such cases but takes them right away and there is all reason in it for when a man committs an offense he is as able to excuse himself ordinarily in the time of it as ever he will be if he has any excuse that is just and good. But that is not the case with you. You have had a great while to think of it and your affair was fresh and publishd in such a manner that you canot but know that there was a necessity of taking cognizence of it unless we would give up all rule and government in the church. For my own part I can assure you I have no hatred or ill-will toward you and shall be heartily glad if you have a reasonable excuse and plea to make for yourself and shall be ready to make all possible allowance for you that can be reasonable and I am perswaded that every one of the church council can say the same. Therefore dont now turn your face towards the wilderness but submitt yourself and be injenuous.

You will not repent it I give you this advice as your souls friend and if you were my own brother I could not advise you better.

I am your real friend and well wisher

E. Wheelock.

Verdict on Samuel Sprague.

Having considered the evidences and his reason we are of opinion 1. That he has not paid that deference and respect to the authority of Christ in his church in not taking sutable care to give the reasons of his not appearing before.

2. It appears that he has given people occasion to think that it was obstinacy and contempt of the authority of the church by often disputing against it, but inasmuch as he pleads that his design to appear and was necessitated unexpectedly to be absent and that he could not appear without great heavy loss and that the time when he heard of the meeting that he could not come without breaking a promise that he had made to pay money which he pleads that he thot that he ought to fulfill rather than to appear before the pastor and church council especially considering that he had not been cited and had only heard of it transiently. He declares his submission and subjection to the authority of the church and had never any design to slight and contemn it.

Upon the whole we are of opinion that he may be dismissed with an admonition to consider more the importance of subjection and obedience to the authority of Christ in his church, and also that he be more cautious for the time to come that he dont by any discourse or disputing against the authority of the church give people occasion to think that he has light thots of it and that he evidences declaration of submission and subjection to be hearty and sincere by practically paying greater deference to it for the time to come.

And whereas the council were informed that when N. L. read the citation to him to appear here he took it of him and refused to let him have it upon interrogation he acknoledges that it was a rash and imprudent thing in him and the fruit of a bad temper that he was then in that he did not consider that he did and dos not justify but condemn it.

49

ELEAZAR WHEELOCK

Testimony

At a meeting of the pastor and church council July 21, 1743 upon a publick report that Mr William Gager a brother of this church was scandalously guilty of drinking strong drink to excess sometime about the beginning of this month he appeared pursuant to a citation and pleaded not guilty.

John English testifies and says that on the 1st day of July towards evening I was riding up the street and heard Mr. Gager calling the sheep he spoke with an uncommon (*mutilated*) to take more notice of him. When I lookd upon him I saw him real as he walkd and seemd to go crosslegg'd. So much that I expected that he would fall. His countenance was more reed than common.

Sarah Wheelock testifies that on the day above said towards night she saw Mr Gager walking thro' the green and falterd in his going. He walkd as tho his joynts were very weak and calld the sheep with an unusual voice loud and drawling. After some time he came up to a rock towards Mr Englishes and sat upon a rock sometime and calld the sheep after the same manner. Jos. Clark testifies that on the day above said in the afternoon I went with John Maltby and Moses Gun to repeat our lessons to Mr Gager. When I came in I observed his countenance lookd very reed and his breath smelt of strong liquor. When we askd him if he could hear us recite he said yes. His speach was not as usual. His words were drawling and his talk all the while we were there was inconnected. When we came to recite he could not keep the line. We went several times to shew him where the place was. His sentances he would repeat several times. We did not say half our lesson to him by reason of what I thot was the fruit of strong drink in him. I dont remember that I observed anything amiss in his going. His treatment of the children seamd odd, stampd loud and said nothing for a good while and then said something that I thought was neither Lattin nor English.

John Maltby testifies to all that Joseph Clark has said above. Moses Gun testifies to the same that the Joseph Clark dos excepting *as usual* for he never saw him so as to know him before and says that he thought nothing that Mr Gager was in drink before Joseph Clark intimated it to him.

Qn. What drink did his breath smell of: put to Clark and Maltby.

A. I cant say what sort but am satisfied that it was rum or cyder. To these Mr Gager refusd to make any reply.

Having considered the evidences we are of opinion that the evidences are sufficient to support the charge of scandalous drinking against him and we think that he ought to make publick Gospel satisfaction for it.

Testimony Regarding Captain Smalley and his slave, Phyllis

Jacob Spafford testifies and says I was at work for Capt. Smalley in his pasture in July, 1745. His negro girl Phillis came up to bring us some drink. I ask'd him why he did not yoke up his negros, and told him they would play the rogue together. He said that he hated her like a toad and said she was a lying creture and represented her as such a lying creture that there was no dependence upon her and he intended to sell her upon that account and I have divers times heard him say she was a lying creture.

Rebeckah Spafford testifies and says that four years ago last summer Capt. Smalley or his wife sent their negro Phyllis to Father Smalleys upon an errand neither father nor mother were at home. She never did the errand which was to borrow something but went home and as we were inform'd, told at home that she could not have the thing she came for, and said that she had been much abused by us. My parents were concernd about it and soon after Capt. Smalley came to my fathers house. My father (as I remember) told him that he heard about Phyllis's lying and was afraid he would believe it and be offended with us. He replied Coz. Smalley I would not have you be a bit concernd about it. She is such a lying creture that there is no trust to be put to what she says. I don't know what to do with her. Said he I have lickd her for lying a great many times and he didn't see as it signifyd anything, for she will lie while I am thrashing her for lying. Said he I was thrashing for lying once, and she said Master dont strike me one blow more and I will give you a 1,000 pds. Said he, I said you lying creture where do you think you shall get a 1,000 lb. The girl replid, I have it by me now in my pockett. And it was comminly known and talk'd by their family viz. Capt. Smalleys, that she was a lying creture. This is to the best of my remembrance the truth.

ELEAZAR WHEELOCK

To Ephraim Loomis Junior a Brother of the Second Church of Christ in Lebanon

Whereas there is a publick report that you have been scandalously and very repeatedly guilty of breaches of the 9th Command viz. lying, in that on or about the month of July, A. D. 1752, you declard and said that you had been (meaning in a late journey you had taken) togather with Leiut. Edgerton and his son, Mr. Joseph Bingham Mr Cleaveland & others of Norwich and with Sam Davise a negro to Plumb Island, and that you there with them had found and taken out of the earth a golden candlestick of great value which you was assisted in finding by said Samuel Davise, and that you with them had brought it to Norwich and had taken out the stones of the cellar wall of said Leiut. Edgerton and made a place for said candlestick and wrapped it in a quilt and put it in, and put up the stones of the wall so that none could discover where it was placed. And that said price was to be divided among said parteners and that said negro was one and to have a larger share than the rest because it was by his intelligence principally that it was found, and many other circumstances and that you have repeated this story or to this effect to divers persons and at many times for many months togather, and that in so solomn a manner as that thro' the advantage of your Christian profession you gaind full credit with diverse persons insomuch that they trusted to your word and dealt with you according to that beleif that you were true and honist in what you had so solomly and repeatedly asserted, whereby they have been greatly injured in their outward estate, and whereby you have also been scandalously guilty of a breach of the 8th Command, in that in all these reports and practise agreable to them beforementiond you have gone contrary to your light, knoledge and conscience, with a wicked design to deceive and defraud your neighbour. Whereby God has been greatly dishonoured and great reproach brought upon the holy religion of which you are a professor. And the glory of God the reputation of our holy religion and your good require that said reports should be enquired into that your innocence or guilt therein may publickly appear.

These are therefore to require and command you to appear before the pastor and church council at my dwelling house in Lebanon on Thursday next at one of the clock in the afternoon then and there to hear what evidences shall testify against you and to offer what you have to say in your own vindication.

By Eleazer Wheelock Pastor of the Second Church in Lebanon Dated, May 27, 1754

Disturbing news came to Wheelock from his birthplace. As he wrote to Stephen Williams (August 18, 1737):

> It is common talk at Windham that old Goody Fullsom (the woman that Mr. Clap has had so much difficulty in the church about and at last excommunicated), is a w--ch and indeed there are many stories which Mr. Clap has told me of her that look very dark. Esquire Abbies widow has been and is still very sick and sometimes delirious has been very much tormented with her as well as many others that have been sick about there. Mr. Clap told me yesterday that on last Sabbath there came in an ill looken dog into the room where Mrs. Abbie was sick and her brother that was there took up a broom staff and gave it a blow as hard as he could strike. The dog went away very lame. At the same instant as near as they could come at it the old woman being at meeting at Scotland[1] roard out in the meeting house with a pain in her sholder and when Sherriff Huntington the bonesetter come to feal of it the next day he found the bones much broken insomuch that he could hear them rattle in the skin.

Wheelock probably exceeded the paternalism that was allowed a pastor even in the eighteenth century. In 1750 a church council of five ministers was assembled at Lebanon to consider eight charges brought against him by his parishioners. The statement of the findings is unfortunately not explicit on all the charges, and the document itself is badly mutilated. We learn that in the opinion of the council Wheelock did not have a right to act as he did (the action is not specified); that he was not blamable in objecting to the disputes and debates among his parishioners; that Captain Smalley and his family were too prejudiced to give unbiased evidence; that Wheelock had a

---

[1] Originally part of the neighboring town, Windham.

right to judge when it was his duty to judge, but in view of the division in the church, the council advised dropping the Smalley case. The council also concluded that Thomas Lyman, one of the pastor's accusers, "was much to blame in reflecting upon Mr. Wheelock as if he kept false records, and that his preaching did more hurt than good," and finally advised the brethren to "bury and overlook what they have taken grievously in time past from one another, and to be at peace among themselves."

In 1755 Thomas Lyman, abetted by Abel Holbrook, complained to the Windham Association that Wheelock had affirmed that there was a vote of the church against one Amos Woodworth, whereas "not one single brother acted in the matter"; that he had charged his people with the sins of the rebellious Corah, Dathan, and Abiram, as recorded in the sixteenth chapter of Numbers; and that he had been remiss in two instances of admitting members to the church and in one of baptising. One is inclined to hope that Wheelock did indeed compare these carping critics to the insurgents mentioned in the accusation. Again, a female parishioner objected to the ordination of Oliver Noble because he had called a modest young woman "soft or softly, thereby intimating and insinuating that she was indiscreet and unlernt and of an awkward or clownish behavior." And in 1769, having informed a certain Hannah Dunham that "your tongue if not your heart seems to be set on fire of hell," Wheelock received from her an incoherent letter condemning him, and a still more incoherent poem to this effect:

> I cant my fathers hous come near
> my shepards tent pass by
> but hell and potash give a smoak
> and igin arrors fly.

Bitterness of this type is displayed often in the extensive correspondence of the period preserved in the archives of

Dartmouth College; the foregoing represent only a small part of the accusations and counter-accusations. Now and then we find a pleasant note: school children invite him to preach to them ("we are very young and very ignorant"); and Ronald Marvin "out of that plenty of creature comforts wherewith God hath been pleased to bless me" bestows on Wheelock "a certain horse herewith delivered unto him to use as absolutely in all respects as if he were his own for and during the whole time of their existing together here in this animal life." Finally, from his parishioners trying belatedly in 1767 to placate their pastor and to retain the charity school in Lebanon, comes the phrasing, "our minister the light of our eyes and joy of our hearts under whose ministrations we have sat with grate delight—whose labours have been so acceptable and we trust profitable for a long time." But Time, alas, in cataloguing the features of the parishioners has omitted many of the kindlier lineaments. And many of the pastor's, too. It is not easy to think of Wheelock, in the words of the historian Trumbull, who was his close friend, as possessed of a "mild and winning aspect."

In spite of his difficulties with the parish, Wheelock stayed on; not that he wished to, but his parishioners were unwilling to grant him a dismissal. Nevertheless, Wheelock was determined to move; his Indian school required a site other than Lebanon could offer. In January, 1765, he relinquished his salary, that is, he freed his parishioners from their legal obligations to him, and expressed himself as content, pending the installation of a successor, to accept "none but what the church and society are pleased to give me of their own accord." Strangely enough, the parish did not know that he had offered to give up his salary: on December 2, 1766, the church committee asked him whether he was willing to relinquish it if they agreed to accept a supply minister. Wheelock now tried to find a successor, although his letter to James Thompson, whom the parishioners were considering, was hardly encouraging: to him Wheelock wrote that the church had been criminally negligent in not paying him. Thompson decided not to accept. In regard to Ephraim Judson, another candidate, fresh trouble arose: church members accused Wheelock of falsifying his word concerning the obtaining of Judson on trial. At last, in April, 1770, Wheelock was dismissed, and soon after migrated to Hanover, New Hampshire. But as late as August of that year Bezaleel Woodward wrote, "Parish people continue in statu quo—revilings dont yet cease."

CHAPTER IV

WE turn abruptly from Eleazar Wheelock, pastor, to view him as a householder and farmer in the town of Lebanon. Our information is derived largely from his correspondence and his other private documents. Of itself this writing was a heavy task. Now and then, when his duties became too much for him or his hand pained him so that he was unable to use a quill, he employed an amanuensis; but the bulk of this material is written in his own hand, a fast, sloping handwriting, the letters usually neatly formed and incredibly small, with interlineations so closely packed that often a reading-glass is necessary and good eyes soon tire in deciphering them. First and second drafts of many letters have been preserved, as well as verbatim copies, also in his handwriting, of letters, minutes of church and school meetings, recipes, business receipts, and proposed charters. Herein are to be found the data from which we can reconstruct his life. Data of fact, of event, abound; important, too, is the light which Wheelock sheds on his own personality; he who was accustomed to probe in public the hearts of his parishioners was equally ready to express in letters the emotions, and often the bad temper, which business dealings aroused in him.

He had a numerous family. By his first marriage at the age of twenty-four to Mrs. Sarah (Davenport) Maltby he became the stepfather of a son and two daughters: John, Sarah, and Betty. In addition he had by this marriage six other children, three of whom died in infancy. The stepdaughter Sarah was an ailing child and suffered from severe headaches for which not much could be done: "she has been helped by her wearing jewels but it may be it is only because the weather has been of late more cold." The account of her death is contained in the letter which Wheelock wrote to Stephen Williams on March 28, 1745.

Reverend and very Dear Brother

The within written[1] has been by me ever since the date for want of an opportunity. for conveyance. The king of terrors broke the prison doors for our dear child, and set her dear soul at liberty, in the world of spirits (and, I trust and beleive) the spirit of the just made perfect, whither it had been before reaching and longing to go, on the last day of Feby. about 3½ o'clock P. M. The conflict was very short death had but little to do when it came to lay on its cold hand. She had the free use of her reason to the last and met death with the utmost composure, presence, and calmness of mind. God had before by many visits of His grace and clear scriptural fruits of the spirit sweetly forcd her to beleive and know her intrest in his favour and love there was no appearance of a boasting bragging assurance which we sometimes see in some, but full of humility, self abasement, charity, meekness, patience, &c. Some of her last words were. O! how good it will be to sleep in Jesus. Well I am going to leave all sin. O how sweet is the tho't I shall leave all my bad here, &c. I trust we have had and shall have the sympathizing sorrows and prayers of you both our dear brother and sister and yours. We salute you all most affectionately. I am

Your very unworthy brother

Eleazar Wheelock

P.S. Please to present our sincere regards to dear Mr Reynold, and Madam.

Yours of last month which is the only one since I saw you, came to my hand but 3 or 4 days ago. I hear you are to be this week at Suffield &c. We have found here that when people begin to leave councill they leave God and God leaves them. Things in this place thro' the pure mercy of God are comfortable. I'll imbrace the first good opportunity to send your book &c. I ask your pardon for detaining it so long.

Yours E. W.

[1] A consoling letter to Wheelock from Benjamin Pomeroy.

I am much exercised with my old pain and distress in my head whereby I am much unfitted for any service. Betty is much out of health, I think her sisters death has been sanctified to her. She has had, I trust, truly the consolation of God, &c. I shall send your book by Mr. Oliver Warner of Hadley.

Yours E. W.

John Maltby, the stepson, entered Yale College in 1742, having taken with him a letter of introduction from Wheelock. It is evident from this letter, and from other documents as well, that Wheelock and President Clap were not sympathetic to one another; in this same year Clap had refused to let Wheelock preach at Yale.

Reverend Sir

I have herewith sent my son whom I committ to your care under God. I beleive you will find him (and the young man, viz. Clark who comes with him) studious, sober, peacible, and orderly. It is with no small concern that I send him, cheifly on religious accounts, being credibly informd of the prevalency of Arminian principles in college which, I know, exceedingly suit the pride and corruptions of the carnal mind. And also I cant but think your princpls and practise in some respects contrary to the natural rights and liberty of all mankind, and especially to what has been boasted as one of the glories of our college, that they breathe a catholick air. You know Sir that my principles are catholick and that I hate everything in religion that has the least shew or appearance of tyranny and oppression and therefore will pardon me in writing as I do. I have a great desire that these young men should have the liberty of hearing such ministers of Christ as they desire to hear when they have convenient opportunities of it. When I consider how fruitless the request has been when made by others who have more interest in yourself than I have my hopes are cutt off at once.

After I saw you I had some encouragement of their boarding at Mr. Cooke's. If that should fail you may remember I spoke to you for the south garrett. I earnestly desire they may live togather and if they should live in college, may I begg one favour of you, viz. that my son may be waiter in the Hall. It may be of advantage to me, and I think my poverty demands it if that be the rule (as I suppose it is) that you go by in that matter. My outward circumstances are very strait and difficult by reason of a very numerous and chargeable family, and also you know, I am deprived of my living, at least of the benefit of a law to secure it to me[1] (with how much justice and righteousness the world will see another day) whereby I have suffered much allready and am like to suffer more as religion declines among us.

My son has been very infirm and can bear but little hardship. I dont know but he will need to ride sometimes. If his state of health should require it I begg the favour of you that he may have the liberty. Reverend Sir I heartily wish your prosperity and the presence of God with you in your important concerns. And tho we have the unhapiness to think differently in some things yet I am Reverend Sir

Your assured friend and very humble servant

Eleazar Wheelock

P.S. I have seen a copy of Mr. Eliots letter to you and yours to him. And as to one clause in his viz. respecting my advising you not to go to college[2] it is an absolute ——. I never said so nor thot so but the contrary and allways manifested to you that I thot it your duty to go. And I have appeald to the whole association who have judged that Mr. Eliot was wrong in that matter.

Wheelock's first wife died on November 13, 1746, and of her death he wrote poignantly:

She is gone, the dear wife of my boosom, my lover and friend, the desire of my eyes, the dearest enjoyment on earth, the dear partner of all my joys and sorrows, hopes and fears. The most dutifull, compassionate, and tenderhearted and faithfull of all women now sleeps in Jesus, and every apartment in my house mourns her ab-

---

[1] Wheelock means that he is *liable* to be deprived of his salary because of the law against itinerants.

[2] Thomas Clap was minister of the Congregational Church at Windham (1726–1739). He was installed as rector of Yale College in 1740.

sence. Oh! how empty, empty now is this world. Oh! that the Lord would now fill up this vacancy. Oh! that His Righteous Holy Hand might be sanctified to me and mine. I beleive she was struck with death before my neighbour English went from home last Thursday and after the greatest agony and distress of body breathed out her dear soul about 3 o'clock P. M. and was interred after the Rev. Mr Meacham had preachd a sermon Friday towards night. Pitty me pitty mine and my dear friend, for the Holy Hand of the Lord hath touched us. I and mine salute you both and dear children most heartily and affectionately. And ask your prayers and the prayers of your people. I am

Your sore broken, afflicted brother and very humble servant

Eleazar Wheelock

Nov. 17th 1746.

Wheelock's grief was soon assuaged by his courtship of the woman who was soon to become his second wife, Mary Brinsmead. Just what the difficulties of the courtship were cannot now be known, but that there were difficulties is clear from a passage in a letter of William Gaylord, pastor at Wilton: "I rejoyce greatly to hear by Mr. Bill that thro divine goodness you have so far recovred your health and hope, by what he tells me, that you may yet thro the same divine goodness yet tast much of the sweetness of that invaluable blessing and wish above all things that your soul may be in health and prosper. I am sorry for any difficulties that you meat with in the pursuit in the very sweet and desirable blessings of another kind, but I hope you are likely to succeed and get over all of them. They will perhaps but only make it sweeter when obtained, and convince you that there is more truth than you was aware of in the vulgar saying *difficilia qua pulchra*. I am glad to hear that you bear these tryals very chearfully and well and hope in short time to hear of a good conclusion of the whole matter."

In the meanwhile Wheelock had married Mary Brinsmead,

on November 21, 1747, three days before Gaylord wrote his encouraging note. A local versifier, Martha (Wadsworth) Brewster paid her tribute. In *Poems on Divers Occasions,* published in 1757, we find in the midst of poems on the four ages of man, on the Last Judgment, on Braddock's defeat, and on the noble man, a wedding posy, which she had enclosed previously in a letter to Wheelock:

Reverend and Honored Sir

Trusting your clemency will pardon whats amiss and accept of a sincere wish I venture to present the inclosed lines (tho rude and indigisted). They bring only a faint lineament of her heart who is with all dutifull respect and affection

Yours

Martha Brewster

> All sweet fruition now betide
> The venerable groom and bride
> Fresh olives by a noble vine
> May bless the world for future times.
> And may the King of Glory grace
> These nuptials with His heavenly rays
> Of joy, and happiness sublime,
> Converting water into wine.
> Your mutual loves let still increase
> And we be blest with truth and peace.
> Still guide us as you've ever done
> And late recieve a glorious crown.
> Serraphic love your hearts inspire
> In consort join the heavenly choir,
> The fairer palm the higher crown
> The lower will ye lay it down.

Of this second marriage five children were born. Consequently by 1759 Wheelock's family consisted of two stepchildren, three children by his first marriage, his second wife, and five children by her. John Wheelock, the third child by the second marriage, succeeded his father as president of Dartmouth College.[1]

There were other members of what Wheelock called his "family." According to the custom of the time, Wheelock accepted certain students at his home and prepared them for college, and principally for Yale; just how many, cannot now be ascertained.

Various slaves also formed part of the household. There was a negro, by name of Fortune, described as being twenty-two or twenty-three years of age, whom Wheelock bought in 1743 for two hundred and forty-five pounds. (Six years later Fortune is listed in Wheelock's handwriting as one of "those who dont desire an alteration of our church constitution.") Four bills of sale serve to identify other slaves:

To all people to whom these presents shall come, know ye that I William Clark of Plymouth in the County of Plymouth, yeoman, for and in consideration of the sum of fifty pounds lawfull money to me before the ensealing hereof paid, or securd to be paid, the receipt whereof I do hereby acknowledge and myself therewith satisfyed, and paid, do by these presents bargain sell and convey unto the Revd Mr. Eleazer Wheelock of Lebanon in the Colony of Conecticutt, clerk, my negro man named Ishmael, being a servant for life, to hold to him the said Eleazer and his heirs executors administrators and assigns; against me and my heirs executors and administrators and against the lawfull claims of all other persons whatso-

[1] The children by the first marriage were: (1) Theodora (b. May 23, 1736). She married (a) Alexander Phelps (b) Capt. John Young, and died in 1810. (2) Eleazar (b. Aug. 14, 1737), who died young. (3) Ruth (b. 1740, d. Dec. 5, 1831) married Rev. William Patten, June 9, 1758. (4) Ralph (b. August 18, 1742, d. Feb. 7, 1817), an epileptic. (5), (6) two children who died unnamed.

The children by the second marriage were: (1) Mary (b. Oct. 9, 1748, N.S., d. March 26, 1807). Her marriage to Bezaleel Woodward (1772) was the first recorded in Hanover. (2) Abigail (b. Dec. 21, 1751, d. 1818) married Professor Sylvanus Ripley of Dartmouth College. (3) John (b. Jan. 28, 1754, d. April 4, 1817); (4) Eleazar (b. Aug. 17, 1756, d. Dec. 7, 1811); (5) James (b. March 5 or 6, 1759, d. Jan. 14, 1835). I am indebted to Doctor G. D. Frost of Hanover for this information.

ever, hereby covenanting that the said Ishmael, servant for life, is well and sound and free from any incumbrances, and I the said William, do hereby warrant the said Ishmael as a servant for life to the said Eleazer Wheelock and his heirs and assigns against all persons whatsoever. Witness my hand and seal February the 7th 1757

William Clark

Signd sealed and delivered
in presence of
  Silas Morton
  Benj. Warren

Know all men by these presents that we Timothy Kimbal of Coventry in the County of Windham and Elisha Wales of Ashford in said county for a valuable consideration received of Mr. Eleazr Whelock of Lebanon in said county have given granted bargained and sold and by these presents do fully freely and absolutely give grant and bargain sell and confirm unto him the said Eleazr Whelock and to his heirs and assigns forever a certain negro man named Sippy being the same which said Kimbal bought of said Whelock the 22nd day of April 1760, to have and to hold the said negro man to him the said Whelock his heirs &c. as a slave for life against all claims and demands whatsoever as witness our hands and seals this 27th day of October 1761.

Timothy Kimball

In presents of us
  John Huntington   Elisha Wales
  Nathl Wales Jr

Know all men by these presents that I Peter Spencer of East Haddam in the county of Hartford and Coloney of Connecticut in New England, for and in consideration of Sixty-five Pounds Lawful Money paid to my full satisfaction by Eleazar Wheelock of Lebanon in the county of Windham and Coloney aforesaid have given granted bargained sold and by the presents do give grant bargain sell convey and confirm to the said Wheelock his heirs and assigns for life my negro man servant named Brister aged about twenty-one years, to have and to hold the same as a good indefeasible estate, to his and their own proper use and behoof. And furthermore

I do for myself my heirs &c covenant to and with the said Wheelock his heirs &c that at and untill the signing and sealing of these presents I am well serv'd of the premises and have good right to bargain and sell the same as is above expressed and that he said Brister is of a healthy and sound constitution and is free from any distemper or disorder of body or mind that may prejudice his usefulness in the capacity of a slave. In witness whereof I have hereunto set my hand and seal this 26th day of April AD 1760.

Test   { Hobart Estabrook   Peter Spencer
        { Jerusha Estabrook

Know all men by these presents that I, Ann Morison of Hartford in the County of Hartford and Colony of Connecticut in New England for and in consideration of the sum of seventy five pounds lawfull money of said Colony to me in hand paid by Eleazar Wheelock of Lebanon in the County of Windham and Colony aforesaid Clerk the receipt whereof I do acknowledge and myself therewith contented have and by these presents do bargain, sell, make over and deliver in open market a negro man named Exeter of the age of forty eight years a negro woman named Chloe of the age of thirty five years and a negro male child named Hercules of the age of about three years, all slaves for life. To have and to hold the above described negros unto him the said Eleazar Wheelock and to his heirs and assigns for and during the term of their said slaves natural lives free and clear of all incumbrances whatsoever. And furthermore I the said Ann Morison do hereby covenant by these presents to warrant and defend the said negros unto him the said Eleazar Wheelock and to his heirs and assigns against the legal claim or claims of all persons, whatsoever. In witness whereof I have hereunto set my hand and seal this thirteenth day of May AD 1762. Signed sealed and delivered

George Smith   Ann Morison
Benj. Payne

Memorandum, May 13th 1762. That the said Ann Morison doth covenant and agree that whereas the above said negro woman hath been sometime past affected with a rheumatic difficulty, that if that difficulty should return upon her, by means whereof she be disabled from business that then she shall abate five pounds lawfull money on the note given for the above sum of seventy five pounds of even date with these presents.

George Smith   Ann Morison
Benj. Payne

In some notes jotted down just before his death, Wheelock recorded his intention of bequeathing Brister, along with certain other slaves, Archelaus, Selinda, Anna, "and the infant child," to his son John as part compensation for John's care of his mother. Brister had already been promised his freedom and a farm provided he could find a wife; in 1779, six months after Wheelock's death, Brister inquired from Hanover about a negress in Connecticut by name of Selinda Wealch. To him she wrote: "Sir, I understand by Marster Bingham that he rec'd a letter from you concerning me &c. I am very well contented here but should be more happy to enjoy my freedom which I hope to obtain soon by your assistance. I pray you to come down as soon as you can conveniently and settle matters with Marster Bingham. I am very well at present. Please to give my love to all." Whether or not the pair married is not known.

Exeter, called *the Spotted African* because "upon his face were several spots of a copper color of more than an inch in diameter," was put on the market by Wheelock in 1765, together with his wife Chloe and their children. As Wheelock describes them:

These certify that the bearer, Exeter, negro man, servant to the subscriber, has liberty to seek him a new master, for himself his wife and little daughter about or near two years old. Said Exeter is a well healthy man and as good a man for business, will do as much as any man I ever imployed, and understands all parts of husbandry work well, has a fine resolution, and is as great a stranger to weariness as ever I saw, and I had rather have him in my business than any of his colour I ever knew; excepting on account of the violence of natural temper.

He is honest, manly, kind, neighbourly when out of his passions. And is a fellow of truth so far as ever I have discovered excepting when in his passions, and at such times he will lie, and sometimes swear. He is about fifty years old. His wife is about thirty-eight years old and is good tempered and understands woman's business well. The child is very likely. Whoever will give for said negroes sixty pounds shall have them, provided a Christian education be secured for the child, and the parents be not deprived of the full enjoyment of the means of Grace, or if the payment be good I will take something less. I have also a son of his in his 7th year whom I have kept at school till he is almost become a good reader, with a design if his abilities and disposition shall prove such than I can do it with safety, to give him his freedom at the age of 28 years and accomodate him to live in the world, and take care of his parents if they shall need; if any desire to purchase said boy with his parents they may.

Further information about Exeter's temper is gleaned from a warrant issued in Lebanon against him, citing him as "giltey of grate abuses to your wife Cloe and you let your bead temper rage, so that you are trublesom to His Majestys good to people." In spite of his temper Exeter was known in the village of Hanover as a "man of piety and respectability." There both he and Chloe died in 1783.

Brief mention is made of a slave named Peggy, bequeathed in 1767 to his daughter Mary, and of Dinah, whom Wheelock bought in 1769 for fifty pounds sterling, on condition that the purchase price plus interest be returned if she should "die or prove lame or useless." Of another slave Nando, in whom Wheelock seems to have had a share, it is recorded that he abused his wife and thus forfeited in Wheelock's opinion any claim to freedom. In 1775 Wheelock offered to provide for Nando's wife if the other part owners paid him a weekly sum, and he was willing to give Nando a farm or employment—"but he must expect to be under the laws of Christ and this province and not live lawless as he pleases." And, finally, in 1776 Wheelock agreed, but reluctantly, because he had "heard much of setting them free," to buy a slave on deferred payments.

Wheelock treated his slaves well. As is evident from the references already made, he provided a secular and religious education of a sort for them, and was on occasion ready to give a slave his freedom if the slave proved competent and law-abiding. And several times in his letters he sends his love not only to the members of his family but also to his slaves.

The farm motif runs throughout Wheelock's life. As a boy he had been brought up on a farm; he was installed in a parish of farmers, and during his pastorate in Lebanon, lived on a farm. He insisted on training his charity students in "husbandry," and after he had removed to Hanover he farmed extensively.

Wheelock's landholdings in Connecticut were considerable. In Lebanon he owned about two hundred acres, including the twenty-five which he had received when installed. From his father he had inherited a three-hundred-acre farm in Windham, and by his first and second wives he had acquired various tracts which have not been fully identified. One can therefore readily appreciate why he continually urged his parishioners to pay him not in farm goods but in currency.

Much of the farm work Wheelock himself superintended, and without slackening his attention to his clerical duties. Today we hear so much about the rush of modern life and the lack of time that there is a tendency to look back on this eighteenth century minister as a man of comparative leisure, going about his duties in an unharassed manner. The contrary is true. Wheelock was hurried, and he felt that he was hurried. Frequently we come across comments such as "I have but a moment to write," "I am in the midst of affairs," "I am in addition to my hurry about haying a harvest, oblig'd to cover my barn at Windham before the man can put his grain into it which stands in the fields much expos'd." Undoubtedly the engagements of a modern minister in a country town make much less demand on his time and on his energy.

At times Wheelock rented his farms, writing out in detail the terms of the lease:

The conditions upon which you shall have my farm in Windham are nearly these following, viz.

I will put on team sufficient for the business to be done upon the farm, of which team I propose a breeding mare shall be part. Also five or six cows, when I can get them. Also 40 sheep or more. Also husbandry tools, viz. cart, ploughs, harrow and chains, and will pay all the taxes for the whole.

I will let you have yearly an acre of land for flax. And the labour of a good hand a fortnit in the spring to assist in making fences. And also yards for all sorts of sauce to be used in your family. I will also put on swine sufficient stores and fatting.

You shall manage and improve the whole according to rules of good husbandry, and render me the one half of the produce of the farm of all sorts excepting as aforesaid and what is necessary for the support or fatting the stock, also seed for the land. And the one half of the meet of all sorts, and the one half of the wool and increase of the sheep yearly.

You shall have liberty to use the team for your own profit off from the farm. And you shall keep the stock and tools in repair and return them as good as when you received them. And you shall be at the expence of getting and securing hay enough to keep the stock through the winter I providing the grass abroad till there will be enough cut upon the farm and pay for cutting and securing the hay in labour upon the farm.

I will have liberty to use the team in my own business as much as you shall use them more than in the business of the farm if I shall need them. And if I don't you shall not be accountable for your use of them. Liberty to keep (*torn*) for your families use, and after two years experience on the premises eithr party shall have liberty to ask for an alteration of any circumstances, and come to a new agreement.

ELEAZAR WHEELOCK

In one of the most delightful letters of the Dartmouth archives Wheelock unburdens himself to Benjamin Pomeroy regarding an unkindly neighbor who had mistreated Wheelock's oxen. Could charity be sweeter than this of the orphan calves which cheerfully resigned their hay to the starving oxen? These creatures are not mere beasts of burden to Wheelock: they are abused colleagues, although his solution, tentatively offered in the last paragraph of the letter, seems drastic.

Jan. 3^{d} 1757

Dear Brother

We find a law of God Deut 25:4 *Thou shalt not muzel the ox when he treadeth out the corn.* Which law I suppose has a foundation in the nature and fitness of things, and that in point of justice and gratitude such liberty is due to the ox for his own support, comfort and refreshment, while he labours. And there appears a fitness in it, as well as pointed out in the precept, that all who labour should live of the things about which they labour, and I think the precept also shews of what account justice and gratitude are with God; even towards the brutal creatures, from whom we receive (tho' comparitively small) advantage. The Apostle referring to the same law, says 1 Cor. 9. 10. *And doth God take care for oxen.* In the light of these Scriptures, I have tho't on the case between me and my neighbour, as impartially as a party and an interested person can. But being willing to support that my judgment is more or less biased, thro' my relation to the cause, chuse to submit it to your disinterested and impartial censure. My neighbour was in absolute necessity of a yoke of oxen; his situation was such, that he had no possible way of support for himself and family but by tillage, and his tillage such, that it was impossible without oxen. I was under no previous obligations at all to him, nor would his poverty admit of his being one under any, not so much as the prospect of a reasonable reward for the favour he wanted. However out of compassion to him and his, and as a mere courtesy, I let him my oxen only in this condition; that he should not muzzle them, but that they should have a full support and for my greater certainty, we aggreed, and he bound himself, that they should have such a quantity of

70

fodder, as would weigh so much in the spring, and of such quality, that they should have it for their support, and consequently in season. And he promised if that were not enough, they should have more. My cattle went to work for him in good spirits, they loved the work, and for some time did 2 days work in one. The man had that gain indeed by it; an hundred or a *1000* fold. My oxen expected no more of him, than a support according to their labour. And just while his gains were flowing in he was something more liberal in throwing out fodder, tho' even then not equal to their labour. Whereupon thro' their abundant labour, (which was at least two-fold the ordinary labour of oxen) they grew very poor and continued declining, till the time that his extraordinary gains were over, when they could not rise alone. My cows and calves were aware that it was coming to this, and did what they could to help them in plight. But notwithstanding all they coud do, it came to such extremity. And it was judged that it would cost not much less than the price of a yoke of oxen to recruit them. When the man came to see them, he thot it would signifie nothing to try to raise them, shewed some disaffection, and displeasure at the oxen, and at the cows and calves, and thot they might have done better; but never considerd that the oxen had labourd day and night, and had no opportunity to graze at all, nor did he at all enquire into or consider the care, toil, and expence which the cows and calves had already been at, and that only from a regard to his interest, without any other obligations more than lie upon all in common, to prevent the evil. He left the oxen in that case without any care for them, he indeed threw them one lock of hay, but never looked to see whether they eat it. And indeed it was thrown at such a distance that they never reach'd more than a handful of it; and there they must have dyed, had it not been for some hay which was left to a few of my calves, who had lost their dam, and was what and all they depended upon for their support; seeing the necessity of my oxen they cheerfully resign'd it up, tho' with many tears, being then pinch'd with hunger; and considering they are now stripd of all they depended upon for support in time to come. When they had seen their fodder eaten up, they were turn'd out agrazing as sad necessity constrained them for a living; and went away with resentments of my neighbours ingratitude that they never desire to see his face or come into his yard again. Thus my neighbour notwithstanding his great gains by my oxen, and his solemn engagement to support them, has not been at more than half the expence requisite to this great profit. But a large part of it hath been at the cost of my cows and orphan calves.

The man instead of doing by my oxen as was stipulated and expected, has all along treated them after this sort, viz. he will give them no more than the same weight in the fall as was agreed to be in the spring, and he says it is as much and as good. They are foddered by many hands, some children who throw out rye-straw instead of hay; some are so weak that they can't carry so much, and yet it passes, and some none at all and the oxen bear it; and they never have it in season but commonly a day or 2 or 3 too late. And he has never once look'd to see if their bellies were full, nor how they are foddered, and yet complains, they are very greedy oxen, they work for him still, but under vast discouragements, are grown dull, not because they don't love the work as well as ever, but thro' discouragement. They see no profit of their labour, the soil is become quite barren, which was so very fertile but a few years ago; not one handful of produce for all their labour since, and they think there is a blast in judgment; and their labour which otherwise they could as free as ever expend for him is on this account painful to them. The man can see nothing but that his treatment of me, my oxen, my cows and my orphan calves, has been just and grateful enough, and the least dislike of mine is imputed to a bad cause. And when I talk with him I can get little or nothing from him but resentment.

And now dear sir, unless prejudice blinds me (and it is the point in which I want your judgment) I think the man unworthy of my favour any longer: and that it is high time to take my oxen from him or some way maim, or disable them for service, in testimony against his ingratitude. My oxen now labour in fear of the consequences to them, knowing that I have no need of them, and that their lives and limbs are of no account with me compard with proper expressions of my displeasure at the mans injustice and ingratitude. They don't know why I let them alone. The end of their being there seems to be frustrate by the fatal bar which his ingratitude has laid in the way to the success of their labours. Please to consult the prophets and apostles in the perplexed affair, and let your thoughts be ripen'd on the subject, against your next interview with your perplexed brother and fellow servant.

The account books which have come down from Wheelock cannot be said to have been tidily kept but they are legible enough for us to learn of the many details which he supervised: "Janne Machray spun fourty four yards of lennen yarn"; "John Gibbs Dr if the metheglin not good, in the spring £2"; "Abigail Alcock necklace 2/4"; "Molle Finney saith that she thinks she must have 5s or 6s which I think is little enough"; twelve shillings for four weeks' board for a workman, three shillings a day to another for making a fence, four bushels of oysters for six shillings. Some one has stolen Wheelock's steelyard, which some one else has finally tracked down; and, as a grace note strayed to the margin, "sweet secssaly steepd with rum and molasses maketh a good cordial."

Wheelock and his friends now and then exchanged medical information. Thus Whitaker suggested that Wheelock wear a small bag of herbs at his waist to rid him of his "hypochondriac flatulence"; Wheelock asks a missionary to find out what medicine the Indian women use to ease them in childbearing, and reference has already been made to his stepdaughter Sarah, who wore jewels to cure her headaches. A doctor in Windham sent the following direction: "I understand that you have the measels in your famely it will be most safe for the sick not to force the distemper if it be 4 or 5 days before it coms out it is most safe for the sick, it gineraly take that time to seperate from the blood. I seldom use anything more forceing than barm and marygoulds. Sum times the fevir is too low I give a dose or two of the lupis contragerva or very weak flip but in gineral if they have a fever let natuer alone with the deseas only such drink as is goon to quench thirs as barm and burnil (*illegible*) have sum times a little milk and water a weak assed made with the

juice of lemons and water or barbary or crambarys but orde-
narily they will do without the use of asseds." Or again: "directions for the childs coħmon drinck: when wanting to drink between using the surup take a handfull of brook liverwort and a
handfully of bitony, short bitony, and a handfull of comfre
leaves and some elder flowers and if you cant get elder flowers
get maple tops: put said yerbs into an earthen pot and power in
boyling hot water in to said yerbs and cover said pot till the
steem has don rising: then to give the child to drinck when
wanting to drinck between using the surup as above mentioned. Directions for blooding your child: blood your child
in the right ear when the sign is in the head: blood the child in
the left ear when the sign is in the brest: blood the child in the
right ear when the sign is in the reaigns of the back. Give John
if the flux continues of rattlesnakes gall 4 or 5 gr. twice a week."

Wheelock's lay duties were in themselves sufficient for the
ordinary man. But so, too, was each of his other occupations.
As a minister of the North Society and as a preacher much in
demand, he was, it would seem, fully occupied; or as tutor of
white students and headmaster of Moor's Charity School he
might have considered himself a busy man. But from the sixth
decade of the century he carried on all these activities con-
comitantly. Some sacrifice was essential. Wheelock chose to
give up the life of a scholar. As a result there are only the scanti-
est references to reading in his many letters. He was an administrator and not a scholar.

CHAPTER V

THE FOUNDING OF MOOR'S CHARITY SCHOOL

MY dear, dear brother, I feel in behalf of the poor, savage, perishing creatures like a covetous, craving beggar, as though I could not tell them when to ha' done, or how to leave begging for them, till the Great Design of their being brought to Christ be accomplished." In these words Wheelock expressed himself to George Whitefield in the year 1756. He knew, as his contemporaries knew, that the Indians were fast decreasing, and he was fearful lest he delay his efforts to the time when there would be no more Indians to convert. The obligation to convert them was imposed, so he believed, from Heaven on him as one of God's Covenant People. "The heart of the Great Redeemer," he wrote in the first of his nine *Narratives,* is set upon this project, and God's displeasure at the failure of his people to convert the Indians is manifested in His "permitting the savages to be such a sore scourge to our land, and make such depredations on our frontiers, inhumanly butchering and captivating our people."

But to think of Wheelock as one who considered himself compelled by the commands of the Deity, and by those commands only, is to limit the extent of his reasoning on the problem. His mind was not so centered on the distant Judgment Day when savages would be accepted as of the elect that he failed to appreciate the immediate economic and political advantages of converting them to Christianity, and to Christianity as he, a loyal subject for the time being of the Crown, and a Congregational minister in Connecticut, construed it. Thus in justifying his prosecution of the "Great Design" he curiously mixes mundane incentives with heaven-sent obligations.

France and England had long been competing for the allegiance of the Indians. Even before the middle of the seventeenth century the Jesuits had begun to proselyte in the province of New York; by living with the savages and enduring hardships they had insinuated themselves into the affections of the Indians and had made French allies of many of them. At the beginning of the eighteenth century the influence of the priests had begun to wane—in 1700 the Legislative Council of New York had banished them from the province—but even at the time of their banishment their power was felt. The letters of the early Protestant ministers who had dealings with the Indians are replete with hostile criticisms of the Jesuits; Wheelock was at one with them in his antipathy toward not only the "hellish rites of the Jesuits" but their political influence as well. In his opinion, the savages if converted to Protestantism would not only become English allies against France, but would abandon their raids on white settlements. If one half the money, he argues, that had been for so many years expended in building, manning and supporting forts had been disbursed for missionaries and schoolmasters among the savages, the converted Indians "would have been a far better defence than all our expensive fortresses." These, he writes, were some of the considerations which influenced him, "though I did not then think much of any thing more than only to clear myself, and family, of partaking in the public guilt of our land and nation in such a neglect."[1]

Wheelock was only one of a numerous company which had been striving for years to win over the Indians to the Gospel. The history of the efforts of predecessors and contemporaries is in general one of failure; failure in that the Indians frequently refused to accept the religious teachings of the whites or, if they did accept them, were all too likely to acquire much of the viciousness of the traders and soldiers with whom they dealt. Disease, too, killed off many promising students, and

[1] *Narrative*, I, 14.

rum, arousing their savagery or debilitating them, added to the failures.

New England ministers seem to have been most successful with the Indians in the seventeenth century. Gookin estimated that in the fourteen towns of "praying Indians" in Massachusetts Bay there was a total of eleven hundred converted Indians.[1] After King Philip's War the number was much reduced; by 1684 the fourteen towns had decreased to four, and in the following century disease, war, and removal to other colonies reduced still further the number of Christian Indians in Massachusetts Bay. The colony of New Plymouth contained (in 1685) one thousand four hundred and thirty-nine Indians; by 1763 these had decreased to nine hundred and five.[2]

These early missionaries of the seventeenth and eighteenth centuries were of course encouraged by the civil authorities. John Eliot, the Mayhews, and Abraham Pierson, as examples, were supported from time to time by the Commissioners of the United Colonies, and enjoyed the sanction of the General Assemblies. The Commissioners informed the President and Society for the Propagation of the Gospel in New England (founded in 1649) that they had disbursed for mission work in 1650 between three and four hundred pounds of the Society's funds, and in the following year the Commissioners voted that a "coat of about 3 yards of the coursest cloth bee made up and given to the Sagamore of Aggawam to incurrage him to learn to know God and to exsite other Indians to doe the like."[3] And more than a hundred years before Wheelock began his Indian school, the authorities of Harvard College asked the Commissioners for Massachusetts to order the building of "one intyre rome att the college for the conveniencye of six hopfull Indians

---

[1] *Mass. Hist. Soc. Collections*, I, 180 ff.   [2] *Idem*, 201.
[3] *Records of the Plymouth Colony: Acts of the Commissioners of the United Colonies*, I, 161 ff.

youthes to bee trained up there." A small brick building, known as Indian College, was erected in Cambridge, but the project was a failure. "Change of diet, lodging, apparel, and studies" proved harmful to the Indians, of whom some died and others were discouraged. Gookin states that he was acquainted with two of the most promising of the attending Indians: one, Joel, was shipwrecked and killed a few months before he was to receive his degree, and the other, Caleb Cheeschaumuck, who was graduated in 1665, died of consumption shortly thereafter. The building was torn down in 1698.[1]

Closer to Wheelock in place and time than the missionaries already mentioned were James Fitch, who labored at Norwich, Connecticut, until his death in 1702, and Jonathan Barber, who succeeded in converting Ben Uncas, sachem of the Mohegans. This not quite "last of the Mohicans" was rewarded with a hat and coat, English style, at public expense.[2] Eliphalet Adams and David Jewett, both personally known to Wheelock, had preached for many years to the Mohegans at New London, and at Stratford the catechetical lecture of Samuel Johnson, later first president of King's College (Columbia) was generally attended by some Indians.[3] Names of other missionaries from Wheelock's time abound: Richard Treat, Daniel Edwards, Peter Pratt. Daniel Boardman and Samuel Canfield were appointed to the New Milford Indians; and John Sergeant, to be succeeded by Jonathan Edwards, was well known for his teaching at Stockbridge, Massachusetts. With the work of all or most of these men Wheelock must have been familiar. Lastly, it should be noted that in 1745 David Brainerd, mis-

[1] *Harvard College Records*, I, lxxxii, in *Pub. of the Col. Soc. of Mass.*, XV; Josiah Quincy, *History of Harvard College*, I, 191–192; *Early History of Massachusetts, Lectures by Members of the Mass. Hist. Soc.*, 314; *Mass. Historical Soc. Coll.*, I, 178.
[2] *Colonial Records of Connecticut*, VIII, 72–73.
[3] Pascoe, 46.

sionary in New Jersey, had sent Wheelock a copy of his journal, the record of his work among the Delawares.

Wheelock decided that he would have to remove the Indians from their native surroundings to Lebanon, where they would be free during their formative period from the evil example of traders, the lure of the hunt or of warfare or of wandering, and where they would be exposed to the better example of his religious community. In the suitable environment of Lebanon Indian boys and girls were to be educated by charity for missionary work among their own tribes. They in due time would accomplish much more than white missionaries because the unconverted Indians would not be prejudiced against them. Furthermore, the cost of educating an Indian would be one half that of educating a white man. The boys were to be trained in the rudiments of a secular and of a religious education, and in "husbandry." The girls would substitute *housewifery* for *husbandry,* and were to be trained in "whatever should be necessary to render them fit, to perform the female part, as housewives, school-mistresses, tayloresses, &c. and to go and be with these youth, when they shall be hundreds of miles distant from the English on the business of their mission."[1] A few white scholars were also to be educated at the school, and on charity funds; from this early association they would quickly learn the Indian speech, and thus save the cost of an interpreter when they entered the missionary field. All this seemed very promising, on paper.

Wheelock had formed a false notion of the receptivity of the Indians, probably from his success with Samson Occom. This Mohegan, who in time was to be the most important non-combatant Indian in New England, had been converted during the

[1] *Narrative,* I, 15. Wheelock was here following the example of John Sergeant, whom he quotes (*idem,* I, 34, fn.) on the value of educating Indian girls. Sergeant also combined study and labor.

Great Awakening, perhaps by James Davenport. Wheelock had accepted him as a private pupil in 1743 (Occom was then about twenty years old), and with some aid from Benjamin Pomeroy had instructed him in English, Latin, Greek, Hebrew, and in such other subjects as were necessary for college. His studies impaired Occom's sight, but his progress was surprising. Wheelock undoubtedly hoped to find other Indians equal to him.

At Wheelock's request John Brainerd, who had succeeded his brother David, sent two Delawares from New Jersey. They arrived at Lebanon December 18, 1754: John Pumshire, aged fourteen, and Jacob Woolley, aged eleven. As Wheelock wrote to George Whitefield: "They left all their relations and acquaintance, and came alone, on foot, above two hundred miles, thro' a country in which they knew not one mortal, and where they had never passed before, to throw themselves for an education upon a stranger, of whom they had never heard but by Mr. Brainerd."

About a year and a half after their arrival Wheelock wrote proudly that they were well-behaved and contented, and that they "read well, have learnt the Assemblies Shorter Catechism thro with the proofs, and have made some entrance into the lattin tongue. They appear seriously inclined for their salvation. The younger almost persuades me that he was converted last spring." Unhappily, Pumshire began to ail, and was sent back to Brainerd on November 14, 1756; on the twenty-sixth of the following January he died. Brainerd wrote to Wheelock: "I was with him the Sabbath but one before, and had some discourse about the concerns of his soul, but he was so very deaf that it was extremely difficult to converse at all with him. His whole behaviour was Christianlike, and he has left us, I think, some grounds for a comfortable hope concerning him." The death of Pumshire was instructive to Wheelock; from this point on he was convinced "more fully of the necessity of special care respecting their diet; and that more exercise was necessary for them, especially at their first coming to a full table, and with so keen an appetite, than was ordinarily necessary for English youth."[1]

It is not surprising that many of the Indians at the school failed in health. Even before the Indian children came to Lebanon their habits of living tended to weaken them. We are inclined to imagine the Indian as feasting bountifully in his forests on venison and other wild game whenever he wished. The contrary is true. In general food was not abundant, and famines frequent. At times they were obliged to travel long distances, in one instance seventy miles, even for their fish, and as some of the excerpts to be given later show, they were often unable to supply the Indian missionaries with sufficient food to keep them in health. The noble savage of the *Leatherstocking Tales* was actually an impoverished creature, often "hungrybelly," often badly clothed, dirty, and ignoble.

In common with eighteenth century educators Wheelock knew little about the physical (or mental) needs of his charges. Even the sturdiest child of today would not be subjected to the severe discipline of that time. School hours were long or otherwise badly arranged. In 1729 a schoolmaster at New Haven agreed to keep the grammar school in session for seven hours in the winter season and eight hours in the summer, "and not to exceed twelve play days in the year."[2] When Nathan Hale kept a school at New London he wrote (1774) that the hours for "young ladies" were from five to seven *in the morning,* and in Norwich, Connecticut, toward the close of the century, the same hours were given over to the girls.[3]

Wheelock was following tradition therefore when he convened his boys early and dismissed them late. They were

[1] *Narrative,* I, 30. [2] Small, *Early New England Schools,* 379.
[3] *Idem,* 288–289.

obliged "to be clean and decently dressed, and be ready to attend prayers before sun-rise in the fall and winter, and at 6 o'clock in the summer. A portion of Scripture is read by several of the Seniors of them, and those who are able answer a question in the *Assembly's Catechism,* and have some questions asked them upon it, and an answer expounded to them. After prayers and a short time for their diversion, the school begins with prayer about 9, and ends at 12, and again at 2, and ends at 5 o'clock with prayer. Evening prayer is attended before the daylight is gone. Afterwards they apply to their studies, &c."[1]

No schoolmaster today could hope to keep his scholars docile under such a system; when one considers that these youngsters were not long removed from their Indian environment before they began the study of Latin and theology, and were in addition subjected to an over-emotionalized, soul-probing religion, the wonder is that any of them were docile—or survived. Happily, Wheelock does not seem to have been brutal to his Indians; in spite of some criticism of his flogging one of them, David M'Clure referred to him as the "gentle and affectionate father of his tawny family."[2]

But we have gone ahead of chronology. We left Wheelock with only one Indian, Jacob Woolley, his companion Pumshire having returned to New Jersey. Seven months after their arrival in Lebanon, on July 17, 1755, Colonel Joshua More, a farmer of Mansfield, Connecticut, deeded to the school certain property variously described as a "messuage or tenement," a "mantion-house," a "small dwelling-house and a shop or school-house," and two acres, adjoining Wheelock's land in Lebanon. From him the school derives its name.[3]

1 *Narrative,* I, 36.   2 *Memoirs of the Rev. Eleazar Wheelock,* 24.

3 The spelling of the name varies, but when applied to the school is usually given as *Moor.* In 1758, because of flaws in the original deed, More's widow reconveyed the property, to Wheelock, personally. Chase states (16) that the school

FOUNDING OF MOOR'S CHARITY SCHOOL

The next Indians to come to the school were two young Delawares, sent by Brainerd: "the eldest is Joseph Wolley, a child that has behaved himself soberly, of a middleing good capacity, naturally modest, and something bashful. He is not the boy I intended, but being disappointed of him, this is the best I could send, and perhaps may answer as well as the other. The younger is the same you had an account of, and for whom you wrote. He is a smart little fellow, but will want taking care of. He loves to play, and will have his hat in one place and his mittens in another. Your wisdom will direct: you will soon find out their tempers and know how to treat them." Joseph was a cousin of Jacob Woolley; the other boy was Hezekiah Calvin. Sad days were in store for each: Jacob was to become an outcast, Joseph to die young of consumption, and Hezekiah to be imprisoned for forgery.

Other Indians were gradually added—from New England and from the Six Nations—so that by 1763 Wheelock had instructed "five since April, 1759, and seven since November, 1760, and eleven since August 1st., 1761, and after this manner they have encreased as I could obtain those who appeared promising. And for some time I have had twenty-five devoted to school as constantly as their health will allow, and they have all along been so, excepting that in an extraordinary crowd of business, I have sometimes required their assistance. But there is no great advantage, excepting to themselves to be

"was known thenceforth only by Wheelock's name." In 1771 Wheelock declared (*Narrative*, VI, 35) that it should be called *Moor's School,* but on the title pages of his *Narratives* (even of those published after 1771) he uses *Indian Charity School.* In an act of the New Hampshire Legislature (1807) by which the status of the school was defined, occurs the phrase "which was formerly and still is known by the name of Moors Charity School, as well as Moors Indian Charity School," and the confusing clause is added that the school "may and shall be known and called hereafter by the name of the President of Moors Charity School." (The Act is given in Chase, 622–623.) To avoid confusion, and in conformity with present usage, I have used *Moor's Charity School* throughout this volume.

expected from their labour, nor enough to compensate the trouble of instructing them in it, and the repair of the mischiefs they will do, while they are ignorant of all the affairs of husbandry, and the use of tools."[1]

More intimate details are given by Wheelock to George Whitefield (July 4, 1761): "None know, nor can any, without experience, well conceive of, the difficulty of educating an Indian. They would soon kill themselves with eating and sloth, if constant care were not exercised for them at least the first year. They are used to set upon the ground, and it is as natural for them as a seat to our children. They are not wont to have any cloaths but what they wear, nor will without much pains be brot to take care of any. They are used to a sordid manner of dress, and love it as well as our children to be clean. They are not used to any regular government, the sad consequences of which you may a little guess at. They are used to live from hand to mouth (as we speak) and have no care for futurity. They have never been used to the furniture of an English house, and dont know but that a wine-glass is as strong as an hand iron. Our language when they seem to have got it is not their mother tongue and they cannot receive nor communicate in that as in their own. It is a long time before they will learn the proper place and use of the particles, *a, an, the,* &c. And they are as unpolished and uncultivated within as without. However, experience has taught us that it may be done. And they lie as open to conviction of the truth of their state, when proper matter of conviction is communicated to them as any, and there is as much ground to hope for their conversion. And I am still of the opinion that the time of Gods mercy is now near at hand."

It was a curious program, this induction of Indians into the culture of scholarly white men. The original hope of bringing

[1] *Narrative,* I, 33.

salvation to the Indians, or them to it, persisted in Wheelock's mind, as witness the last sentence in the otherwise despondent passage just quoted. But why, one wonders, subject young Indian boys to the study of Greek, Latin, and even Hebrew? From white paying scholars a knowledge of the classics was reasonably required: they were to enter college later, and become, many of them, ministers. With them Wheelock lumped the Indian and white charity scholars. He made no distinction, in subjects taught, between students who would settle in Connecticut and those who would go out to mission posts among the Six Nations. Hence we have his statement that Joseph Woolley and Hezekiah Calvin "will now read Tulley, Virgil, and the Greek Testament very handsomly"—after they had been four years at the school. The Indians, the expectation seemed to have been, would ultimately return learned in the classics to their kin. So they were coerced into studies that were valueless in fitting them to deal with the problems of drunken, roving savages, or in helping their unconverted brothers to gain a living by a craft.

That the Boston Board, representing the Society in Scotland, did not favor this ill-adapted program is shown in a letter from Charles Chauncy to Wheelock (February 15, 1762): "And as to their education, we would have it intirely confined to their learning English. To be more explicit, we would have none of their time taken up in learning so much as the rudiments either of Latin or Greek. We imagine it will turn to much better account, if they are taught to *speak, read* and *write* English, as those who have a thorow understanding of the language.—So far as the knowledge of Latin, or Greek, or Hebrew, may be proper for a missionary to the Indians, we should chuse to have it in the mind of one that is not himself an Indian."

Husbandry, we know, was included in the curriculum, and

if it had been properly taught, would have been of great value to the missionary Indians; but husbandry was only a dignified word for farm-chores. The Indians, as might be expected, were disgruntled with the enforced manual labor. John Daniels, a Narraganset and father of one of the students, complained to Wheelock: "I always tho't your school was free to the natives, not to learn them how to farm it, but to advance in Christian knowledge, which wear the chief motive that caus'd me to send my son Charles to you; not that I'm anything against his labouring some for you, when business lies heavy on you: but to work two years to learn to farm it, is what I don't consent to, when I can as well learn him that myself and have the prophet of his labour." Daniel Simon, another Narraganset, the only Indian educated at the school who received a college degree during Wheelock's life, wrote bitterly to Wheelock: "I now make bould to write to the most Reverend Doctor, when I came frist to this school I understood that this school was for to bring up such Indians, as was not able to bring up themselves, but the doctor is to learn them to work, but I have been to work ever since I have been able; and therefore if the doctor will let me follow my studys, I shall be thinkful, as I understood the doctor when I talked with him, that we must work as much as to pay our way, and if we should, what good will the charity money do the Indians, which was given to them, if we poor Indians shall work as much as to pay for our learning, we can go some other pace as good as here for learning, if we are ablie to work and pay for our learning, and I say now wo unto that poor Indian or white man that should ever come to this school, without he is rich—."

I have quoted earlier Wheelock's statement of the daily routine. The reader may be interested in seeing the school through the eyes of a friendly Boston merchant, John Smith, who reported his impressions to "a Friend" as follows:

FOUNDING OF MOOR'S CHARITY SCHOOL

In rideing last week to New London I turned some miles out of my way to see Mr. Wheelocks Indian School; nor do I repent my trouble. I had heard in general that it consisted of twenty or more Indian boys and girls of the Mohawks and other tribes of Indians and that a number of the ministers of that province had spoken well of Mr. Wheelock and of this undertaking of his, but this I thought was seeing with the eyes of others and therefore chose to use my own.

My first observation in travelling through the towns was the different acceptation of both Mr. Wheelock and his enterprize there, from what some in Boston had entertained.

Here because of his lively adhering to the doctrines of grace he was not accepted by *some;* and when this is the case you are sensible both enterprize and executior of it are too apt to be viewed by an eye of surmize and sometimes of carping: but in Connecticut I found charity and candor and every where in passing Mr. Wheelock had the reverence of a man of God, and his school was had in high esteem.

I reached his house a little before the evening sacrafice and was movingly touched on giveing out the Psalm to hear an Indian youth set the time and the others following him, and singing the tenor, and base, with remarkable gravity and seirousness, and tho' Mr. Wheelock, the schoolmaster and a minister from our province (called as I was by curiosity) joined in praise; yet they unmoved seemed to have nothing to do but to sing to the glory of God.

I omit Mr. Wheelocks prayer and pass to the Indians in the morning when on ringing the school house bell they assemble at Mr. Wheelocks house about 5 oclock with their master; who named the chapter in course for the day and called upon the near Indian who read 3 or 4 verses till the master said Proximus, and then the next Indian read some verses and so on till all the Indians had read the whole chapter. After this Mr. Wheelock prayes and then they each Indian perse a verse or two of the chapter they had read. After this they entered successively on prosodia and then on disputations on some questions propounded by themselves in some of the arts and sciences. And it is really charming to see Indian youths of different tribes and languages in pure English reading the Word of God and speaking with exactness and accuracy on points (either chosen by themselves or given out to them) in the severall arts and sciences, and especially to see this done with at least a seeming mixture of obedience to God; a fillial love and reverence to Mr. Wheelock, and yet with great ambittion to excell each other and indeed in this morning exercises I saw a youth degraded one lower in the class who before the exercises were finished not only recovered his own place but was advanced two higher.

I learnt hear that my surprize was common to ministers and other persons of litterature who before me had been to visit this school or rather colledge for I doubt whither in colledges in general a better education is to be expected and in mentioning this to a gentleman in this town who had visited this seminary, he acquainted me that he intended at his own charge to send his son to obtain his education in mixture with these Indians. There were 4 or 5 of these Indians from 21 to 24 years of age who did not mix with the youth in these exercies—These I learnt were perfected in their literature and stand ready to be sent among the Indians to keep scools and occasionally to preach as doors open.

On my return Mr. Wheelock accompanied me a few miles and on passing by one house he said here lives one of my Indian Girls who was I hope converted last week; and calling to the farmer he unperceiv'd to her brought the young girl into our sight and the pleasure was exquisite to see the savageness of an Indian moulded into the sweetness of a follower of the Lamb.

In passing some days after this through the Mohegan country I saw an Indian man on horseback whom I challenged as Mr. Occum and found it so. There was something in his mein and deportment both amiable and venerable and though I had never before seen him I must have been sure it was he. He certainly does honour to Mr. Wheelocks indefatigable, judicious, pious intentions to send the Gospel among the Indians. I heard Mr. Ashpo was then among them but at a distance and I being hurried and tired lost the opportunity of seing Mr. Wheelock in him and more especially of seeing Christs image in this tawney man but I wont tire you.

The first Indian girls had come to the school in 1761: Amie Johnson, a Mohegan, and Miriam Storrs, a Delaware. By 1765 ten girls were attending the school, in addition to twenty-nine Indian boys, and seven whites, all supported by charity. The girls, it will be remembered, were to be instructed in *house-wifery,* and to that end they were placed in homes in the neighborhood of the school. There they helped with the house chores, and were, in all likelihood, not much better than servants. Instruction in reading and writing was given them at the school on one day a week; a letter of 1766 indicates that Wheelock was about to hire a white woman as tailoress for three months and that she was to teach the girls; and by vote of the parishioners the girls were given liberty to attend church and "to sit in the hind seat on the women's side below."

In general these girls were backward and recalcitrant, subject to despondency, and wayward. Strong drink enticed them frequently, as is evident from the confessions, many of them written out by Wheelock, himself, for them. Hannah Nonesuch, a Mohegan, acknowledged "with shamefacedness" that "on the evening of the 8th Inst. I was (by the enticement of Sarah Weogs) guilty of being at the tavern and tarrying there with a company of Indian boys and girls for (what is commonly called) a frolick, where was much spirituous liquor drank, and much dancing and rude conduct and in tarrying to an unseasonable time of night, with much rude and vain company, all which conduct I am fully sensable is much to the dishonour of god and very prejudicial to the design and reputation of this school and to the good of my own soul, and the souls of my mates for which sinful and wicked conduct of mine I am heartily sorry, and desire to lie low in the dust and do now beg forgivness of God, the Revd. and worthy Doctor Wheelock, his family and school, and all whom I have hereby offended, and I do promise that by the grace of god I will never offend by the like, or any other misconduct for time to come, and I desire and warn all my mates not to take occasion by this misconduct of mine to commit the like or any other evil."

Mary Secuter, a Narraganset, confessed with Wheelock's

help, "I have been repeatedly scandalously guilty of the sin of drunkeness and particularly last evening being the evening following the Lords Day Dec. 27, 1767, I went into the school while I was intoxicated with liquor and there behaved myself in a lude and very immodest manner among the school boys, I also in a vile manner profaned the sacred name." She and Hannah Nonesuch in the following year fell from grace again, and at last in despair she begged to be dismissed from the school: "I am not insensable of my obligation to the Doctor for his patarnel cair over me ever sense I have been the school. My faults have been overlookd with tenderness when they have deserved severity—I am quite discouraged with myself. The longer I stay in the school the worse I am—dont think I shall ever do any good to the Cause, and it will cost a great deal to keepe me here, which will be spending money to no porpose. I have been more trouble to the Docter then all my mates. Dont think I desarve the honour of being in your school, if agreable to the Doctor I should be glad to leave the school next week and be no longer a member of it."

Wheelock's labors would have been much simplified if he could have kept his Indians from liquor. To the end of his life he was writing confessions for the fallen or combatting the influence of taverns in the neighborhood of the school or college. Not that he wished courtesy "to invent some other custom of entertainment." On the contrary, he believed with his contemporaries in a moderate use of spirits, and his account books show that he often bought liquor. He even agreed, although "with trembling heart," (in 1767) to buy enough rum from a prospective tavern keeper to launch his business, and he did order a nephew to bring a barrel of rum along with the household goods when the school was removed from Connecticut. Poetic license has played about this subject, and now we are to understand, in the words of Richard Hovey's song, that "he mixed drinks for the heathen, in the goodness of his soul"! As for the *"five hundred* gallons of New England rum" all that can be said is that they fit the exigencies of the meter much better than the cramped space of an eighteenth century vehicle, wending its slow way from Lebanon, Connecticut, to Hanover. It is a pleasant Paul Bunyanesque fancy, however, this of a migrating divine's loading such a tun on an oxcart. But the records bring us back to the actuality which disquieted Wheelock and nullified much of his discipline. Samuel Ashpo, although licensed to preach, was suspended from his mission at Chenango, New York; Joseph Johnson repeatedly fell, and in 1769 was to Wheelock a "drunkard and apostate"; even Samson Occom, after his return from England, was reported on two or three occasions as indulging too much.

They misbehaved in other ways. That we might expect when two score Delawares, Mohawks, Oneidas, Montauks, Mohegans, and Narragansets, to name some of the leading tribes represented, were gathered in a school. They had never lived in a decent house, some of them could not speak a word of English when first admitted, and certain of the Mohawks on arrival were almost naked, and as Wheelock wrote, "I might have added also that they were very lousey." They had been used to wandering and to scenes of violence. How different then the environment of an orderly Connecticut community, and how irksome the long school day and the discipline. A vivid and quaint description of a brawl at the school, participated in by John Wheelock (in time to come, the second president of Dartmouth), by an illegitimate son of Sir William Johnson and a squaw, by Isaiah Uncas, the Mohegan heir-apparent, and by others of less note, has survived the years. It was written by David M'Clure, then about seventeen years old, who lurks behind his initials and the peace-maker's (and tattle-bearer's) title of *Animus Quietus.*

ELEAZAR WHEELOCK

Lebanon Sep. 25th 1765.

Rev^d & much Honour^d Sir

Permit me humbly at your feet, to take the freedom of troubling you with a letter from your ever dutifull servant.

On the one hand, never with more regret did I take pen in hand. and set down to write to a gentleman of your exalted station than at present I am obliged to do. But on the other hand I am elivated with the assurance, that, the reigns of goverment are in his hands who (under God) is both able and ready to exercise that disipline over his houshold, as is necessary to preserve peice and good order. this consideration is that, which banishes all fear, and helps forward my trembling pen.

What I would be permission lay before you, is the disorder and misconduct of some of the Indian boys, in your absence to Norwich. —which I shall endevour to describe.

On Tuesday last, sun about two hours high, Johnson, and John Wheelock, were standing near the woodpile, great William by the gait, William and John Wheelock were chatting togeather calling one a nother names. at last John challanges William to fite Johnson, calling him spekkle face white eye &c which Johnson repeated. William being run upon by Johnson's threats, advances up to Johnson and offers to fite him. whereupon they both strip of their waistcoats, and prepair for an incounter, and in the mean time the most of the school boys were greather'd around, Johnson call'd William Son of a Bitch, and I think, Indian Devil, at last they came to blows, immeadetly I stept between to part them and advised them to desist, but I was soon push'd of by them, I being apprehensive of the event while several people of the parish pased by and saw them in such a condition. but still they continued dominearing over each other till sun down, when they went in the house and put on their waistcoats, but they were not cool'd they went at it again with more fury, tore each other's shirts of their backs. finally, one nation seem'd to be at variance with each other. Uncas was inraiged among the rest, put on his new coat and I heard threatned to go home, (for what reason I know not) Uncas, David and Little William came out to the cyder mill. Uncas told me that David threatned to kill him Little William said that David would fight with him in the house, and they begun to go at it in cyder mill, and would have gone had I not

parted them, and told them that Mr Wheelock would have no fight-
ers in his school, and that if they did not behave better they must
go home to their own country, and that they must be whipt when
Mr Wheelock comes home &c. Next morning they seem'd beetter
composed. But I must desist (fearing I have already worn out your
patiance, and almost distracted your mind with my story) humbly
beging the boldness to indite myself,

Your ever Dutifull &
Obeidant Servant,

Promoter, of Peice Tranquility & Good order.
Animus Quietus. D.M.C.
The high Study Septr 25

P.S. Please Sir, not to expose me, William & Johnson and all of
them seem'd to be better agreed, and I believe are sorry for their
conduct. [but I believe the Devil was in them all last Tuesday
night].

And finally, to have done for the present with these accounts
of temptations and personal weaknesses, let a Delaware girl
tell of her trip from Lebanon, Connecticut, to New York, during which her religious training, and perhaps a modicum of
native modesty, kept her inviolate from the roguery of a fellow-
traveler:

New York Novbr 24 1768

Revd & Honrd Sir

Sir I arrived here 19 of this month and I am to go this week from
here but I keep good courage hopeing to be where I shou'd be. I
have been sick some of the time but nothing to what I deserve I
was well treated I have work enough people would have be tarry
with them but I have got long so far but the Doctr will need the
Greeke to read my writing. if I had common sence I should form
this writing better Sir I have heard but one prayer since I went from
Norwich. Since I went from thy house instead of prayers filthy
talk &c.

I found no rest till I put my whole trust in god who was my best
presever then was I lifted up above any temtation I have been un-

der many trials but god was my deliverer heavy temtations, prest down to the dust which caused me soo to weep nights and hours when I saw every one out of my sight Dear Sir I want see the Doct again. I lay many a night and for fear of one mans bad intention in his heart as I thought and he told me after he went to shore that was his end and aim but he found he was mistaken he owned but I did keep clear of him which I have reason to praise my redeemer for all my days and hope to go to him in due time. May God of infinite grace grant me it for his sake. No more from your

unworthy Subject

Miriam Storrs

PS to Remember to all the family I am in health and to the school.

CHAPTER VI

WHEELOCK SENDS MISSIONARIES AND SCHOOLMASTERS TO THEIR POSTS

FROLICS, homesickness, carnal appetites, and ineptitude were not as yet the despair of Wheelock. Of the faults of the Indians he was quite aware; these, though, were but trials from Heaven, and could not be permitted to frustrate the "great design." Persistence in his ambition was typical of him. He held as tenaciously to his plan of converting the Indians as to his theological doctrines. The idea was fixed in his mind: the Indians were dwindling, they should be saved *now*, he as one of God's Covenant People was obliged to save them. And the medium of salvation was Moor's Charity School. In the early seventeen sixties he would not allow any discouragement to deflect him from his plan.

The first missionary sent out by Wheelock was Samson Occom, whom, it will be recalled, he had helped to educate privately and before the establishment of the school. On June 10, 1761, Occom departed from Lebanon with David Fowler, a Montauk, to visit the Oneidas, in the province of New York. Occom stayed among them for nine weeks, trying too rigorously to transform them according to his notion of civilized men and women: he aroused ill-will by insisting that the Indians dispense with their ornaments and abandon their feasts at weddings, births, and baptisms. His companion returned in August with three Mohawk boys for the school. In 1762 Occom visited the Oneidas for the second time, remained for a short while, and during the following year returned once more, but was forced to withdraw at the outbreak of Pontiac's War. In the same year (1763), Samuel Ashpo, a Mohegan, was obliged to leave Chenango, having been there only six weeks; and the white missionary of independent means, Charles Jeffry Smith,

95

who had gone, with Joseph Brant as interpreter, to the Six Nations, also withdrew because of hostilities. Wheelock therefore had to suspend all missionary work for this year.

In 1764 Wheelock sent out young Joseph Woolley, a Delaware of some seventeen years, one of the gentlest of the Indian scholars, blameless in his conduct, and of fair intelligence. Between him and his master was a genuine affection. As illustrative of the pupil's attitude I quote the first letter we have from Woolley to Wheelock:

Lebanon Nov. 2 A.D. 1761

Rev^d & Hon.^d Sir

I now with pleasure set down to congratulate myself, and shall imploy myself in writing these following lines. and I would inform you in the first place that I am in good state of health, nor I never felt so hearty sence I came to live with Mr. Wheelock hoping you are the same, I dont mean sence you came to live with Mr. Wheelock. And also I would beg leave of you to let me go and visit my friend at Mohegan and from thence to Lime that is about six miles beyond New London, Now as soon as possible before the vacancey is up, it may be by that means my mind may (will) be loosend from home. for they expect to see me there some time this fall and they desired me to come. I told 'em I should come if I could get leave, and nothing would happen more then common, but I must conclude. Thus have I said.

Yours in reality

Joseph Woolley

Woolley was installed as schoolmaster at Onohoquaga by Samuel Kirkland, and soon reported, "I keep a school, upwards of 20 schollers, with some decency and regularity, and there is a daily addition." But Woolley was ill with tuberculosis, the progress of which was hastened by bad food and inadequate clothing. He died in the latter part of November, 1765, and by his death Wheelock lost one of his most promising Indian teachers.

MISSIONARIES AND SCHOOLMASTERS

Because of the importance of Samuel Kirkland, to whom reference has just been made, as a missionary, it is fitting at this point to discuss him more fully.

Kirkland was born in Norwich, Connecticut, December 1, 1741 (N.S.), the son of a minister. He entered Moor's Charity School in 1760, and two years later became a member of the sophomore class at the College of New Jersey (Princeton). In 1764, having installed Joseph Woolley, as stated above, he remained with the Oneidas for six weeks, and then undertook the dangerous task of visiting the intractable Senecas at Canadasaga. Fears for his safety were well founded. Soon after his arrival, and by an unfortunate coincidence, the chief at whose house he was lodged died, and the Senecas saw in his death the evil influence of the visitor. He was protected from violence, however, by the very family affected, and before he left the Senecas a year and a half later had been adopted as a brother by the chief sachem.

On his return to Lebanon Kirkland was ordained (June 19, 1766) and on the same day was commissioned by the Connecticut Board of Correspondents as Indian missionary. He resumed his work, this time with the Oneidas, among whom he labored for forty years, supported partly by funds which Whitaker and Occom had raised in England and Scotland (*see chapter X*), and partly by the New England Company.[1] In 1769 he married Jerusha Bingham, one of Wheelock's nieces. His service under Wheelock officially terminated in 1770.[2]

[1] See McCallum, *The Letters of Eleazar Wheelock's Indians,* 92, for a detailed statement.

[2] During the Revolution Kirkland aided in keeping the Oneidas and the Tuscaroras loyal to the colonies, and after the war induced the Senecas to accept the terms of the government. In 1793 he obtained a charter for Hamilton Oneida Academy; in the following year the Oneidas requested that he be removed from his position, but an investigation of the charges proved favorable to him. He died Feb. 28, 1808, four years before the Academy became Hamilton College. (Lothrop, *Life of Samuel Kirkland;* Sprague, *Annals;* McCallum, *The Letters of Eleazar Wheelock's Indians;* and Wheelock's letters.)

The Providence of God in directing the affairs of the school, a school which Wheelock considered "of more consequence than any in America," was clearly shown, according to his thinking, on March 12, 1765. On that day the Connecticut Board of Correspondents[1] met at Wheelock's house. While they were sitting, there entered Good Peter, an Oneida, sent by his tribe to petition for a missionary. He had come three hundred miles "through a deep snow, and reached Mr. Wheelock's that very day, and at the very hour that several ministers met to examine two young men for the ministry; one of which was designed for them. And so remarkable was the Providence of God, that an interpreter came in at the same instant, who had lived with these Indians for ten years, by whose assistance we were able to understand them, and they us. Thus all these three parties met together in less than half an hour, from places three hundred miles distant, and without any previous appointment, or the least knowledge of each other's design."[2]

As a result of this meeting the Board of Correspondents approved two white scholars as missionaries, three Indians as schoolmasters, and six other Indians as ushers, that is, as assistant schoolmasters, all to serve in the province of New York. They were shortly sent to the Six Nations. Thus Abraham *Primus* and Abraham *Secundus,* Mohawks, returned to their tribe as ushers. David Fowler, Montauk, began (June 3) to teach at Canajoharie, whence famine drove him in a few weeks. Theophilus Chamberlain, a white scholar and now an ordained minister, settled in Butlersbury, and from that town as a center, traveled among the neighboring towns until June, 1767,

---

[1] Representing the Society in Scotland, and established July 4, 1764, at Wheelock's desire. It acted as a board of trustees for the school. Composed as it was of Wheelock's relatives and close friends, the Board was more sympathetic to his plans than the Boston Board of the Society was, and being nearer at hand, more easily convened. Wheelock was actually the dictator of it.

[2] *Narrative,* III, 30.

when he left Wheelock's service. Titus Smith, another ordained white missionary, went to Onohoquaga, with an interpreter; there he learned that the Indians had gone to Lake Otsego because of famine, and having followed them to the lake, he installed a young Mohawk, Moses, among them as a schoolmaster, who was soon reported as conducting his school "with the gravity of a divine of fifty or threescore." In this same year of 1765 Hezekiah Calvin, he of the scattered cap and mittens, began to teach at Fort Hunter, where he remained for two years. Altogether these schoolmasters and ushers were teaching one hundred and twenty-seven Indian scholars during 1765.

Throughout the next year Wheelock sent still more "graduates" from the school. Aaron Kinne was installed at Cherry Valley, but had to give up his school because of poor health. Samuel Kirkland, as already mentioned, began his work among the Oneidas, a work which he was to continue for forty years. David M'Clure, Joseph Johnson (a Mohegan), David Fowler, and Nathan Clap (a "Cape Cod Indian") were teaching at Canajoharie, and Samuel Johnson and Jacob Fowler (the latter a Montauk), took over the schools formerly conducted by the two Abrahams. Samuel Ashpo returned to Chenango and remained until 1767, when he was suspended for drunkenness. In all, one hundred scholars were reported for this year.

From these field-workers Wheelock received many communications in the form of letters and journals. The story told by the teachers is in general a story of hardship and ultimately of failure. Nevertheless Wheelock adhered to his original plan, for a number of years at least, and in spite of the disappointing accounts sent to him by whites and by Indians, continued to write to his friends in this country and abroad that "things wear a smiling aspect." Not that Wheelock failed to appreciate the problems of his missionaries or later to feel to the full the effect of Sir William Johnson's disapproval. But to Wheelock a disappointment was a goad, and when conditions in the province of New York became too unfavorable, and when he saw that his confidence in the Indian as a messenger of the Gospel and of learning was misplaced, he adapted himself to the conditions—and remodeled his plan.

The Indians whom he had sent to the Six Nations were themselves problems. Wheelock had brought some of them up from childhood, had instructed and disciplined them, and had observed them beset by vicissitudes caused by their lusts or their stupidities. Many of them he had pardoned more than once and with a liberalism and patience that belie the picture we have in our minds of the colonial minister. And now that they were in the field they continued to harass their master.

Let us follow in detail the history of two of these Indian teachers. As we know, Hezekiah Calvin entered the school in 1757, and in 1765 he began to teach at Fort Hunter. In the next year he sent this report to Wheelock:

I have now eighteen schollars which come very steady, but it his very hard to bring them too I do my best that I can and yet the Indians will complain that I am not severe enough will it do for me to be a thrashing them continually, how oft have I corrected them within a week sometimes twice or thrice a day I hate forever to be a whipping, whipping too much wont do. I told them if I was not severe enough they must in consequence get a severer one but I hope Sir in time to bring them too by the help of God which I cannot do without, all these means wont do, they are stubborn people sometimes I am ready to give out with these Indians and with the pains I have, I have a hard head ache certain time in the afternoon which sometimes is so hard that I hardly know what I am about &cc The Indians say that I shall not come home these three years they think that I am their servant and are obliged to keep school for them and yet they wont send their children It is true I should be glad to keep school here all my days but all these things makes me faint hearted together my wanting to see my father mother and relations

Oh! how glad should I be if I could do but a little good among these savages, but yet I think Indians will be Indians they will still follow their evill practices. &c.

Within two years Hezekiah was asking forgiveness: "It is enough to plunge Mr. Wheelock into a great greif, if an unfeigned promise of a good behaviour would in any wise move you for a farther trial and forgiveness of all my misconducts (I am sorry for my putting upon you by saying that I was a devil after Mr. Wheelock, which I knew not the meaning of at first) I would most humbly beg it,—And if their is no prospect of my doing any good to the design you have in view, doing good to my poor brethren, I desire to leave this school and not tarry to bring reproach upon this design any more, I have brought too much already—."

About this same time he fell in love with Mary Secuter, a Narraganset scholar at the school, to whose father he wrote coyly: "It may be no small thing that I have to acquant you with, the design that lay, between your daughter Moley, and me, pardon me if I blush to name it, that is matrimony but I shall not attempt it without your consent and approbation." The young schoolmaster (he may have been eighteen years old) was much worried about himself. He thought that he ought to go home, and he admitted that he was in love and that he would like to marry "and so follow farming business, to maintain me and my companion &c." Now and then, however, "the state and condition of my friends and fellow brethren would be hovering in my mind daily." The responsibility of leading a decent life, not to mention the responsibility of conducting a school in the wilderness, was too much for him. So we find him on December 26, 1767 (by this time he had returned to Lebanon) promising never to drink liquor again, and on the following January 29 writing out this abject confession in phrases much superior to those used by his fellows:

Honoured Sir,

The spirit of gratitude lays me under an indispensible duty of thanking you for all the care and pains you have taken in my education.

Tis true I have been guilty of drunkeness, but be assured the misfortune which occasioned me to depart so, was my being in liquor, or I never would have done it. I came to myself when or after I had got to Lebanon Plains. And after I found myself I was so ashamed of myself that I did not want to show myself in the school no more, But designed fully in my mind to follow the seas or go home. But I concluded to follow the seas, I went to Seabrook and their I found my me a sloop going to Virginia and intended to gone of with her, but as I was considering what I had been about, their came in my mind somthing as if I could not go, before I had given thanks to the Doctor for my education and then leave to depart from his school and presence,—and then after this I concluded to come back and see Mr. Wheelock before I could go with clear conscience &c Tis true I have been guilty of drunkenness now twice and of going away without leave numberless and it is with shame I put pen to paper, after having so notoriously abused your goodness and have brought a scandalous reproach upon the school by being scandalously drawn aside with liquor, thus to abuse thee, and thy school, for which I heartily beg pardon, promising double diligence in watching against any such evil practices for the future but having promised so many times, I would not, that you should any longer be deceived—I am now returning from my evil ways, to come home, and lay myself on my bended knees at thy feet, that I may wholly submit myself to the resentment of a master unjustly abused. If the acknowledging my crime can have any influence on your goodness, I am sure of success, I have incurrd your displeasure by my ill deeds on the eighteen day of January in the year of our Lord 1768. A weakness in me that is always attended with a hearty contrition and therefore ashamed of that action I leave the judgment of my weakness to you all who are present and am willing to suffer the judgment that you will pass upon me, having wholly condemned myself already worthy of great punishment and then to be turned away from the school with all the disgraces that can be. You know that our first motions are so arbitrary in their violence, that in spite of reason they will undergo no law but their own, therefore I beg you would consider that in the faults I have committed, there was more contributed by nature, than my own free will but as all mankind are subject to failings, and none perfect, I am consequently liable to step aside in liquor and commit errors. tis therefore I am heartily sorrow for being thus drawn aside from my reasons, but laying myself low at the feet of a just displeased superior imploreing thy compasion and acknowledging my fault with contrition, subscribe myself thine unworthy servant

Hez. Calvin

From now on his plaint is that he wants to go home, "but I beleive I should soon be tired of home and yet my mind is all the while cleaving to go home, and somtimes it excite a motion in my breast to go without leting the Doctor know of my intentions, when I am alone I am almost crazy I will catch my hair and pull and cry, for to go home." The next step in his downfall was his slandering of the school to the Narragansets at Charlestown, Rhode Island. In 1769 Wheelock reported him as a "drunkard and apostate" and a prisoner for having forged a pass for a negro. The story of Hezekiah Calvin's life ends with Wheelock's words, "and it is probable that he will fare badly."

The history of David Fowler's life parallels in passages that of Calvin, but the ending is happier. He was a Montauk, and had entered Moor's Charity School in 1759, at the age of twenty-four. Two years later he accompanied his brother-in-law, Samson Occom, to the Six Nations, in quest of recruits for the school. In 1765 he had been approved by the Connecticut Board of Correspondents, and had settled in Canajoharie, as has been stated.

The letters from him begin with a confession: he had left the school without permission. The next letter (1765) is one of his matrimonial letters regarding Amy Johnson, a Mohegan, and one of Wheelock's scholars:

Rev^d and Honoured Sir.

According to your desire I now send you a few words of our transaction.—I have determined to have Amy for my companion: I shall marry her as soon as I return from Onyda, if I find all things well betwixt us—We have settled all those things I told you of. some she confesd and some not: I suppose some were fals.—I hope, Sir you will take the best care you can of her. She wants a gown very much, handkerchief, also I wish you would let her have some fine linnen to make her &c. Don't know what else she wants, it is likely you will when you come up.—I know if you love her as much as you do me, all what she desires will be given: It is strange (if Mr. Wheelock, don't love my rib as well as my whole body.—I have given her a gold ring, which cost two dollars:—I hope Sir, you won't be displeased with me for that, I think it will do her good; now she sees my sincerity towards her. therefore she will put more weight upon what I say to her, it will also serve to keep her back from those things. She has been apprehened too often; though not once since she came here. She tells me that she is quite contented here and hopes to tarry all summer.—Do let her tarry the bigest part of this summer, if you dont design to send her to Boston. Sir you know, Woolly don't want one so dexterous as I do, at least he can do better with poor one than I can: for I want one that is handy in every thing: I expect to do great deal in reforming my poor brethren both in spiritual and temporal things; also I shall be always crowded with guests: I believe, you seem to see how it will be. from these reasons and many others I can produce had I time, you may see that I require one that can turn her hand to any thing that belongs to houswifry.

After I had some conversation with Mirs. Bull about Amy I understood that she han't had one well day since she came here: I suppose she cetch'd cold when I brought her up: she has continual pain in her side and head. I am afraid she is in a consumptive way: she should go to some skilful physician.—Sir, you dont know how much it disheartens me, when I consider her weakness it strikes such heaviness in my heart so that I am unwilling to leave her; for fear, you wont try to get her healed. O pray for her in secret and private, that God would give her health and strenght also all the graces she stands in need of and continue her a long and rich blessing in the world, that he would make her a pattern of piety and virtue to all her poor kindred, who will be about her. I am cut off from my expectation, I thought I found one that was able to go through hard work: but I see now I am in the same difficulty as before; but I hope for the better not for the worst.—

I did not hear of her illness till after I wrote you one letter, so I was obligd to writer another, that is the reason why I put it in the last place.—Poor girl I cant help loving her, she is indeed a pretty girl. And therefore from this time I shall keep clear from all girls whatsoever.

Having arrived without Amy Johnson at Oneida, New York, he informed Wheelock (May 29, 1765) that "I live like a dog here, my folks are poor and nasty, I eat with dogs, for they eat and drink out of the same as I do," and that "here are great number of children, but I cant tell you how many scholars I shall have. I beleive my singing school will exceed the other in number." In the next month he wrote this vivid, if not very pretty, description of conditions at Canajoharie:

This is the twelfth day since I began to keep this school, and I have put eight of my scholars into third page of the spelling book: some almost got down to the bottom of the same third:—I never saw children exceed these in learing. The number of my Scholars are twenty six when they are all present togather: but I cant keep them togather: they are always roving about from place to place to get something to live upon. provision is very scarce with them.

I am also teaching a singing school: they take great pleasure in learning to sing: we can already carry three parts of several tunes.

My friends are always looking for the ministers there is scarce a day passes over but that some body will ask me when will the ministers come: all that I can tell them, is, I expect they will come middle of this month. I have been treated very kindly since I came to this place,—I beleive I should want for nothing if they had wherewith to bestow it.

I find it very hard to live here without the other rib, for I am oblig'd to eat with dogs, I say, with dogs because they are continually liking water out off their pales and kettles; yea, I have often seen dogs eating their victuals when they set their dishes down, they'll only make a little noise to show their displeasure to dogs and take up the dish. finish of what was left. My cooks are nasty as hogs; their cloaths are black and greasy as my shoes. their hands are dirty as my Feet, but they cleanse them by kneading bread; their hands will be very clean after they have kneaded three of four loves of bread. I am oblig'd to eat whatsoever they give me for fear they will be displeas'd with me; after this month I shall try to clean some of them. for I must move along by degrees, if they once get out with me it is all over with me.

I shall have a house built me next week, then I shall have my victuals cleaner.

I think 30 lawful money per annum as the least that will be necessary will not be too much for my support for the three first years: It is very costly to live here, because it is so far from an English settlement; and I determine to live better than a hog, for my food now is not fit for any man, that has been used to have his victuals drest clean: I am almost sick now for want of some refreshment that is nourishing. I wish I had some of Mrs. Wheelock's bread and milk, little sweet cake and good boild meat. I could eat those things gready as a hog that has been kept in a pen two Days without it's swill.

Less than a year after David Fowler had resolved to "keep clear from all girls whatsoever" he had set his heart on another Indian girl, as he informs Wheelock:

I have wrote a large letter to Hannah Pyamphcouch which will iether spur her up or knock her in head.—I therefore ask a favour as a child from kind father or benefactor, that this letter may be sent to the supperscrib'd place as soon as you get it into your hands. For I shall be down about the 13 or 15 of June and in very great hast. I must tarry at your house a week or ten days the longest to shed my skin. for I am almost nached now. I want all my cloaths to be blue and that which is godd: The reason why I want this letter to get down so soon is, that she may have some time to think and dress herself up. and another which is the greatest that I may clear myself from those strong bonds wherewith I bound myself to her and which could not let me rest night and day from the time I left her till I returnd to her again. what I mean about clearing myself is if she denies. If she won't let her bones be joined with mine. I shall pick out my rib from your house. ———

Sir. Dont be angry with me for write so bold and foolish. I hope you will not expose me.

Whether the letter to which David referred was not sufficiently amatory or was unduly minatory is not known; we do know that he failed to win Hannah Pyamphcouch. But he quickly solaced himself by marrying Hannah Garret, a Pequot maiden resident among the Narragansets: "I find great profit by having the other rib join'd to my body for it hath taken away all my house work from me, but I had very hard spell geting it up here rocks and hills almost broke it into peices two or three times. But this topic will not answer to dwell on long."

By this time David Fowler gave promise of being one of the most successful Indian teachers sent out by Wheelock. But difficulties cropped up. Fowler was proud of his standing as a teacher and resentful of what seemed to him an assumption of authority on the part of Samuel Kirkland. He therefore warned Wheelock: "I speak calmly and sincerely not in ruffle. Another favour for Mr. Kirtlands comfort, which is this. Dont try to give him so much authority as that he would persuad or take upon himself to goven me or order me about. as soon as he try to do that he wont be so comfortable here; for he cant order me, nor no missonary that shall come into these parts. As I am an instructor I am able to act for myself, without having a master over me, &c."

Further complaints from Fowler: Wheelock has not supported him adequately, has treated him like a negro slave, has failed to write "when others received folio's after folio's," has called him harsh names. Far be it from Wheelock to receive

such complaints without returning a brisk reply. The answer
from Wheelock is given here without changes; this version is a
first draft or a copy of the letter sent, and is difficult to read because of the abbreviations which Wheelock habitually used:

Lebanon 26th Augt 1766

David Fowler

I this Minute received Yours and Sorry to find that you are not
yet come to your right Temper of Mind. Who has calld You a Devil,
or Said you are as proud as the Devil Since You came here? Who
has ever said that you have not behaved well in the Main since you
lived with me, or that I have not sat as much by You and expected
as much benefit to ye grand Design as by any Indian I ever Educated or there has there been any Indian y^t I ha' been mo. friend^y to
y^n to y^o & y^r Charact^r.—ha' I ev^r S^d y^o ha' not done mo. for my Benefit y^n all ye Indians I ever had &c. and now y^o say I am too bad to
live in ye House for one of my mySteps y^{r}efore I must leave y^o & y^r
School y^s very day & go weep^g in ye Road Homeward—Now David
cons^r a little. Is this Just comely and reasonable Treatment of me.
ha' I s^d worse of y^o or to y^o y^n y^t I was afraid y^t ye Prid of y^r ☉^{1} aspird
aft^r such Grand^r as was not for ye Gl^y of G. & cod not consist with y^e
good of ye gen^l Design in view. y^t w^n I had given y^o leave to get every
thing y^t y^o wanted for ye Design & told y^o I begrutchd y^o noth^g y^t was
necess^{ry} for y^o.—y^t y^o shod affect to cloath yslf & Hannah like Cour-
tiers & w^n y^o knew y^t I had been already reproachd thro' ye Country,
as I ha' been only for lett^g y^o Wear an old velvet Coat y^t was given to
y^o—I told y^o y^t ye Eyes of all Europe & America w^{re} Upon y^o & me
too. & ye Eyes of thousands w^o are unfriendly & will not fail to Catch
at any occasion to reproach me & ye Design—I told y^o it was no Interest of mine but only y^r Hon^r & Interest of X^2 y^t I was plead^g for,
& ye Success of y^t Cause w^c has been so long an (—?) & in w^c I ha' So
much labourd & Worn out myself—& w^c certainly so nearly concerns
y^o as me to Lab^r to promote—did y^o not w^n I was only Enquir^g w^t it
was prud^t & best for y^o to ha' so many as 4 p^r of shoes at once rise up
& wth a very unbecom^g air go out of ye Room & Say I w^{ll} ha' no shoes
I'll wear Indian shoes—& how y^o & Hannah ha' Spent y^r prec. Hours
yesterday & t'day I know not—Or how y^o will live or w^n y^o will serve

---

^{1} A symbol for "heart." ^{2} Christ.

tog^r I know not I wish y^r Sett^g out w^{re} mo. in ye Meekness & Humility of X—as for my own p^t great as ye prospects of y^r Usefulness are, (and y^e are very great if y^o will take G.[1] with You) I don't at all des^r you shod return to Onoida wth y^r present Tempers—nor am I at all afraid but I can fully vindicate my own Reputation, take w^t Course y^o Will—I suppose y^o cant reasonably think it unjust if ye Whole & plain Truth comes to ye Light of ye World, if I am put upon my own Vindication—nor do I think y^o can feal very Easie if y^o sho^d go 'till y^o return to me again. w^c I promise myself y^o will do as Soon as y^o return to God. my Heart is ye Same and as full of Kindness & Good Will tow^{ds} You as ever it has been. and I am as ready to do any thing y^t will Hon^r Christ && promote ye Salv^n of ye Souls of ye poor Indians as ever I was—but I ha' no notion of Send^g any Man w^o is aiming to set up himself instead of XJ.[2] as ye obj^t of y^r W^p & w^n y^o will app^r ye Same as y^o ha' heretofore done y^o will find me ye same

I am

Y^r Sincere Well wisher

Eleaz^r Wheelock

The letter did not conciliate Fowler, and he soon left Wheelock's service for good to teach at Montauk, Long Island. Ultimately he settled with the Oneidas, among whom he was a respected leader and an industrious farmer, until his death in 1807.

So many names of relatively unknown teachers have been mentioned in this chapter that the reader may welcome a summary of Wheelock's work from 1761, when the first missionaries left Lebanon to begin their preaching among the Indians, to the fall of 1768, at which time they were forced from the province of New York.

During these seven years Wheelock had sent eight white missionaries[3] to New York, all of whom had received their elemen-

---

[1] God. [2] Christ Jesus.

[3] David Avery, Theophilus Chamberlain, Phineas Dodge, Samuel Johnson, Aaron Kinne, Samuel Kirkland, David M'Clure, Titus Smith.

tary training at Moor's Charity School, and a ninth, Charles Jeffry Smith, whom Wheelock had not trained. Their terms of service as missionaries, whether under Wheelock or not, ranged from a few months to forty years.

In addition, Wheelock had sent at least thirteen, and perhaps as many as fifteen, Indians as missionaries, schoolmasters, and assistants, all likewise educated on charity at the school, with the exception of Samson Occom. The proportion of Indian students deemed capable of teaching is surprisingly large. While we cannot write with finality, it appears that Wheelock and his assistants had taught between forty and forty-five *male* Indians from 1754, when the school proper begins, to 1768. Two of these had died not long after their coming to Lebanon, half a dozen had left the school for various reasons with less than a year's schooling, and some had attended the school for less than a year before this phase of the missionary work ended in 1768. Of the remainder, approximately forty per cent were delegated to posts among the Six Nations. These whites and Indians preached and taught at Cherry Valley, Chenango, Canajoharie, Canadasaga, Onohoquaga, Butlersbury, and Fort Hunter.

Nor can we write with desirable accuracy of the number of students under these schoolmasters. Certainly they amounted to several hundred. And no guess at all can be hazarded regarding the many Indians to whom the missionaries preached.

Wheelock was to be much embittered by the defection of some of these men whose training had added an enormous burden to his regular ministerial and teaching duties, and we today sympathize with him in his disappointment. On the other hand, his success with them did not terminate as soon as they had left his service; he had given many of them the groundwork for better lives, whether they were to be laymen among the Indians or ministers established in New England parishes. Viewed in this light the "great design" contributed appreciably to the development of American culture in the eighteenth century.

CHAPTER VII

IT is not clear at what precise date Wheelock first planned to remove from Lebanon; roughly, the date may be given as 1761.

There were various reasons for his desire to find a new location. In the early years of Moor's Charity School Wheelock had insisted on the necessity of bringing Indian scholars from their native surroundings to the civilized community of Lebanon. He was soon to learn how difficult it was to bring young Indian boys and girls a distance of some one hundred and thirty miles, and to restrain them from returning to their homes. Furthermore, the journey was expensive for schoolmasters and missionaries, and communication was slow and irregular.

Other causes operated also. In spite of many efforts he had not been able to obtain a charter for the school from the Connecticut General Assembly. Lord Halifax (President of the British Board of Trade), to be sure, had suggested that Wheelock "get a law in this (*Connecticut*) government establishing the same" and had promised to have it ratified in Council, but the General Assembly raised objections: the forming of a corporation within a corporation might endanger the peace and unity of the government; the undertaking might prove a burden to the colony; such a corporation could not extend beyond Connecticut; "to send it home to be enlarged will be such a precedent as we do not chuse"; the neighboring governments are already envious of our charter privileges—.

Perhaps, too, the many frictions between Wheelock and his parishioners played their part. For years there had been trouble about his salary. His parishioners frequently rebelled against his discipline. And on Wheelock's part there was a diminution of zeal; never again was he to display, as a preacher, the energy which had characterized him during the Great Awakening.

Friends, and some not quite friends, made suggestions. Former students pointed in the various directions of the compass. If Wheelock had investigated all the locations suggested, he would have traveled as far north as Nova Scotia, south to South Carolina, and from the center of the province of New York to the Mississippi River, with many side trips in most of the New England colonies. "We can have the pick of America" is the phrase used in his correspondence, and if the statement was exaggerated, it was *reasonably* exaggerated.

Not many offers came from within his own colony. Lebanon offered to sell Wheelock five hundred acres, and to give him about eight hundred pounds, lawful money, and as convenient seats in church for the students as possible. Hebron promised a thousand pounds. George Whitefield favored Hebron or Lebanon, "on your own land." And it was thought that Wheelock's birthplace, Windham, would offer two thousand pounds, sterling. But not only was none of these offers alluring enough to offset the disadvantages of remaining in Connecticut: combined they were trivial compared with the grandiose scheme which Wheelock had evolved. He had set his heart on the Wyoming Valley in northeastern Pennsylvania, a territory which had been purchased by the Susquehanna Company, composed of Connecticut citizens, from the Six Nations in 1754. Here Wheelock hoped to obtain a tract of land large enough to accommodate not only his school but three or four towns!

This plan he broached to Sir William Johnson (Superintendent of Indian Affairs) in 1761; not having received a reply by August 20, 1762, he again asked Johnson for his aid in obtaining the tract. On September 8 he wrote a third time, and in the following October received Johnson's discouraging answer: "Whilst the Indians remain in their present sentiments it will be highly improper to attempt any establishment in their country, as they are greatly disgusted at the great thirst which we all seem to show for their lands, and therefore I must give it as my opinion that any settlement on the Susquehanna River may prove fatal to those who should attempt to establish themselves thereon, as the Indians have all declared not only their great aversion thereto, but have also threatened to prevent any such settlement, so that I hope the dangers to which they may be exposed, together with your Governours proclamation against the same, will induce those concerned to drop their undertaking."

Johnson's forecast, which proved to be correct, did not deter Wheelock. In 1763 he petitioned General Amherst for a tract along the Susquehanna of fifteen or twenty miles square, one thousand acres of which he wished for the charity school. To this request Amherst replied that the land was not at his disposal and that a petition to the king was necessary.[1]

Once more, however, Wheelock had reason to believe that he might get a patent for part of the Wyoming Valley, this time with the help of Eliphalet Dyer, born as was Wheelock, in Windham, Connecticut, a lawyer, and one of the original members of the Susquehanna Company. Because the Pennsylvanians had challenged the title to the Wyoming Valley of the Susquehanna Company, Dyer had been sent to England in 1763 to have the title held by the company confirmed. To him Wheelock had, by invitation, outlined his new plan for the school. Unfortunately, Dyer failed in his mission, and with his failure vanished Wheelock's hope for land in northeastern Pennsylvania.

The next person from whom Wheelock sought aid was General Phineas Lyman, a citizen of Connecticut and a notable commander of Provincials during the Seven Years' War. In

[1] *Documentary History of New York,* IV, 210, 212.

1763 he had gone to England to obtain land for his soldiers in order to establish colonies along the Mississippi and the Ohio rivers; to Wheelock he promised that he would try to obtain a royal patent for land.

Now that Wheelock had, as it seemed, a valuable ally to plead for him, he enlarged his scheme, as set forth in the following *Proposal for Introducing Religion, Learning, Agriculture, and Manufacture among the Pagans in America:*

That a tract of the late conquered land 30 or 35 miles square, conveniently situate in the heart of the Indian country, be granted in favor of this design, that every third township be given and so secured to the Indians and their heirs, that it may not be in their power to sell it to the English. That a large farm of several thousand acres of and within said grant be given to this Indian school. That the school be an academy for all parts of useful learning; part of it a college for the education of missionaries, schoolmasters, interpreters &c; and part of it a school for reading and writing &c. And that there be manufactures both for males and females for all needful trades, and they so situate that all may attend the worship of God in the same place; and the whole be supplied with proper officers, tutors, masters, and mistresses. That there be a sufficient number of labourers upon the lands belonging to the school, and that the students be obliged to labour with them, and under their direction and conduct so much as shall be necessary for their health, and to give them an understanding of husbandry, and also those design'd for trades to be instructed in husbandry. And those designed for farmers after they have got a sufficient degree of school learning to labour constantly upon said lands 'till they come to an age and ability sufficient to set up for themselves, and introduce agriculture among their brethren; and the school to have all the benefit of these labours. That the two thirds of said tract belonging to the English be peopled with a chosen number of inhabitants, of known honesty, integrity, and such as love and will be kind to, and honest in their dealings with the Indians. That the several towns be furnished with ministers of the best character, and such as shall be of ability when incorporated with a number of the most learned and judicious of the inhabitants, to conduct the affairs of the school, and of such missions, as they shall have occasion, and ability for from time to time. And that so fast as Indians appear willing to come into such a way of living, they be assisted by the English on both sides them in setting up husbandry and settling the Gospel, and schools among them. And that there be a fund in the hands of trustees for the support of the whole design. That the whole granted tract be a borough indowed with such privileges and immunities as may be necessary and beneficial to the success and progress of the whole undertaking. And that in order to obtain a fund, the corporation be speedily existing of such as live so near to one another, that they may conveniently meet as there shall be occasion on the affair, and when all matters are prepared such as dont design to remove with the school may resign their places to those who do.

Such a manner of introducing the affair, with so many of their own sons already in the school, and many of them well fitted for missionaries, schoolmasters &c will be the most likely mean to convince the savages of the sincerity of our intentions, conciliate their friendship, render our cohabitation with them safe for us, and invite them to a complyance with the design proposed and likely after an entrance on the design is made the school may be supported for less than half the expence. Also vast expence for the support of missionaries, now occasioned and necessary on account of our great distance would be prevented, our missionarys be much better and more agreably provided for, than can be at present; and have the advantage of council and direction in difficult occurrances, and yet always the melancholly thought that they are so far out of the world, as to friendly assistance in case of sickness, or suspicion of peril and danger &c.

The whole is humbly submitted to the censure or correction of all the judicious who love our Lord Jesus Christ in sincerity, and long for the inlargement and prosperity of Zion.

General Lyman also was unsuccessful; indeed, he had to wait seven years (until 1770) before he obtained any land for himself. Before the end of that period Wheelock had not only obtained land in New Hampshire, but had founded Dartmouth College.

It is of course futile to speculate on how Wheelock's plan would have developed if he had obtained any of these tracts. But it is certain that if he had settled in the Wyoming Valley he would have become involved in the so-called Pennamite-Yankee Wars (the conflicts between the citizens of Pennsylvania and of Connecticut), and disaster would probably have been his fate during the Wyoming Massacre of 1778, when the Indians drove out or slaughtered the white men in the Valley.

A few details regarding other locations will show how zealous Wheelock was in bringing about a removal from Lebanon. In the spring of 1766 he inquired by letter of the mayor of Albany regarding that city as a possible location. To this inquiry the mayor replied that "we esteem ourselves peculiarly happy that an opportunity is offered us, to show how much we are inclined to promote a plan so universally countenanced, and so deservedly applauded." In praise of Albany the mayor and the aldermen stated that it was not exposed to Indian warfare, that it is located on an important waterway, and that the Mohawks were only forty miles away. As inducements they offered six and a half acres of land, on which was a sixteen room house; and commonage for his cattle. All this they valued at £2,300, sterling. In return they would expect Wheelock to educate the children of the city at a reasonable charge. The correspondence continued for about two years—at one point Wheelock stated that he had heard rumors of immorality among the citizens of Albany, a charge strongly denied by the mayor—and terminated after the ire of Sir William Johnson had been aroused at the Fort Stanwix Congress against Wheelock's agents. Regarding this episode details will be given later.

The South did not attract Wheelock, mainly because he was unacquainted with it. With the exceptions of George Whitefield, who conducted an orphanage in Georgia, and of Charles Jeffry Smith, formerly one of Wheelock's missionaries, who had preached among negroes mostly in Virginia, he knew of no one who could give him first hand information about a section of the country which he had never visited. Hence Wheelock could not take seriously Sir William Johnson's suggestion, made also by Smith, that he remove to North or South Carolina. Even less likely to suit Wheelock was the proposal that he merge his school with the College of New Jersey! The begetter of that idea knew little of Wheelock's disposition. And Occom's recommendation of Long Island because of the abundance of fish, oysters, clams, and salt hay was not weighed seriously.

From Colonel Oliver Partridge came a promise of "something handsome in the western part of Massachusetts," an offer that became more definite in 1768 in the form of two thousand acres in Pittsfield. Governor Francis Bernard was reported as willing to charter a *college* provided a Massachusetts site were chosen; proprietors of Stockbridge offered a thousand acres (of which the Indians there were to give five hundred), and money and materials estimated at £220 sterling.

But of all the New England colonies Massachusetts appealed to Wheelock the least. For years he had known that many in Boston were opposed to him both as a preacher and as an educator; Charles Chauncy had strongly criticised his preaching, and in company with other ministers of Boston had objected to Wheelock's teaching the Indians more than the rudiments of learning; and a group in Boston had tried to discredit Samson Occom as a *bona fide* Indian convert. As Wheelock wrote to the Reverend Timothy Woodbridge (November 12, 1768), "All the known opposers of this school are in the metropolis of Massachusetts, . . . you have a college for the supply of the churches &c., which will likely have a jealous and envious eye upon this school . . . it will never be patronized if so much as favoured." In contrast Wheelock set forth the advantages of

118

New Hampshire: a favorable reception to the school, a larger grant of land, soil as good as or better than that of Massachusetts, and an abundance of cheap provisions.

At the time of his writing this letter Wheelock had been searching for seven years for a favorable location. Much of the search had been conducted by correspondence, much also by agents: Benjamin Pomeroy, Ralph Wheelock, Ebenezer Cleaveland, and others. But, as has been shown, for one reason or another Wheelock's requests had been refused or he had rejected offers. This search had been carried on, of course, in order that he might more efficiently convert and educate the Indians of the Six Nations, in particular. He was now (in 1768) to be rejected by those very people. This termination of the work of Wheelock's missionaries in the province of New York was effected by the hostility of Sir William Johnson and the bungling of stupid agents acting for Wheelock. To this repulse we now give our attention.

CHAPTER VIII

FOR years Wheelock had counted heavily on the goodwill of Sir William Johnson toward the school. In 1756 he had applied to him for aid and had been answered favorably. Five years later Johnson sent five Indians to Moor's Charity School, and in 1762 wrote to Benjamin Pomeroy: "I have always entertained the most favorable sentiments" toward Wheelock, and "I shall at all times be glad to promote so useful a design."[1] Johnson showed his interest in other ways, also, by granting supplies from the King's stores to some of the missionaries, by his friendliness to Kirkland, and by sending medicine for Ralph Wheelock.

But as superintendent of the Indians Johnson viewed with disfavor the efforts of New Englanders to acquire land among his wards. To Lord Amherst he wrote that the Mohawks were much disturbed at the thought of a Connecticut settlement, and that the people from that state "may prove a means of oversetting all our good measures hitherto taken to satisfy the Indians."[2] And as a member of the Church of England Johnson was not sympathetic to Congregationalists and Presbyterians. Five months after he had informed Benjamin Pomeroy of his "favorable sentiments," he wrote Henry Barclay that "all those Indians who are instructed by the Dissenting ministers (who are the only clergy in these parts) have imbibed an air of the most enthusiastical cant (*crossed out:* and are in short intermixed with the greatest distortion of the features and zealous belchings of the Spirit, resembling the most bigoted Puritans. Their whole time being spent in singing psalms amongst the country people, whereby they neglect their hunting and

[1] *Doc. Hist. of N.Y.*, IV, 205, Oct. 16, 1762.
[2] *Johnson Papers*, IV, 71, March 30, 1763.

most worldly affairs, and are in short become very worthless members of society.)"[1] To Samuel Johnson (formerly the first president of King's College, and at this time rector at Stratford, Connecticut) Sir William wrote: "Mr. Wheelock's plan for a school at Lebanon would not have answered any extensive purpose, as the distant and most numerous nations are a very jealous martial people unlike those of New England having an utter aversion to sending their youth at any distance amongst white people so that the very few who might be persuaded to come down the country would relapse into their original barbarity on their return from the contagious example of the rest."[2]

Let the reader not hastily infer that the man of the world was completely hoodwinking the man of God. Clearly Johnson was not straightforward in his letters to Wheelock, but the latter was shrewd enough to know that letters need not express the writer's whole intention; some inkling Wheelock must have had of Johnson's plans, because he wrote to Nathaniel Whitaker (in 1767) that Johnson no doubt "designs the Six Nations shall be supplied with Episcopalians."

Wheelock's surmise was correct. So desirous was Johnson of accomplishing his plan that he informed the Society for the Propagation of the Gospel (sponsored by the Church of England): "I would rather take upon myself the sallary than suffer so good a design to drop."[3] A year later, in answer to a letter from Wheelock asking for information about a rumor to the same effect, Sir William ingenuously replied that "by the accounts I have received from the Venerable Society, and by other letters[4] I am informed of their having an establishment

---

[1] *Idem*, IV, 72, March 30, 1763.

[2] *Idem*, V, 439, Dec. 2, 1766.　　　　[3] *Idem*, V, 414, Nov. 8, 1766.

[4] His interest in establishing missionaries and ministers from the Church of England is shown in his own letters: *idem*, IV, 72, March 30, 1763; V, 27, Feb. 1, 1766; 388, Oct. 8, 1766; 413, Nov. 8, 1766; 438, Dec. 2, 1766, to cite only a few.

much at heart and of their resolutions to put the same immediately into execution, to which end I understand that proper clergymen were forthwith to go upon the charge—. I flatter myself you are fully persuaded of the countenance I have always given to your endeavors for the instruction of the Indians, and you may always rely on the continuance of it, wherever it shall appear necessary, from the persuasion that your pursuits will be wisely dictated by a disinterested zeal and a becoming prudence, especially in affairs respecting the Nations who have received the first principles of religion from ministers of, and according to the rites of the Established Church of England, and I am convinced that the clergy of that church as well as the Society will equally approve of all undertakings which appear to flow from generous principles of charity, without any views tending to prejudice the Indians, against the religious forms, or civil manners of that church—. The countenance which I have afforded the gentlemen you sent on this service, as it has been their principal introduction and security will remain as so many manifest proofs of my regards, and the continuance of it you may firmly rely upon, wheresoever it shall be deemed necessary for these laudable purposes."[1]

Eleazar Wheelock could never have overcome in his negotiations with Sir William the handicaps of his Congregationalism and of his Connecticut citizenship. To Sir William the Dissenters were actual or potential enemies of the Crown and from his point of view the New Englanders were intent on acquiring land for selfish purposes. These animosities are clearly expressed in a letter to Daniel Barton: "I cannot but think that the members of that Church (*the Church of England*) are the surest supporters of the Constitution, and that they are the faithfullest subjects of the Crown an argument which may be particularly applied to America where the number of the Dis-

[1] *Johnson Papers*, V, 683, Sept. 19, 1767.

senters and the measures they pursue threaten more than our religious libertys if not timely prevented—. Mr. Wheelock's plan seems a laudable one but give me leave to remark that many of these schemes which had their birth in N. England have soon appeared calculated with a view to forming settlements so obnoxious to the Indians who have repeatedly declared their aversion to those who acted on such interested principles; all the good lands in N. England being thick settled they are extremely desirous of migrating and have created much disturbance by attempting it, another objection is that those brought up under the care of Dissenting ministers become a gloomy race and lose their abilities for hunting &c., spend their time in idleness and hanging upon the inhabitants for a wretched subsistence having lost those qualities which render them usefull to us without acquiring any others in their place worthy the name of Christians to which indeed they have little or no pretensions all which discountenances religion with the rest of the Indians."[1]

Thus even before the Fort Stanwix Congress of 1768 Wheelock was practically debarred from forming permanent settlements among the Indians; his proposal for a tract of land in the Indian country was likely to be opposed by the savages, and because of Johnson's hostility, political and religious, would certainly be rejected.

The Congress had been called to establish what lands should be reserved for the Indians and what territory should be open for settlement by the whites. The Indians were present in great numbers, and Johnson and the assembled governors had laden bateaux with goods and rum to facilitate negotiations. No time could have been less propitious for furthering Wheelock's plans. Yet Wheelock's first representative to arrive at the Con-

[1] *Idem,* V, 388, Oct. 8, 1766.

gress, David Avery, petitioned Sir William to stop the projected sale of land!

The second representative from Moor's Charity School was the Reverend Jacob Johnson, whom Wheelock had accepted only after better choices had failed. He was eccentric. According to an account written by one of his descendants,[1] he wore a "girdle of hair" in imitation of John the Baptist, was a seer, had a premonition of his own death, prepared for his funeral, dug his own grave, and died on the day foretold. To him Wheelock's future success among the Indians had been entrusted.

Jacob Johnson at once set about dissuading the Indians from parting with their land. Seemingly, the Indians threatened him with violence, because he felt obliged to write to Sir William for protection against them and "the priests," adding, "As I am a seer, I may be knowing to some things your Excellency possibly may not which occasions me thus to write."[2] In addition he proposed a toast, the exact nature not known, which gave offence to the dignitaries at a banquet, and offered a stupid explanation of it in an effort to exonerate himself: he would continue to drink the health of the King as long as the King ruled justly, but if the King began to rule with a rod of iron, he, Jacob Johnson, would seek a retreat elsewhere or join with the discontented in founding an empire distant from the British. And having warned Sir William that "we are quite unwilling to be circumvented in any way whatsoever being assured our design is good," he proceeded to address the savages, asking them to donate a tract of land on or near the Mohawk River for the use of the school!

Whatever of high seriousness there may have been in these efforts of David Avery and Jacob Johnson, and however much the public events of the next decade may be taken as justification of Jacob Johnson's rebellious political sentiments, the

[1] F. C. Johnson, *Rev. Jacob Johnson.*   [2] *Doc. Hist. of N.Y.*, IV, 247.

position of Moor's Charity School could hardly have been strengthened by actions and speeches offensive to the white leaders at the Congress, and by demands that were construed by Indians and whites to be as selfish as those which the representatives of the school were opposing.

As soon as Avery realized how eccentric Jacob Johnson was, he sent a messenger to Wheelock. In an effort to save the school, and his own reputation, Wheelock dispatched two other representatives (Ebenezer Cleaveland and Allen Mather) about the middle of October. They might as well have spared themselves the laborious journey. Sir William had had enough of emissaries from Lebanon: to him they were guilty of treason, and were liable to be sent across the Atlantic to stand trial. To General Gage he wrote that a desire to gain land rather than to advance the cause of religion had been the main aim of the missionaries.[1]

Perhaps it was because he was unwilling to learn anything more from Jacob Johnson that Wheelock wrote to him at the beginning of 1769: "You need give yourself no uneasiness at all about the affair of the Congress; all is right, and well. I han't so much concern about it as to spend time to hear it, if you were here." In a letter to Sir William in the same year he asserted that Jacob Johnson had no commission for any one step which he took, that he was supposed to request countenance for the school, and nothing more. He condemned, too, his agent's "total deficiency as to common sense." And to Hugh Wallace of New York he complained, with a sad lack of Christian charity (and clarity), that "the animal had been delving in a swamp to fit it for mowing before he went on his mission, and it seems he had never got of the mire, or if he had, he had got quite out of his eliment by it."

All this was sufficient of itself to eliminate Wheelock's mis-

1 *Idem*, IV, 249, Nov. 24, 1768.

sionaries from the province of New York. But still another agent was helping to sever relations between the Six Nations and the school: Wheelock's oldest son, Ralph. One would like to be charitable to him. He was an epileptic and felt keenly his physical handicap. For three years previous to his entering the College of New Jersey he had suffered so much that, to use his father's phrase to President Finley, he had been unable to read even a chapter in the Bible at a sitting. After two years at the College of New Jersey he transferred to Yale, by the advice of his tutor, graduated in 1765, and taught for two years at Moor's Charity School. He undoubtedly tried to make something of himself, but will power could not make him a well man. To this extent he enlists our sympathy. But for his blustering, his arrogance, his stupid, tactless conduct toward the Indians he deserves nothing but condemnation.

Ralph Wheelock visited the Indians three times: in 1766, in the company of Benjamin Pomeroy, in the following year, and once again in 1768. Wheelock refused to believe ill of Ralph, and as proof of his confidence had named him as his successor. It was not until 1771 that he learned the truth about Ralph's harmful influence. In that year Wheelock sent David Avery to report on the attitude of the Oneidas toward his missionaries, and from Avery's report of Ralph his father finally learned that his confidence had been misplaced.

As Avery reported, the Oneida spokesmen, assembled at Canajoharie, were at first mild in their comments. Thus, referring to Eleazar Wheelock, then living in Hanover, one of them answered Avery in the following words:

Our great father is really to be pitied! He resides yonder at a great distance, in the woods as well as we, and knows nothing what is done and doing here among us Indians. There he sits and thinks, and longs to have all the Indians become an holy people, and does not conceive or imagine any great obstacles in the way, because his heart is so full of benevolence towards the Indians, and thinks that they must view his good design in the same light as he does.

At a later meeting (June 5, 1772) they were more outspoken:

English schools we do not approve of here, as serviceable to our spiritual interest, and almost all those who have been instructed in English are a reproach to us. This we supposed our father was long ago sufficiently appraised. And as to our neighboring towns, there is not, at present, the least gleam of light, even no appearance at all which embraces such a proposal.

Our father does not know the mind of Indians: their minds are invincible; they are strongly attached to other things. We don't say to what our minds are most strongly attached, but of this we are confident, that they are not disposed to embrace the Gospel, for here we are upon the spot, with open ears, ready to receive such intelligence.

Moreover, we are dispised by our brethren, on account of our Christian profession. Time was when we were esteemed as honorable and important in the confederacy, but now we are looked upon as small things, or rather as nothing at all. Now, may we not conclude that they don't favor your designs? Or would they speak well of us instead of reproaching us for embracing this religion you are endeavoring to publish among them?

As to your expectations of a favorable answer from the Onondagas, we must desire you to cut off your hope, and not protract it to any farther length, for we know by experience that hope defered is very painful.

Father, we must tell you. Your former speech there, by your son, made so little impression and has left so few marks, that we have never been able since to find any traces of it, tho' we have often discoursed with one another upon the subject. We never conceived that the least expectation should be at all excited in our great father's mind of their acceptance of his proposal, from what past there, if he has been rightly informed.

Up to this point the Indians had restrained themselves. Thomas, an Oneida, now reported the gist of a speech by Ralph, who had accused Samuel Kirkland of running away from the missionary field. Kirkland, to be sure, had returned to Lebanon just prior to Ralph's visit of 1768, but the reason for his return had been the need of medical care and not cowardice. Ralph's accusation was as follows:

> My brethren, I am come here in business of importance, sent by my father. I am surprised that your father (Kirkland) has run away upon my coming. I depended upon his assistance, and so did my father, as he trained him for this purpose. I am bound to Onondaga, to know their minds respecting my father's school. You see, my brethren, my situation. I am left alone. I now ask your assistance. You see your father has run off in this manner and left me. And it seems that instead of helping, he is counteracting my father.
>
> To this, father the less (Avery), we replied as follows: "Your situation, brother, is very difficult; but we wonder that you should expect our father's assistance, when he wants one to lead himself. He has been for a great while scarce able to speak, and be sure, not to run. Moreover, brother, the time was appointed for his removal before you came, and we advised to it: tho' some of us thought he never would be able to perform the journey, and would die by the way."

As the conference proceeded, the Indians gradually lost their patience, and Ralph did not improve in tact. He said:

> I hope you will consider carefully all these things I have told you, as I am sent in consequence of the command of Jesus, and by immediate orders of my father, who is the head of the ministers in New England, and known the other side the waters; and many great ones on this side and the other side are engaged to assist in his instructing the Indians. I act in consort with my father, engaged in the same work; you will therefore consider me here speaking in his stead—and when he dies I shall succeed him, and manage all the affairs of instructing the Indians.
>
> Now, you see I have told you all things. If you do not receive and embrace the message I am upon, I shall wash my hands of your blood. My father also will be clear of the blood of you all. And it may be Jesus is about to return, then we shall all see and know the truth of these things.

To which the Indian spokesman answered:

Brother, we heartily thank you that we now understand the whole of your message, as you are come with the word of God. You have spoke exceedingly well! Very sweet words indeed, as coming from the tongue, from whence we perceive you have spoke!

But, brother, do you think we are altogether ignorant of your methods of instruction? (Then taking and shaking him by the shoulder said) Why, brother, you are deceiving yourself! We understand not only your speech, but your manner of teaching Indians. We understand affairs that are transacted at a great distance to the westward—they are brought here; this is our centering council-house. Just so well am I acquainted with your deportment. I view all your conduct as just by under my eyes. Take care, brother! In the first place, correct yourself. Learn, yourself, to understand the word of God before you undertake to teach and govern others. For when you have come to understand it yourself, perhaps some of our children will like to make trial of your instructions. For the present, brother, I shall watch your future conduct. You have spoke exceedingly well, even to our surprise, that our children should become wise in all things by your instructions, and treated as children at your house, and not servants.

Brother, take care—you were too hasty and strong in your manner of speaking, before the children and boys have any knowledge of your language.

Why, brother, if another hears my dog barking or having hold of a creature and bids him get out, and perhaps he don't obey him immediately, not understanding the voice; upon which the stranger catches up a club and malls my dog—I shall resent it because he is my dog. Brother, I love my dog. What do you think of children then in the like case?

(Here they spake with high elevation of voice, and their answers were loud shouts of contempt. Upon which I desired them to speak more moderately, as Mr. Wheelock was ignorant of their language and in a strange country. I saw he was much affrighted and feared he would go into one of his usual fits. The sachem upon this immediately turned to the speaker, and desired him to lower and soften his voice. This he did, but soon broke off, when they whispered sometime among themselves, and at length proceeded and said):

Brother, you must learn of the French ministers if you would understand and know how to treat Indians. They don't speak roughly, nor do they for every little mistake take up a club and flog them. It seems to us that they teach the word of God and can't see those they instruct naked and hungry.

Thus had gone awry Wheelock's plans for saving the savages in the province of New York. In 1769 the Oneidas had withdrawn their children from Moor's Charity School, ostensibly that they might have them at home for a visit. Sir William Johnson had shown his hostility, and the Indians in conclaves had expressed their antagonism. The last word was probably said by David Avery, who in June, 1772, delivered a valedictory, or maledictory, to the Indians, listing their sins in thirty categories, with subheadings, followed by nineteen remarks and admonitions. According to his notation, their temper seemed "much like that of the Gadarenes when they desired Christ to depart out of their coasts."

The Society for the Propagation of the Gospel established missions at the very locations which Wheelock had selected for his own schools.

CHAPTER IX

DISILLUSIONMENT

AT this point in the narrative it will be well to consider in detail the effects of Wheelock's program on the Indian students. Of course, the results of an educator's efforts are in the main unrecorded and intangible. *This* student he has taught for a semester, for a year, for two years; how is the teaching to be estimated? Are we to count up: so many have become leaders in business; so many, teachers, whose results will also in the main be unrecorded and intangible; so many, too hastily introduced to a new mode of living, to a new manner of thinking, and thus left "wandering between two worlds"? What standard have we by which to judge the efficacy of the instruction?

Wheelock had a standard. He held firmly certain values, and knew what he was training for. All Indians, male, received at Moor's Charity School, so the standard defined, were to enter the missionary field that they might preach the Gospel, impart a knowledge of the rudiments of a secular education, and assist their untutored kin to the better life by their example as teachers, farmers, model Christians. The Indian girls, after their training in Lebanon were, as already stated, "to perform the female part, as housewives, school-mistresses, tayloresses, &c., and to go and be with these youth, when they shall be hundreds of miles distant from the English on the business of their mission."

From confidence, to doubt, to disillusionment: this is the history of Wheelock's attitude toward removing the Indians from their native haunts in order to educate them. That his hopes were high in the early days of Moor's Charity School has already been made sufficiently clear. But by 1763, after nine years of experience, Wheelock began to doubt.

And if one half of the Indian boys thus educated shall prove good and useful men, there will be no reason to regret our toil and expence for the whole. And if God shall deny His blessing on our endeavours, as to the general design, it may be these particular youth may reap eternal advantage by what we shall do for them; and if but one in ten does so, we shall have no cause to think much of the expence. And if a blessing be denied to all, "we shall notwithstanding be unto God a sweet savour of Christ in them that perish."[1]

One-half, one-tenth, perhaps none.

Eight years after Wheelock had penned that statement he expressed (in 1771) his despair in the following manner:

The most melancholy part of the account which I have here to relate, and which occasioned me the greatest weight of sorrow, has been the bad conduct and behaviour of such as have been educated here, after they have left the school, and been put into business abroad: and it is that from which, I think, I had the fullest evidence that a greater proportion of English youths must be fitted for missionaries; and enough of them to take the lead entirely, and conduct the whole affair of christianizing the savages, without any dependance upon their own sons, as leaders, in this matter, or any further, than they are employed under the immediate inspection and direction of Englishmen.

It is with regret I give the account, I should gladly suppress this part of it, did not justice to the public, and the vindication of my own conduct in the affair require it.

Among those whom I have educated, there have been near forty who were good readers and writers, and were instructed in the principles of the Christian religion, and were sufficiently masters of English grammar, arithmetic, and a number of them considerably advanced in the knowledge of Greek and Latin, and one of them carried through college, and was a good scholar, and others carried through a course of learning with not less expence for each of them,

[1] *Narrative,* I, 28–29.

than would have been necessary to have supported an English youth through a course of collegiate studies, and they have generally behaved well while they were with me, and left my school with fair and unblemished characters, and under the influence of every motive I could set before them, and enforce upon them to induce them, to a good improvement of the distinguishing talents which God had committed to them, and many of them have gone immediately from my school into good and reputable business, and such business as they were equal to, and generally to serve as schoolmasters, but some as interpreters, &c., and nothing has prevented their being imployed usefully and reputably in various capacities till this day, but their want of fortitude to resist the power of those fashionable vices which were rampant among their tribes. The current is too strong, and is tenfold more so by reason of the united force of such wicked dealers as are making great gain to themselves by the swift destruction of the poor savages; and by this means the progress of this design has been retarded, and the raised hopes of many, which were founded on those encouraging prospects have been disappointed, for of all the number before mentioned, I don't hear of more than half who have preserved their characters unstain'd either by a course of intemperance or uncleanness, or both; and some who on account of their parts and learning bid the fairest for usefulness, are sunk down into as low, savage, and brutish a manner of living as they were in before any endeavours were used with them to raise them up; and there are some of whom I did, and do still entertain hope that they were really the subjects of God's grace, who have not wholly kept their garments unspotted among the pots. And six of those who did preserve a good character are now dead. . . . These youth have generally done well in their schools for one season, or till their schools have been broken up by a hunting tour, or by some public congress; but I have seldom known an instance of their collecting their children, and reviving their schools after they have so been broken up—the youth themselves seem to be conscious of their own unworthy behaviour, or their not having answered my expectations, that they appear shy of me, and of such as I have sent among them; insomuch that the kindest invitations will scarcely prevail upon them to return to my house.[1]

[1] *Idem*, VI, 18–21.

Specifically, just what had the Indian scholars, male and female, done to cause such despair to Wheelock? Their accomplishments, or lack of them, are recorded in the following list, which gives the status of the Indians up to 1769, in which year Dartmouth College was founded. In this listing no attempt has been made to give a full account of the Indian students; were the list amplified to include details of the seventeen seventies and later years, some of these records would be much more creditable. But that is not the purpose; I wish merely to find justification for Wheelock's disillusionment, for his writing that "the current is too strong." The name of Samson Occom has been excluded from this list because he was not a member of Moor's Charity School. As for the others, the date which is given at the left is the date of their enrollment in the school.

1754 John Pumshire, Delaware, died January 26, 1757.

Jacob Woolley, Delaware. In his senior year at the College of New Jersey he suddenly developed a loathing for study, lamented his confinement at college, and became enamored of a Princeton girl. He was reported as a ne'er-do-well, in rags, picking up scraps of firewood, and despondent.

1757 Samson Woyboy, Pequot. After nineteen weeks at the school he withdrew to become a schoolmaster, and died, probably, in the late seventeen sixties.

Joseph Woolley, Delaware. A sprightly and promising boy, sent in 1764 as a teacher to Onohoquaga, New York, where he died of consumption in a year.

Hezekiah Calvin, Delaware. After his schooling, he was appointed to Fort Hunter, New York. His health and morals weakened. In 1769 Wheelock characterized him as a "drunkard and apostate." He was imprisoned for forging a pass for a negro.

1758   Joseph Johnson, Mohegan. At this time he also was a "drunkard and apostate."

1759   David Fowler, Montauk, was an Indian of high repute, in general. About 1767 he left Wheelock's employ, and was therefore a disappointment to him.

1760   Aaron Occom, Samson's son, was a very poor student and almost unmanageable.

Isaiah Uncas, Mohegan. He was so deficient as a student that he was "taken to work on the farm" by Wheelock.

1761   Amy Johnson, Mohegan, after about five years of training under Wheelock, became a servant in a tavern at Hartford, Connecticut.

Joseph Brant, Mohawk, remained two years at Moor's Charity School, and later acted as interpreter for Wheelock's missionaries among the Six Nations. His later career does not concern us here.

Negyes, Mohawk, after several months at the school, returned to his tribe, "was captivated by a young female and married." His record ends with that notice.

Center, Mohawk, entered and returned with Negyes, and died soon after.

Miriam Storrs, Delaware. Nothing is known of her, of any value, except that she stayed three years at the school.

Moses, Mohawk, was approved as an assistant schoolmaster in 1765, and later was reported as conducting his school (at Lake Otsego, New York) "with the gravity of a divine of fifty or three-score."

1762   Sarah Wyog, Mohegan, was an incorrigible girl, given to "much dancing and lude conduct." She was rusticated in 1764.

Enoch Closs, Delaware, ran away in 1765.

Samuel Tallman, Delaware, became a carpenter, and migrated westward with the New England Indians.

Daniel Mossoch, Farmington, remained only a few months at the school.

Abraham Primus and Abraham Secundus, Mohawks, were sent as schoolmasters to the Mohawks. Nothing more is known of them.

Patience Johnson, Mohegan, was dismissed as incorrigible.

Samuel Ashpo, Mohegan, was in his forty-fourth year when he entered the school, and had already been a schoolmaster. In 1763 he was appointed as missionary to Chenango, New York, and was suspended in 1767 for drunkenness. When Wheelock wrote his despairing account quoted above, Ashpo was apparently a total loss.

Jacob Fowler, Montauk, after three years at the school, was appointed to Canajoharie, New York, where he taught acceptably.

1763 Emmanuel Simon, Narraganset. Nothing is known of his career.

Hannah Poquinatup, Niantic, "went away a few months after."

Hannah Garret, Pequot, married David Fowler in 1766.

Mary Secuter, Narraganset, was incorrigible; she remained five years at the school.

1764 William Primus, Mohawk, reputed to be a natural son of Sir William Johnson, was sent home in 1766.

William Secundus, Mohawk. Except that he entered in this year, nothing is known of him.

Elias, Mohawk. All that is known of him is that he was hit on the head by a "ballstick" and was reported as recovering.

1765 Susannah, Katharine, Mary, Mohawks. The two latter

went home about January 9, 1767, and from them, and from the third, nothing more is heard.

David, Oneida, returned to his tribe in 1766, without having finished his schooling.

Jacob, Oneida, attended for two or more years, and was probably withdrawn by his parents in 1768.

Mundius, Oneida, probably was teaching in the Oneida country.

Sarah Simon, Narraganset, attended the school for four years, and then is lost to us.

Charles Daniel, Narraganset. His father complained that his son had to perform too many farm chores, and withdrew him in 1767.

1766 John Green, Seth, Mohawks, left the school after a year.

William, Oneida, went home in 1768 with his sister Hannah.

Paulus, Mohawk, went home in a few months.

John Shattock, Narraganset, after a year at the school, went to Edinburgh, where he died of smallpox.

Toby Shattock accompanied his brother abroad, and on his return served as schoolmaster in Stonington, Connecticut, but not under Wheelock's supervision.

Toby Shattock's wife and child withdrew from the school with her husband.

Margaret, Mohawk, went home after a year.

1767 Abigail, Martha, Narragansets, have not left any record.

John Secuter, Narraganset. Nothing is known of him.

James Simon, Narraganset. Nothing is known of him up to 1769.

Nathan Clap, a "Cape Cod Indian." Wheelock had sent him to assist Samuel Kirkland, whose report from Oneida, New York (Dec. 29, 1768) is damaging: "Elder Joseph (Johnson) and Prophet Nathan kept their strumpets here nigh two months last spring—drank up near three gallons of wine (sent up for me in my sickness) and between six and seven gallons of rum, disposed of sôme household furniture and wasted no small quantity of provisions."

James Niles, Narraganset, has not left any record.

Hannah Nonesuch, Mohegan. Her record is a blank except for a confession of drunkenness in 1768.

Abraham Simon, Daniel Simon, Narragansets, were well-behaved and studious.

Hannah, Oneida, was withdrawn by her parents in 1768.

This is the discouraging evidence which confronted Wheelock just prior to the founding of Dartmouth College. As stated earlier, some of these Indians were to serve creditably in future years, but of that service Wheelock had of course no inkling at the time he wrote of his disillusionment. Casual students of the history of Dartmouth College have wondered why a school dedicated primarily to the education of Indians should have evolved within fifteen years into Dartmouth College, with its relatively slight emphasis on their education. It is indeed a far cry from Moor's Charity School, with its original pair of Delaware Indians to the present Dartmouth College with its more than two thousand students, among whom in a college generation a solitary Indian may be found whose deportment and achievement do not differ essentially from his classmates'. Today in the form of a weather-vane on the spire of the Dartmouth College library, the founder of the college, cast in metal, sits on a pine stump, instructing a metal Indian from whose pipe no smoke will ever come, and shifting, as he cannot truthfully be said to have done in his life, to every wind. So far are we from the original purpose of the eighteenth century divine that this metal artifice, which should be a reminder, arouses query rather than memory. The explanation should now be clear. The Indian "graduates," for one reason or another, failed to *continue,* and many to qualify, as suitable teachers; rival missionary boards had successfully competed against Wheelock; and after the Fort Stanwix Congress the Six Nations were definitely closed to him. Moor's Charity School was still to be maintained, and Wheelock and his successors were to continue the program of educating Indians, but from the school was to develop the immeasurably more important Dartmouth College.

CHAPTER X

FINANCING MOOR'S CHARITY SCHOOL

A T this point the reader is asked to retrace his steps in order to learn how Wheelock was enabled to support his Indians and white charity students in Lebanon and in the mission field. The expense was considerable, and from 1754, ever mounting. With the same industry which he had displayed during the Great Awakening in his own and neighboring parishes, Wheelock undertook to gather from all who were within reach of his pen or voice funds sufficient to carry on his project. Only, whereas during the revival he had fulminated and terrified, he now begged and cajoled. None was too mighty for him: King George the Third gave two hundred pounds; none too humble: "a little girl a copper." A "secret female" is thanked for £10.10, and a friend, for a gift of books, is quaintly promised his reward in the hereafter: "I shall hear it credited (to your acc't) by the Judge himself viz. 3 vol. of Newton on the Prophesies."

As stated earlier, Joshua More of Mansfield headed the list of donors with his gift of a house and two acres of land in Lebanon. Shortly thereafter Wheelock raised by subscription the sum of £500, Proclamation money.

The cost of educating, clothing, and boarding an Indian for a year at Moor's Charity School was about £16, lawful money, according to Wheelock's estimate. In his words: "For their board, washing, and lodging but five shillings per week; the lowest common price in these parts was six shillings, lawful money. What cloathing &c. they got of me, I charged at the lowest cash-price, and what I got for them of our traders, shoemakers, taylors, &c., I charged just as they charged me, without any advance in one instance." The girls cost much less than the boys: four pence a week, for which they were given "one day's schooling and dinner." Instead of being housed in the school, they were placed about in the neighboring farmhouses, as mentioned earlier, where they paid for their care by performing household chores. A schoolmaster was given £56, lawful money, a year, and found as well, although now and then Wheelock was fortunate in having young men who taught gratis.

The first organization from which he received funds was the so-called New England Company, or, to give it its proper title, the Company for Propagation of the Gospel in New England and the Parts Adjacent in America.[1] Through the Boston Board of this society Wheelock obtained in 1756 the sum of twelve pounds, lawful money, less to be sure than the cost of caring for one charity scholar for a year, but gladly received; and in the following years, up to 1767, other sums varying from ten pounds to twenty, to make a total of about one hundred and sixty pounds. These sums had been transmitted to Wheelock by Andrew Oliver, acting for the Boston Board. Typical of Wheelock's letters to him is the following:

Lebanon May 29. 1760

Honored Sir.

Your favor of March 15 by Mr Young came safe to hand. Any thing the Honourable Commissioners shall see fit to contribute toward the support of these Indian boys will be thankfully accepted. Nor did I mean to prescribe how much but only to let them know that the expence for them has been considerable and has much exceeded what has been hitherto given for that purpose. When we first enter'd upon the design it was a time of profound peace. One consideration which induc'd us to undertake it was the criminal neglect of them by Gods professing people in this land, who we apprehend are by many distinguishing covenant blessings

---

[1] For a detailed account of Wheelock's relations with this and other missionary societies see J. D. McCallum, *Letters of Eleazar Wheelock's Indians*, Appendix B.

outward and spiritual laid under many and strong obligations to exert themselves far beyond what they have yet done, that those poor creatures might become fellow heirs with us of the grace of God. And we tho't that presenting them with such objects of their charity might as likely invite to liberality and to as good purpose as any method we could think of but after the war broke out the frequent reports of the perfidy cruelties of the savages evidently wrought in great numbers a temper very different from charity and has vastly obstructed the progress of what we had so fair a prospect of. However we are not discouraged but apprehend there is now a favourable opening and that our prospects are much increasd by the mercifull occurrances of the last year. Yet as the temper of numbers at present is we think it prudent to do nothing which may occasion public talk or provoke such as are incensd to stirr up opposition to it, and therefor have for some time almost wholly neglected to ask the charities of any for them. And if the Honourable Commissioners shall see good to take one or two or all of these boys, under their patronage, and to be at their direction and controul, I am quite willing and should rejoyce much in it, only provided they be educated in this school while they study the languages or are removed to college. I have two who read Virgel and Tulley, and have begun Greek. The inclosd is a specimen of their writing. I have a third who has got about half thro' Castalio's Dialg. a fourth in his Accidence and a fifth (viz. Mr. Occoms son) who begins to read the English Bible. I find much need of care and prudence in conducting and governing them. The elder ones have now almost wholly put off the Indian, and appear seriously tho'tful about their eternal salvation and behave with so much decency humility and good manners that I am constraind to love them. They are so much so pleased with living with me and so much attachd to this school that I apprehend there would be danger in removing them at present. I am Hon^d Sir with most sincere duty and respect

Your Honours Obedient and

Most Humble Servant

Eleazar Wheelock

P.S. Sir I am greived at the heart for Mr Occom. his involvemts thro the necessary expences of his Family and ministry are such as must in a great measure prevent his usefulness unless he has releif. He told me tother day that he was about or near £100 N. York currancy in debt and that he saw no way to extricate himself unless he came and settled upon his lands at Mohegan and betook himself to his trades (viz. of a cooper and book binder) for it. He is forcd to labour hard to support his family, has no books nor leisure to read if he had. His ministry I understand is acceptable to the Indians and those of the English who attend upon it, but he has none to take any effectual care for his subsistance, nor like to have any unless the Honourable Commissioners will do it. If my freedom in what I have written be immodest, please Sir to pardon

Yours (as before)

Eleazar Wheelock

In 1767 Andrew Oliver informed Wheelock that the Board had decided to discontinue its grants to Moor's Charity School because Wheelock had at his disposal the large sum raised in England by Whitaker and Occom, of which an account is given later.

Questing continuously for money, Wheelock lighted on the Sir Peter Warren Fund, originally seven hundred and fifty pounds, accepted by the Massachusetts General Assembly in 1751.[1] All things fitted nicely. Wheelock needed funds for prosecuting his missionary work among the Six Nations: Sir Peter had stipulated that the interest on the fund should be used for educating children from the Six Nations. Andrew Oliver, agent for the New England Company, had long been apprised of Wheelock's needs: Oliver, too, was secretary of the Massachusetts General Assembly. Sir Peter was the uncle of Sir William Johnson: Sir William was superintendent of the Indians. Could any pattern have been neater?

Wheelock's petition to the Assembly was approved by that body, and he was voted (November 23, 1761) twelve pounds a

[1] *Acts and Resolves of the Province of Mass. Bay,* IV, 561.

year for each of six children from the Six Nations. At once Wheelock wrote to Sir William Johnson:

Lebanon Dec. 11, 1761

Sir.

Last evening I was informed of an opportunity by Mr ——— (?) of Albany to acknowledge the receipt of your Honours by Mr. Kirtland and, return you my thanks for it; and also the kindness and respect you shewed him, while he was with you, and inform you, that Joseph and his two boys arived here safe and well on the 28th of last month; and are now well and seem well pleased, and content and hitherto behave well in the school; and I see nothing but that they may well answer the design proposed.

I would also inform your Honour, that I received last evening from Secretary Oliver of Boston, the vote of their General Assembly, passed in answer to a memorial I preferrd, as follows: "That the Revd Mr Wheelock the petitioner be allowed to take under his care for one year, six Indian children of the Six Nations, for education, cloathing and boarding; and that he be allowed for that purpose for said children, or for so many of them as he shall receive under his care, at the rate of twelve pounds pr annum each for one year, out of the interest of the money of Sir Peter Warren's donation; he the said Wheelock laying before this government an accompt of his disbursements on said children, and of the improvement they may have made at the end of the year, when he shall apply for payment.

Sent up for Concurrance.

James Otis Speaker

In Council Nov. 23, 1761. Read and Concurred

A. Oliver, Secy.

Consented to Fra. Bernerd."

Your Honour sees this sum allowed is twelve pounds per annum for each, which as times are this way, will not support them, unless they be females. And perhaps it will be expedient to take some female from your quarter, to be joyned with two which I now have (one from Mr. Brainerd the other of the Mohegan tribe) to be educated in all parts of good housewifery, tending a dary, spining, the use of their needle &c as well as reading writing &c which I have hired proper gentlewomen of this neighbourhood to do, the girls attending the school at my house, to be instructed in writing, one day in each week, and receive copies in order to write four times on each day they are absent, the necessity of which, in order to introduce, the English, or any more decent and easie manner of living among them, your Honour well understands.

I desire, if your Honour pleases, you would add six to the number which I expect by New Year, and if you think proper let two of them be girls. However I wholly submit the matter to your Honours discretion. Your Honour will doubtless think it will be best that they be of as remote tribes as may be. As to the expence of their journey I shall wait for your Honours demands, and comply therewith.[1]

I trust your goodness will pardon the faults of what I write, thus in a hurry. and accept most sincere duty and respect from

Your Honours most Humble and

Most Obedient Servant

Eleazar Wheelock

P.S. I trust your Honour will forward their coming as soon as may be. If the girls cant come in the winter season, perhaps there may be a good opportunity from Albany to Norwich to the care of the Rev. Mr. Whitaker by water next spring.

These donations were generously continued, the Assembly being *memorialized* from time to time by Wheelock with petitions in which he described the progress of the Indians, emphasized the necessity of continuing them at the school, and asked for renewal of the money grants:

To His Excellency Francis Bernard Esqr. Capt. General and Commander in Cheif in and over his Majesty's Province of Massachusetts Bay. The Honourable his Majesty's Council, and the Honourable House of Representatives in General Court Assembled

[1] Crossed out: the boys are not yet out of bed and know nothing of this opportunity.

ELEAZAR WHEELOCK

The Memorial of Eleazar Wheelock of Lebanon in the Coloney of Connecticut (clerk) humbly sheweth:

That your Memorialist still keeps the Indian Charity School which by your kind assistance (of which he retains a grateful remembrance) has been in part for several years last past supported under his care and the number supported by charity is now 22, among which are 10 Indian youth well accomplished to keep an English school, excepting only their want of age and a manly fortitude. of which number are the 5 boys of the Six Nations which your Memorialist has kept pursuant to your order and faithfully instructed them according to your direction. and they have profited proportionable to the expence bestowed upon them. They can all read well in the Bible, and write a good copy hand, and have all learnt their Lattin grammer through and all excepting one near or quite construed and peirced thro' Corderii Colloq. and can repeat the Assembly's Shorter Chatechism well, and have been well instructed in english authography and etymology. Their diligence is laudable, their behaviour in the main exemplary, and they all appear promising. And it seems a pitty they should not be still continued in the school and further encouraged, at least till they arive at an age suitable to be sent forth on public service among their tribes, by which time it is likely several of them may be well fitted for missionaries, or other important business, which it is likely they will fail of if they now leave this school, and not only so, but by reason of their youth, and the influence which their nation will likely have on them, through their want of more knowledge and fortitude than their years will allow us to expect, even the learning they have got will likely be in some measure forgotten, and rendered useless among them.

Wherefore your Memorialist humbly prays Your Excellency and your Honours and this Honourable Assembly to take it into your consideration and still continue the assistance which you have heretofore so kindly and generously granted him towards the support of said 5 boys (and a sixth if he may be obtaind which your Memorialist has some prospect of soon) and Your Memorialist will be ready to account with you when and as often as you shall require it, and as in duty bound he shall ever pray &c.

Eleazar Wheelock

Dated Nov. 16. 1764.

146

Altogether Wheelock received £291 from the Massachusetts General Assembly. These donations were discontinued in 1767 because a fund had been raised in England for the school.

Of undoubted value in spreading news of the school were the nine *Narratives* which Wheelock published from 1763 to 1775. In these accounts he described with considerable detail the state of the school and of the missionaries, and listed many of the contributions which he had received. Of great assistance also was the English evangelist George Whitefield, who in spite of the fact that he was financing an orphanage in Georgia and was otherwise engaged in charitable work, generously recommended Moor's Charity School to friends in England. Thus the Marquis of Lothian gave fifty pounds in 1761, and duplicated the gift in the following year. Forty-five pounds came in from two London merchants, an English minister sent ten guineas, and a "lady, in London, unknown" (probably Selina, the Countess of Huntingdon) gave fourteen pounds. Whitefield himself sent a bell and a set of globes, and in New York City, with the same power that charmed money from the reluctant Benjamin Franklin, raised one hundred and twenty pounds for Wheelock. In 1765 John Phillips, the founder of Phillips Exeter Academy, contributed one hundred pounds, the first of his many contributions to the school.

The following letter from Wheelock to two Boston ladies is representative of his letters of thanks:

Lebanon Augt 24. 1761.

My dear Friends

I hant neglected writing thus long because I dont remember with pleasure that truly Christian, and charitable spirit which you have shewn towards the furtherance of the kingdom of our great Redeemer, nor because I have no abiding relish for that openess and truly Christian freedom, and mutual love which I observed in your conferrences, mixd and temper'd with so much Christian prudence,

and proper caution not to give any occasion to the Adversary to reproach, either you, your friends, or the dear cause which your
hearts appeard so much ingaged to promote. These are not the reasons of my neglect, for much the contrary is true, I have often tho't
of you and your associates with much pleasure, and my soul blesses
you and them. May you enjoy much of God, and your mutual endeavours to promote one anothers sanctification, and spiritual increase, be abundantly blessed of God. But I have been full of business, my corrispondents are numerous, and my cares necessarily
many having now 10 charity scholars vis. 9. indians besides *David*,
who is now with Mr Occom among the Mohawkes and one English.
My family somewhat weakly, and my people poor, which has sometimes obliged me to be much more concernd in worldly matters
than agrees either with my principles or disposition if necessity did
not urge me to it. But I make no doubt, had you opportunity you
would be much gratified to see such a number of blacks so prittily
ingaged in their studies, so willing to be taught, and who have in
such a measure (as some of them have) put of the savage Indian.
And though the service is more laborious, and painful than any,
who are unacquainted with it, seem to conceive, yet such appearances and hopeful prospects of success do abundantly compensate
all my care and fatigue about it. My time seems to me very short,
and I feal in hast to accomplish as much of the great affair as possible, before my Blessed Master calls me from it.

I was sensibly, and greatly encouraged by what I met with at
Boston last spring. The Lord bless those who opened their hands
to encourage the design. What they gave was lent to the Lord and
he will repay them. God has appeared from time to time for my
help in this affair when the case looked (as it did then) dark and
difficult; and I find such gracious appearances sensibly encourage
me still to pursue the design, and trust in God to support it. I have
earnestly desired, and I do desire, if it be not His cause which I am
pursuing, He would stop it soon, and so, as shall be without dis-
hounour to His Name or reproach to religion, or discouragement
to any good charitable attempts in time to come. When I can trust
in God, and refer the whole affair to Him (alass! I blush to mention my doing it I am so defective in it and so unbeleiving), I then
have peace within, and no disquietude on account of any dark ap-

pearances whatsoever. Trusting in God, and believing in His Name (which contains every thing in it we want) will make a dark scene light, and a heavy burthen quite easie to be born. God's thoughts, and ways, and works are perfect, tho' to us He makes Darkness His pavilion round about, and His way be in the sea and paths in the mighty waters where, for the present we cant track Him. Yet He does all things well, and it is sweet living upon Him and having all in Him, and to feal ourselves in His hands and love to be there.

I dont write this because I think it new to you, or suspect you hant experienced these things more fully than I have; but I seem just now to be got into your back chamber with only a few dear souls who have our Lord Jesus Christ in sincerity, and know what walking with God means. And I have confidence in your prudence, that if I use a little more freedom in these things, than is fashionable there will be no ill use made of it.

I bespeak your prayers, and the prayers of all your intimates who love our Lord Jesus Christ, and long for the prosperity of Zion, and not only for myself and school but also for Mr. Occom that under his present full and great sail, he may be made and kept humble, and be preserved from falling. I dont write this because of anything I have seen in, or heard of him but because God has raised him from the dunghill and his temptations to pride are now very great.

please to accept most sincere regards to your selves and your associates, (in which Miss Wheelock heartily joyns)

From, my Dear Friends,

Yours in our Common Lord

Eleazar Wheelock

Miss Hannah Winslow and
Miss Sarah Bethan

His own colony of Connecticut, officially at least, did not equal the generosity of Massachusetts, although by means of "briefs" read in the churches by permission of the civil authorities, about two hundred pounds, sterling, were raised during the seventeen sixties. And in 1763, having been petitioned by Wheelock, the New Hampshire Assembly granted him fifty pounds sterling.

Finally, there was one other source of income, grudgingly given: the Society in Scotland for Propagating Christian Knowledge. Wheelock wrote to the Boston Board of this society on December 1, 1760, describing the origin of his school, alluding to the "ruffle" which the country had lately suffered from and in spite of which he has been able to "scrabble along," and asking aid for Samson Occom and for the charity student Isaiah Uncas, son of the dissolute sachem of the Mohegans, Ben Uncas.

On May 7, 1761 the Society in Scotland through its Boston Board voted twenty pounds to "fit out" David Fowler for a mission to the Oneidas, in company with Samson Occom. According to the terms of the commission, Fowler was to remain for not more than four months among the Oneidas, and to bring back "a number of Indian boys, not exceeding three." Two or three months later Fowler sent three Mohawk boys to Wheelock. They arrived at Lebanon on horseback. Two were at once sent back: one was ill and the other was to accompany him. The third, Joseph Brant,[1] remained in Lebanon. A second pair of Mohawks arrived in November, and they with Joseph Brant made up the trio, authorized, as Wheelock thought, by the Boston Board. But the Board, of which Wheelock's critic of old, Charles Chauncy, was a member, decided in a hair-splitting manner that Wheelock was not educating the three first decided on, and withheld payment. After the passage of some months and the exchange of unfriendly letters (the Board had accused Wheelock of making an excessive charge of four shillings and sixpence for a shirt for Joseph Brant, and Wheelock had offered to rebate sixpence or even a shilling from his own pocket), the Board allowed Wheelock's claim for fifty-eight pounds. This seems to have been all that

---

1 Thayendanagea, the brother of Sir William Johnson's squaw, Molly.

he ever received from the Boston Board; his further dealings with the Society in Scotland through its home office in Edinburgh will be discussed later.

It would be almost impossible at the present time to learn with any exactness the extent of all these contributions from individuals and from organized groups, if Wheelock had not totaled them for us, at least the sum received from "well-disposed persons" from 1754 to 1765. This he states as £1639, sterling. All of this sizable sum he had spent for the charity students; in addition he had expended £280 of his own money, and owed £400 more, for which he was personally liable. He himself did not receive any salary. Friends in England, though, were soon to relieve him; as the Reverend Andrew Gifford in London "said with emotion" when told that Wheelock's estate stood bound for the debts contracted, "The dear man shant pay one penny."

In this strait Wheelock, influenced by George Whitefield, decided to send representatives abroad to collect money for Moor's Charity School. The decision was the most important he had made since 1754, when he had decided to receive the two young Delawares from John Brainerd.

The selection of fitting men to represent Moor's Charity School abroad was not a simple matter. They had to be men of integrity and piety, acquainted with the details of the school and of Wheelock's plans, able to hold audiences by their preaching, acceptable to the Dissenters and to the evangelical group of the Church of England, industrious in carrying out their mission, and approved not only by Wheelock and the Connecticut Board of Correspondents, but by George Whitefield, also. To be sure, the representatives might count on raising some money in England and Scotland without Whitefield's co-operation, but with the leading English evangelist to introduce them properly they were assured of thousands of pounds more.[1]

According to the earliest letter extant on this subject (Sept. 29, 1764), Whitefield had planned from the beginning to take Occom and "another" with him to England in order to raise money for Wheelock. The choice of Occom was obvious: no Indian up to this time had imbibed as much of the white man's learning. He was pious, acceptable as a preacher, acquainted with mission work among the Oneidas, and anxious to further the cause. Nevertheless, certain objections were expressed against him. As a Mohegan and much respected by the remnant of his tribesmen in Connecticut, Occom opposed the claims of the white men to the lands which they had taken (illegally, he believed) from the Mohegans. This litigation (the so-called "Mason controversy") was of long standing, dating from 1640, when Uncas "the great" had sold, as the whites asserted, or had deeded in trust to the whites, according to the Indians, seven or eight hundred square miles for five and a half yards of cloth and a few pairs of stockings. At this period when Wheelock was planning to send representatives abroad (1764), Samuel Mason, a descendant of the original John Mason, was in England engaged in the dispute. The fear, accordingly, was that Occom, too, might take part in the controversy, champion-

[1] L. B. Richardson's *An Indian Preacher in England* is indispensable for a study of this mission. Professor Richardson shows (pp. 14–15) that in the eighteenth century the following American colleges raised money in Great Britain: (1) 1749, the College of New Jersey (Princeton) raised "considerable sums," the vague phrase being not his; (2) 1753, on the advice of Whitefield, the same college raised "over £3,200" in England, Scotland, and Ireland; (3) 1762, Provost William Smith of the University of Pennsylvania went to England, where he joined with James Jay, from King's College (Columbia). Under Episcopal auspices they raised £6,000 for each institution. This sum was increased by separate solicitation so that the University of Pennsylvania received £6,921, including £200 from George III, and King's College received "nearly £10,000," including £400 from the king; (4) 1766, Rhode Island College (Brown University) raised £880 in England and Ireland.

ing the claims of the Mohegans, distracting attention from the purpose of the proposed mission, and by arousing animosities alienate prospective donors.

There were other charges against Occom: of "ill-conduct toward the overseers in the affair of leasing the Indian lands, and some proud and haughty threatnings to turn Episcopalian, and unsettledness respecting the constitution of our churches and infant baptism, and disrespectful treatment of the Revd. Mr. Jewet (minister of the North Parish in New London, Connecticut, the seat of the Mohegans), and illegal proceedings against the schoolmaster at Mohegan."

So loud was the "public clamour" against Occom that the Connecticut Board of Correspondents (the group associated with Wheelock in conducting the school) was called together. The members acquitted Occom of all charges (March 12, 1765) except that of his being engaged in the Mason controversy, and on his expressing regret and promising not to engage in the litigation "unless called thereto and obliged by lawful authority," he was accepted by the Board for the enterprise abroad. Later, further opposition from the Boston Board (of the Company for Propagation of the Gospel) was raised against him, as will be shown shortly.

The first choice for the other member of the mission was the Reverend John Brainerd, missionary to the Delawares in New Jersey, from whom in 1754 Wheelock had received two Indian boys. Brainerd was willing to go to England, but his employers, the Society in Scotland, evidently refused their permission; "evidently," because there is no direct statement that they did refuse. No other conclusion is admissible, however, since Wheelock and his Board were in favor of him, and Brainerd himself had agreed.

Having failed to engage Brainerd, Wheelock unsuccessfully solicited the Reverend Charles Jeffry Smith, a Yale graduate

(1757), a teacher for three months at Moor's Charity School, and a missionary to the Indians, and the Reverend John Rogers, who, however, accepted the pastorate of the Presbyterian Church in New York City.

"What if thou art the man?" Whitefield asked Wheelock (May 11, 1765). Let Wheelock give the answer:

Lebanon Augt 26th 1765.

My dear and Reverend Sir.

Yours from Philadelphia I received after your embarkation for Europe. The difficulty of my leaving the school for so long time as a voyage to England must necessarily take, will be very great, as there are none to be had that I know of both willing and equal to the business, which will always be found to require a good deal of experience, and which seems to be the principle thing which makes the Board of Corrispondants and other friends (who otherwise would be very desirous of my going) rather advise to the contrary.[1] Mr. Whitaker is in many respects well turned for the design, and will improve by any hints which you or other friends shall give him as much as any man, and is more than any other acquainted with Mr. Occom.

Not knowing whether you or Mr. Smith have arrived I have inclosed all to Mr. DeBerdt. Please to accept the copies and all the intelligence given him and Mr. Smith as tho' sent to you. I doubt not of your friendship to the cause, and need say nothing on that head to move you to any expressions thereof within your power. I am every week surprised with favourable occurrances in Providence, and the opening of new and unexpected prospects; something of which you will see in the accounts I have sent, to which I referr you.

I am, my dear Sir, with most sincere respect to you and your dear spouse,

Your poor unworthy though

Very Affectionate Brother &c

Eleazar Wheelock

[1] There are other reasons of great weight as, my age, never having had the small-pox, the danger of jealousy in the Indians, &c.

The choice now fell on Nathaniel Whitaker (Princeton, 1752), pastor of a church in Norwich, Connecticut. Wheelock was cognizant of some of Whitaker's shortcomings: a controversial spirit, a certain instability, an unministerial interest in trade; but he was also aware of Whitaker's zest and industry. Whitaker's parishioners did their best to hinder him from accepting, even though he agreed to give up his salary during his absence: "O how strong is their love!" he wrote sarcastically. And Mrs. Whitaker, too, was loth to see her husband go, perversely, so it would seem, until we learn that she was to have a baby in seven months.

The Connecticut Board of Correspondents finally appointed Whitaker (Sept. 23, 1765). Two matters should be mentioned regarding their document recommending Whitaker to the British. In the first place, Occom is not referred to, because of a fear that if he did break his promise to keep clear of the Mason controversy, the Board would be criticised for sending him. And secondly, since the Board (technically) represented the Society in Scotland, the document was discreetly withheld from English eyes, although Whitaker used it freely in Scotland.

Other credentials were acquired: Occom personally obtained a recommendation of the plan from Sir William Johnson, who stated as his opinion that Wheelock's program of establishing "an Indian school and enlarging the plan thereof so as to enable a number of missionaries to be employed in the Indian country" was "highly necessary and may be productive of good consequences if properly conducted." Wheelock, himself, wrote a recommendation of Occom, the only one the Indian received for the occasion. Whitaker's letter of introduction was signed not only by the Connecticut Board of Correspondents but by "Benning Wentworth, Governor of New Hampshire; Francis Bernard, Governor of Massachusetts;

Theodore Atkinson, Chief Justice of New Hampshire; Theodore Atkinson, Jr., Secretary of New Hampshire; General Gage, Commander-in-Chief of the British forces in America; Governors Franklin of New Jersey and Fitch of Connecticut; Lieutenant Governors Penn of Pennsylvania and Colden of New York; the Chief Justices of Pennsylvania and New Jersey; the President of New Jersey College, and fifty-six other gentlemen of repute in the colonies, twenty-one of whom were ministers, including Samuel Seabury, first bishop in America, and two other clergymen of the Church of England."[1] The Boston Board (of the Company for Propagation of the Gospel) refused to lend its sanction.

Stamp Act riots in Boston postponed the sailing, because stamped papers were not available, but in due time everything was ready, passage on the *Boston Packet* was paid for (£15.5 for both, John Hancock, part owner, having waived his share of £5.5), and the vessel sailed from Boston, December 23, 1765. On February 3 Whitaker and Occom landed at Brixham, England—"very gentle gales, and headwinds, we were not sea-sick" —and on the sixth arrived in London, where John Smith of Boston, a merchant and contributor to the school, conducted them to Whitefield. On the tenth of February Whitefield carried Whitaker and Occom in his coach to wait on Lord Dartmouth, who, according to Occom, "apear'd like a worthy lord indeed," and who was, in Whitaker's words, "a sweet youth full of piety and good works and loves Jesus X."

The "sweet youth," William Legge, second Earl of Dartmouth (1731–1801) was thirty-four years of age. Half a year before Whitaker's arrival he had been appointed president of the Board of Trade and Foreign Plantations. Whitaker's characterization of him agrees with his general reputation. He was a close friend of the pious Selina, countess of Huntingdon, and

---

[1] Richardson, *An Indian Preacher in England,* 72, fn.

because of his sympathy for the Methodists was known as the "psalm singer." William Cowper (in *Truth*) refers to him as "one who wears a coronet, and prays." He nominated John Newton to the curacy of Olney (where Cowper found refuge), and Newton reported to Hannah More that Samuel Richardson considered the Earl of Dartmouth a suitable model for Sir Charles Grandison, except for his Methodism.[1] Because of his piety Dartmouth was able to enlist the aid of the evangelically-minded in the Church of England, and by reason of his political position was of great potential value to the mission.

At once Wheelock's two envoys were in a flurry of sight-seeing, visiting, dining, and preaching. Occom was amazed at the hurly-burly of London on a Sabbath evening: "saw such confusion as I never dreamt of—there was some at churches, singing and preaching, in the streets some cursing swaring and damning one another, others were hollowing, whestling, talking gigling, and laughing, and coaches and footmen passing and repassing, crossing and cross-crossing, and the poor begars praying, crying, and beging upon their kness." They visited Parliament House, where they saw the king putting on his royal robes and crown, the glittering jewels reminding Occom of how glorious the crown of the Redeemer must be; and in the Tower they saw the royal lions, tigers, wolf, and leopards. An English clergyman tried to persuade Occom to take orders in the Church of England: "I modestly told him, I had no such view when I came from home, and added, I had been ordained six years in a Dissenting way." It was hoped, but falsely, that Occom would be presented to King George. Players on the stage mimicked the converted heathen. The Archbishops of Canterbury and of York received them. Whitaker inoculated Occom against smallpox, and after three weeks the patient was well again. And the indefatigable Whitefield carried them

[1] *Dictionary of National Biography,* article *William Legge.*

from one house to another, introducing them to the right people.

The hostility of the Boston Board followed them to London in the form of a letter to the parent society, discrediting Wheelock's claims and Occom, in particular. It all seems very trivial now, but deserves mention. The crux of the dispute was this: (1) Was Occom a heathen when Wheelock began to educate him? (2) Did the Boston Board or Wheelock support him? The Boston Board insisted that Occom had been brought up among Christian Indians at Mohegan, Connecticut, and that he was posing as a savage who had been converted after he had grown up. Against this assertion there is Occom's "affidavit of heathenism": that although occasional sermons had been preached to the Mohegans, his tribesmen and especially his parents were heathen, and that he himself began to think about Christianity only when he was sixteen. Wheelock also wrote that Occom was a heathen until his sixteenth year. The evidence on this point seems to be against the Boston Board.

The question of support is a matter of definition; perhaps the other question is, also. The Boston Board had indeed granted Occom £60 a year during part of the time he was under Wheelock's tutelage in Lebanon (1745–1748). In addition, the Boston Board had given him while he was teaching at Montauk, Long Island, and living at Mohegan (1749–1761) altogether £225. Against the claim of the Board that these sums had supported Occom, he could urge that they had been insufficient and that he had been obliged to eke out his living by farming and handicraft. Further, the expenses of his visits to the Six Nations in 1761, 1762, and 1763 had been paid by Wheelock, and from 1764 he had been dependent on Wheelock.[1]

Everyone concerned was quite incensed: the Boston Board

[1] *An Indian Preacher,* 129, fn. 1.

at Wheelock's presumption, he and his colleagues at what they considered complete misrepresentations. Wheelock demanded a copy of the letter from Andrew Oliver, secretary of the Board, but was refused. Whitaker was allowed to read the letter but not to make a copy. Occom asked Wheelock for a full accounting of the sums paid to him by the Board. There were assertions and denials during the extent of the mission. The Boston Board probably did not harm Whitaker and Occom in their efforts to collect money from the Dissenters; it certainly kept aloof the Society for the Propagation of the Gospel, and the majority of the members of the Church of England.

Both Whitaker and Occom preached many times in London and in the towns nearby the metropolis as well as in those further removed. Every Tuesday Whitefield met with a group of ministers and laymen to consider the progress of the work and to send letters of advice to the two representatives when they were away from London. The collection mounted rapidly: by August 20, 1766, less than eight months after their landing in England, they had collected £3,000.

Whitaker had taken with him a power of attorney, but it now seemed advisable to establish a committee to supervise the management of the fund. Therefore on October 2, 1766, he relinquished his authority to a board of trustees, the so-called English trust, of which Lord Dartmouth was president.[1] This group co-operated with Wheelock until the fund was finally exhausted, that is in 1774.[2]

The confidence of the English trust in Whitaker was soon to be shaken. On March 25, 1767, Robert Keen, secretary, reported that the trustees had reason to suppose that the fund was

[1] The other members of the English trust were Sir Charles Hotham (d. Dec. 1767), replaced by Sir Sidney Stafford Smythe, John Thornton, treasurer; Samuel Roffey, Charles Hardy, Daniel West, Samuel Savage, Josiah Robarts, Robert Keen, secretary.

[2] Wheelock's relations with the English trustees are discussed later (pp. 172 ff.).

being used dishonestly. Specifically, that Whitaker and the Reverend Nathaniel Eells in Stonington, Connecticut, were in collusion to utilize for trading purposes the sums being raised in order that they as well as Moor's Charity School might profit. This the trustees had learned because Whitaker had commissioned Keen to open his letters while he and Occom were traveling in England. Keen demanded that Wheelock explain his relations with Eells, Moses Peck (a Boston watchmaker), and Gershom Breed, a Connecticut trader, and that he certify to the honest use of the fund; and on the same day the trustees threatened to resign unless the clandestine dealings of Eells and Whitaker ceased. Some £700, it was stated, which had been sent over to Wheelock, were being used in trading.

Whitaker, who had also been informed by the trustees, immediately wrote Wheelock: he had answered Keen that he knew of no moneys being so used, that he could not account for Wheelock's drawing such a large amount without sending a statement of disbursements, and added the following sentence: "If you can give a reason why you have drawn for so much without saying anything of my giving leave for Mr. Breed to obtain draughts for £500 I shall be glad."

The Reverend Nathaniel Eells' defense: he believed that by trading with the fund the traders could turn over a larger profit to the school; that his son and son-in-law were to be the traders, and that he hoped to persuade his son to use his profits for pious causes. The school was always his first thought, he averred. And five days later he stated that the trader would expect to receive half the profits and that the school was to have the other half. As for himself, he was glad that the plan had failed, and that he would return the money entrusted to him (£100), or send security.[1]

---

[1] Eells never returned the money, although Wheelock frequently asked for it. In 1778 he deeded a *tenement* to Wheelock from which Wheelock may have realized all or part of the debt.

FINANCING MOOR'S CHARITY SCHOOL

Eleazar Wheelock answered Whitaker: "You know I had run several hundred pounds in the rere before you went away. I used to take goods for the school upon my own credit, and charge them to the school as it wanted, by this means my public accounts appeared as they did, but this year I have taken goods, in part of pay, for the bills I have drawn, and have also paid those arears with them, by which means my debt is become due the school, so that my next public account will appear in such a view which I should not chuse, viz. a considerable balance due to the school, while I shall have nothing in my hands. I am not anxious in the affair, I trust all will come out right by and by."

To Robert Keen Wheelock wrote the following letter to exonerate himself:

Lebanon May 21, 1767

Sir.

I had but just finished my letter to you yesterday when good Mr. Peck of Boston came in with your shocking tho' Christian and friendly letter of March 25th. I hope my account and letter to the gentlemen of the Trust will give you satisfaction as to many things you write. The £100 in Mr. Eell's hands he promised me last week to secure with the intrest. and has prepared a way to pay it to the school and I depend upon it he will do it. I will take the most effectual care I can of it as also of everything else committed to my care for that purpose.

You will find in my account, that the bill you have protested is charged, and I have received the money and to the best of my ability laid it out part of to supply Messrs Kirtland, Chamberlain, and the school missionaries and you have before now or will soon receive amount bill drawn by Mr. Moses Peck of Boston of £49.7.3 in favor of Mr. George Green, which I have also received. And also another of March 24 of £100 in favor of Mr. Breed, which he has also paid. I have sent for no more than I found absolutely necessary in the prosecution of the design, but have not been without fear that my plan has grown too large, and it has been with regrett that I have had any occasion to meddle with the capital at all, but I sup-

161

posed that when you, Mr. Whitefield, and Mr. Whitaker advised me that I might draw freely, and part of the principal. You complained that it would not be a favourable time to beg in these colonies while the report of Mr. Whitaker's success was the topic of conversation thro' the country, 'till they could be informed what was collected and what was wanting. And I supposed that my letters from time to time gave such accounts of necessary expenses that you would be put to no difficulty to find a reason for my drawing as I did.

But I presume a great part of my letters have miscarried or my dear Mr. Whitaker who is certainly able to judge in such matters could never say that 3 or 400 had been transmitted more than I could possibly want, did he know that the mean number who have been supported by this charity at home and in the wilderness has been about 40 all the last year. Has he not been informed of the mission of the Revd Mr. Pomeroy almost 300 miles, and my son the same length to settle the schools &c among the Mohocks. Of Mr. Kinne's mission to the Onoidas from whence he returnd by reason of sickness, of Saml Ashpo's mission to Jeningo about 3 months, the Rev. Messrs Kirtland's and Chamberlains mission the whole term, viz. 20 months, Mr. Chamberlain's interpreter at 15/ per Sabath the whole term, Mr. Kirtland's and others occasionally of 4, 5, and sometimes 7 school Masters in the wilderness. The expenses for Mr. Occom family and house, for Mr. Kirtland, David Fowlers settlement, Tekananda. I might add one sick in the school and under the doctors hand all the last year. The most of these things I have mentioned in one or other of my letters to him, which I think must have miscarried.

No gentlman of penetration who has looked into the affair but wonders to find so much done with so little expence. And take out my expences for Mr. Chamberlain (who has cost me much more than any other, not only as he is very infirm and requires more on that account but also as I have had £49.13.3 Sterling of his college expences to pay for him (which is included in the present account:) and what has been done by the rest, I doubt not will appear to be £50 pr Cent. cheiper than any such services in the wilderness, since Dear Mr. D. Brainerd wore out his precious life in the cause.

I have such caution as to expences that I allow nothing to be bought for my family that is not necessary and if it had not been for the rents and profits of my little inheritance, I could by no means have sustained the weight upon me 'till this time.

But God has made everything I have taken in hand to prosper. Blessed be His holy Name. I write in utmost hast because I would forward this to Boston by Mr. Peck.

Please to remember in your nearest approaches to God

My Dear sir,

Yours in the dearest Bonds

Eleazar Wheelock

P.S. On reviewing the account I find the sum paid for Mr. Occom not mentioned which was £60.6.6 Sterling, and for General Teka-nanda £20.9.1 Sterling how much extraordinary for Mr. Kirtland and David Fowler I cant say as it was so much out of the common stock,—expended promiscuously.

N.B. I have no other connection with Mr. Breed than that I have desired him to provide for Mr. Occoms Family and have sold him bills and taken clothing and money of him when I wanted it for the school. Nor do I know of or suspect in the least any such clandestine scheeme as you feared.

Wheelock also informed the trustees that not one farthing had gone into trade, that he knew nothing of the letters which had passed between Whitaker and Eells, that he was opposed to the original plan of the Connecticut Board of Correspondents to use the money in business ventures, and that as soon as the English trust had been established all talk of trading had ceased.

This was a difficult position for Wheelock. In 1766 he had asked Whitaker to remit his collections in England chiefly in goods, and had requested that three thousand pounds' worth be sent over. Robert Keen had agreed to send goods at cost, without any commission for himself. Then Eells had evolved his profit-sharing plan, and had received one hundred pounds of the English money, Robert Keen having honored his draft.

The trustees were fully satisfied by Wheelock's explanations, and as Keen informed him, hoped that there would "be no more occasion to suspect or so much as mention any iniquitous scheme carrying on by Messrs Eells and Whitaker, as now we take it for granted if any such scheme was intended by them, by your being fully apprized of it, you have and will effectually quash it." The conspiracy, Keen also advised, disqualified each of these two men as Wheelock's successor.

While this difficulty was being settled, Whitaker and Occom were collecting in Scotland. Here Whitaker had planned to use the credentials which the Connecticut Board of Correspondents had given him; such action would mean that the Society in Scotland would control any money collected in Scotland. The English trust was strongly opposed to this plan. As Robert Keen wrote: "If you have any thoughts of collecting monies in Scotland or elsewhere to run in any other channel then this one plan already pursu'd, reject such thoughts, for the gentlemen of the Trust will not be concern'd if any other method takes place—mind this and let all your intentions be upright—." In all £2,529 were raised in Scotland to be used "towards building and endowing an Indian academy for cloathing, boarding, maintaining, and educating such Indians as are designed for missionaries and schoolmasters, and for maintaining those who are, or hereafter shall be employed on this glorious errand." But, to look into the future, alas for Wheelock, who was a party to such an agreement. He assumed that the expenses of *white* students who were to teach the Indians should be debited to the Scotch fund; the Society in Scotland refused to accept this interpretation of the agreement, and furthermore, refused to approve most of Wheelock's later claims for educating Indian scholars. A scrutiny of Wheelock's accounts shows that of the total sum raised in Scotland he received only £190. To be sure, the Society in Scotland paid Samuel Kirkland a salary and charged it to the fund, much to Wheelock's chagrin, since he and Kirkland had parted; and John Wheelock, years after his father's death, obtained twelve hundred pounds from the interest on the fund, and after much difficulty, an annuity of £90 for the school. And it is also true that during the nineteenth century Moor's Charity School received additional aid, also paid from the interest: in 1827 the annuity was increased to £130, and in 1840 to £140. But Eleazar Wheelock gained but little by the efforts of his two representatives in Scotland.[1]

These disagreements were still to come, however. The reception accorded Whitaker and Occom in Scotland was cordial. And in addition to the money received, Whitaker was granted a D.D. by the University of Saint Andrews, and Wheelock was granted a similar degree by the University of Edinburgh.

From Scotland they went to Ireland, landing there July 19 (1767). To their disappointment they learned that the Reverend Morgan Edwards was soliciting funds for Rhode Island College, and they consequently left at once and began again to tour England. By March, 1768, when the mission ended, they had secured a total of £9,497, in England alone.

A few details regarding the contributors will be of interest. The largest donation was that of King George III: £200. A few of the nobility contributed: Lord Dartmouth (£50), the Earl

[1] See *The Dartmouth Indians*, by Professor L. B. Richardson (*Dartmouth Alumni Magazine*, June, 1930, 524 ff.), from which I have taken this information regarding the history of the fund after Wheelock's death. The last word on the fund (from the same article) comes from the secretary of the Society in Scotland (in a letter dated Oct. 7, 1930): in May, 1922, the Court of Session, having been petitioned by the Society in Scotland, which set forth the failure of Moor's Charity School to provide for the education of the Indians, allowed the Society to apply the fund to its general needs. By that time the original sum of £2,529.17.11 had increased to £10,295.

of Shaftesbury (30 guineas), the Marchioness of Rockingham (£10), the Duke of Bolton (3 guineas). As stated already, the members, lay and cleric, of the Church of England, were in general not sympathetic to the mission. Whitaker reported that the Archbishop of Canterbury had requested his friends at Oxford to save their money for the Society for the Propagation of the Gospel, and that since the Dissenters had not helped the Society, it in turn should not help the Dissenters. The Bishop of Gloucester informed Whitaker that he and Occom were inflaming the people, causing dissension, collecting money without authority, and were liable "to be taken up." "He would not give a penny nor ask us to sit down." But the Bishop of Derry gave 10 guineas, the Vice-Chancellor of Cambridge, 10 shillings and sixpence, a professor of music at Cambridge, 2 guineas. These last two donations were all that were received from the University. After the King's gift, the next largest are the contributions of Isaac Hollis, Samuel Savage, and John Thornton, £100 each; Sir Charles Hotham and Charles Hardy each gave £50. But the bulk of the money came from subscribers of small sums. Professor Richardson has counted 2,169 contributors, scattered in 216 communities. Collections were taken in 305 churches.[1] The total collected in England and Scotland was £12,026, from which certain expenses were paid: the support of Whitaker's and Occom's families, traveling and living expenses for each man, and a bonus of £100 to each, leaving a net sum of £11,000.

Having completed their mission so successfully, Whitaker and Occom embarked at Gravesend in March, 1768. Occom was persuaded to return to London to appear as a witness in the Mason controversy,[2] and Whitaker sailed alone, arriving in Connecticut in June. Occom returned to his home in Mohegan about a month later.

[1] Richardson, *History of Dartmouth*, I, 66–67. [2] Blodgett, *Samson Occom*, 103.

CHAPTER XI

THE FOUNDING OF DARTMOUTH COLLEGE

THE causes which led to the founding of Dartmouth College are as follows: (1) Wheelock's strong religious faith and his belief in the urgency of converting the Indians (2) the failure of the Indian scholars to accomplish all that Wheelock had hoped (3) his change of policy to stressing the education of white scholars rather than of Indians for teachers and missionaries (4) the success of Whitaker and Occom in raising the fund abroad. Wheelock was thereby freed of obligations to the Boston Board and to the General Assembly of Massachusetts, both bodies having ceased to contribute to him because of the fund at his command, and enabled to expand his educational program as he wished. That he should remove the charity school and should establish a college with it in a new location were assured. He now had to find the location, obtain a charter for a college, and name it.

Wheelock's attention had been directed to New Hampshire as early as 1763, when Governor Benning Wentworth had offered him five hundred acres in western New Hampshire. This was the first of numerous offers from that province, the inhabitants of which bid more insistently for Wheelock's decision than did those of any other colony. It is not to be assumed that these offers showed a remarkable interest among New Hampshire proprietors in education as education; in general they realized how greatly improved their holdings would be if a college were established on or adjacent to them.

Gradually Wheelock became more and more interested in New Hampshire, and as one after another of the locations in other colonies was closed to him, some spot in western New Hampshire, preferably on the Connecticut River, seemed most desirable because of the easier access to the Canadian Indians.

Unwilling or unable to undertake the arduous task of inspecting the various sites himself, he sent the Reverend Ebenezer Cleaveland, to be joined later by John Wright of Hanover, to gather the information for him. A detailed report, dated December 17, 1768, and signed by them, reviews the most attractive offers; a draft of this report in Wheelock's handwriting, frequently interlineated and differing here and there in wording from the final signed copy, may indicate that Wheelock was responsible for placing the emphasis where it is.

We learn from the report that Cleaveland visited Governor John Wentworth, who had succeeded his uncle, and that the governor, "very favorable to the design," had promised to reserve the township of Landaff for the school, since the proprietors had forfeited their charter. He then spent a few days "with gentlemen in lower towns of New Hampshire who proposed their donations generally where their interests lay."

The agents next consider the offers from Plymouth, Romney, and Campton. In these towns five thousand acres were offered; in favor of accepting them, the agents mention the centrality in New Hampshire of these towns; against accepting them, that they are twenty-seven miles farther from the Canadian Indians than a site along the Connecticut River.

It is clear from the report that the agents were most attracted to Haverhill and Orford, and particularly to the former. They praise, and their praise is still merited, the beauty of the locations, and they found the lands "so much improved and so fertile that there is already a sufficient supply of provisions for the school." At Haverhill they were shown an excellent farm of about six hundred acres, with barns, gristmill, and sawmill, all of which could be bought for £450 sterling, or about the cost of improving the farm up to that time. Furthermore, 5,600 acres were already subscribed at Haverhill and 2,100 acres at Orford.

Cleaveland and Wright stress the generally favorable situation of New Hampshire: about two hundred towns chartered, settled, or about to be settled; the religious habits of the settlers and the demand for ministers, and the lack of any college or "public seminary" in the province. They conclude this section of the report by mentioning that Haverhill and Orford are forty miles nearer to the Six Nations than is Lebanon, Connecticut (the hopelessness of working among the Six Nations was as yet not fully apparent), and about sixty miles from the Saint Francis Indians on the Saint Lawrence River. If Doctor Wheelock, they added, were to remove to either of these towns, the population would doubtless increase and "their lands will soon bear a great price."

To be inclusive the agents comment on the offers from Massachusetts: at Hatfield they found the "prospect very beautiful," the soil good, but not equal to that at Haverhill or Orford. At Albany, the mayor and the alderman showed them the six acres and house (132 x 42), "beautifully located on a hill," but unfinished; and as a postscript they refer to the desire of the people of Lebanon to retain the school there.

This document and letters of his own bearing on the subject Wheelock sent to Robert Keen, the secretary of the English trustees, stating that he himself was so pleased with Haverhill and Orford that if the trustees "shall fix upon that as the place for it, I shall be well satisfied." Accordingly, the trustees voted unanimously in favor of either of those towns, leaving the choice between the two to Wheelock: "we think you may possibly give the preference to the former."

With this problem of location finally settled, as it seemed, the next move was to obtain a royal charter for a college. Inasmuch as New Hampshire was the colony selected for the site, it was inevitable that Wheelock should apply to Governor John Wentworth. To him, on August 22, 1769, Wheelock sent a let-

ter outlining the main points of a charter, adding in a postscript the important sentence, "Sir, if you think proper to use
the word *college* instead of *achademy* I shall be well pleased
with it." Ralph Wheelock and Nathaniel Whitaker attended
the Governor to learn his views, and reported that he was insisting on having the Bishop of London as a trustee "on both
sides of the water," that is, as a member of the American board
of trustees as well as of the English, and further, that the
Bishop of London should control the English fund.

Wheelock at once rejected the reported suggestions, and was
ready to give up all thought of New Hampshire unless the Governor withdrew his proposals. So averse was Wheelock that he
asked Hugh Wallace of New York "in the most aggreeable
manner to propose the affair to Governor Colden, and know
if he will grant a generous charter for this school in that part
of your province. I propose to have one as free from cloggs and
embarrassments with any names as the charter of New Jersey
College is. The place for the school being fixed in the vicinity
of Cowas, a charter from either government will equally consist with the determination of the trust." In a bold letter to
Governor Wentworth, typical of Wheelock when he wished to
express himself without ambiguity, he wrote (Oct. 5, 1769) as
follows:

Doctor Whitaker and my son who applied to Your Excellency in
my name for an incorporation for my Indian achademy, inform
me that you proposed to them that the Bishop of London should
be a trustee &c but I would humbly offer to your consideration
whether such a step would not very greatly disoblige the greater
part of the generous benefactors on both sides the water; and especially the greater part of the inhabitants of your new country who
expect special benefit by it. It is publickly known that Your Excellency proposed only the governor of the province for the time
being as a non-elective trustee in the charter, which you generously
proposed to give. And upon that plan, they and I have proceeded

to bring the matter to the present ripeness for an incorporation, and I think sir that not only they will be disobliged, but that I myself shall be liable, on both sides the water, to the imputation of forfeiting my honor and betraying my trust if I should consent to accept a charter with such an addition, and I also apprehend there would be reason to fear that it would overset and ruin the design. I have had opportunity to know the minds of a number of gentlemen of character and penetration who are well acquainted with the minds of people in general and they are fully agreed with me in the same sentiments respecting the consequents of such an alteration from what has been proposed.

Your Excellency well knows the controversies of the present day, and what a formidable idea our country in general have of a bishop; and how jealous people are of their religious rights and priveleges, and of every thing that has the least look towards an infringement upon them. I am sorry with all my heart that the Church of Christ should be disjoynted by party names, but Your Excellency is well sensible that the evil cant be cured by force.

The prospect of attaining the great end, proposed by this school, at present appears to me most incouraging, and the inhabitants of your new country have their hopes and expectations much raised, and it would be a great cross no doubt to them to be disappointed and you may easily conceive not a very small one to me to give up the affair after I have waded through such a scene of labour and expence to accomplish it, but Your Excellency will easily believe great as the cross would be I shall rather chuse another situation for it than suffer the consequences which I may reasonably expect from a complyance with such a proposal, but I have confidence in your candour and stability which are so universally known, and justly admired, that though you think proper to try me in this matter, you will not persist in it so far as to give me occasion to shew a fortitude in refusing, which I think my own honor and fidelity to my trust will oblige me to.

Wentworth answered reasonably and courteously: his desire, he wrote, was to serve Wheelock, and he was certain that there must have been a misunderstanding. He had heard of rumors that the proposed college would train sectaries to the discouragement of the Church of England, and to offset this tendency he had proposed the Bishop of London *as a member of the English board only,* to serve with the consent of the English trustees.

Colonel Alexander Phelps, Wheelock's son-in-law, acting as Wheelock's agent, after having consulted Wentworth expressed the same understanding of the Governor's proposal. Phelps added that the trustees in England could refuse the recommendation if they wished to, and hoped that this "bare circumstance" would not cause Wheelock to break with one who could be very helpful. The avowal from Wentworth and the interpretation from Phelps mollified Wheelock, who now suggested that Wentworth "Christian the house after your own name." This honor Wentworth declined.[1]

The last obstacle in obtaining an incorporation was now removed. The charter was drawn up in its final form, letters patent in the name of George III were issued, and Governor Wentworth affixed the seal of the province of New Hampshire.

The charter for Dartmouth College is dated December 13, 1769. Phelps returned with a copy of it the following March, and Wheelock then for the first time gave the English trustees details of its final form. Dartmouth's name had been used, he informed the members, without the Earl's consent because to have waited for it would have caused delay. That clause in the draft of the charter which had given the English board power equal to that of the American in nominating and appointing a president had been rejected on the advice of Governor Wentworth. To Robert Keen he expressed the hope that the English trustees would look favorably on the suggestion to include the Bishop of London in their number, a mere gesture, of course, for Wentworth's satisfaction. It must have shocked Wheelock

[1] Mayo, 108 ff., presents evidence which *may* be construed as showing that Governor Wentworth secretly wished to further Episcopal interests by means of the proposed college.

to learn in the course of time that the English trustees had agreed to the suggestion, and his relief must have exceeded his shock when he learned still later that the Bishop of London had refused to serve.

Whether or not Wheelock expected the English trustees to be pleased with the charter cannot be definitely answered; considering the nature of the negotiations, one concludes that he hastened on the incorporation with the hope that it would be acceptable. That the trustees were chagrined and strongly disapproved is clear from their letters to him. The fund of which they were trustees had been raised to educate Indian boys and girls in the charity school and to defray their expenses in the missionary field. That school was now assimilated into Dartmouth College—in the words of the charter, "enlarged and improved to promote learning among the English"—and although the charter states that Indian and English youths should be instructed there, it was evident that the number of Indians prepared for a college education was trifling and that the emphasis would be placed on training white students. Furthermore, the governing of Dartmouth College was vested in the newly constituted board of American trustees, thus leaving the English trustees in control of a fund which was to be used for Dartmouth College on the recommendations of the American board.

The English trustees at once expressed their dissent. Robert Keen wrote that "it was certainly a very wrong step for you to take without consulting us. It is the sentiments of us all that by lodging the power in other hands, it has superceded the trust here (*in England*) and we shall desire to have done with it." John Thornton, another English trustee, informed Wheelock: "I am afraid the step you have taken to get a charter will prove the ruin of your school to all valuable purposes. I wish it may prove otherwise, but you seem to have taken it out of the hands of the trust here to put it into those that I wish may not oppose instead of forward your design. As soon as it takes place I shall be very ready to relinquish any further say in the affair which I think necessarily must be the case with Lord Dartmouth and every one of us." Thornton added a fable in verse of a paper kite that longed to break its string and rival the eagle, and was as a result plunged into the tide:

> Beware of self, beware of pride;
> When you are prone to build a Babel
> Recall to mind this little fable.

The first step necessary in removing the fears of the English trustees was to convince them that they were not being deprived of their authority. Consequently, at the first meeting of the trustees of Dartmouth College (October 22, 1770, held in Keene, New Hampshire) "it was proposed to them to do something to perpetuate the memory and act of Mr. Moor who was the first considerable benefactor to the school while it was small and contemptible. And they the trustees all with one voice declared it to be out of their province, that they had no jurisdiction or right in that matter and refused to do anything about it." Assurance on this point and on other details of the charter Wheelock conveyed to the English trustees on November 9, 1770, as follows:

I acknowledge the receipt of your favour of July 19th in which you say Ld. Dartmouth, Esqr. Thornton as well as the other trustees see clearly that by the affair of the charter the trust here is ment to be annihilated, but I have now the pleasure to assure you that no such thing was ever ment or desired by one of the trustees in Connecticut but the contrary they all look upon it a singular favour of heaven and a token of God's gracious design towards this institution that it has such a reputable, wise, godly and zealous patronage in Europe, and not only so but they also desired that the trust in England should have not only the patronage of the school but of the college too so far as to have an equal part in the choice of the president so long as they should think fit to persist with their board. And so the charter was drafted when it was sent to Govr. Wentworth, nor have I ever heard that one of the trustees in this province objected against it but the Governor apprehending it would be a burden you would not be fond of and that it would make the body too unwieldy rejected that clause in it.

The charter means to incorporate the school[1] with the college and give it possession of the donations and grants made in this province to it, and make it capable of holding the same against all claims whatsoever and we know of no other way in America to secure real estate to such a body but by charter. And the obtaining this appeared to be of such importance and absolute necessity that I was advised by all judicious friends to accomplish it as speedily as possible as there was just reason to expect great opposition from the potentates of our country as soon as the design should be talked of as a reality.

The charter was never designed to convey the least power or controul of any funds collected in Europe or any jurisdiction over the school to the trustees of the college. The charter grants them jurisdiction only over the college. If I resign my office as president of the college I yet retain the same relation to the school as ever.

If I resign the charter I resign all the fund in this province with it.

The English trustees finally accepted Wheelock's statements regarding the division of authority between the two boards, and cautioned him to keep distinct the expenses of the charity school and those of Dartmouth College. That he was unable to carry out this admonition will be seen later.

The charter for the college has been granted; the location,

---

[1] In addition to the information given in this volume (p. 82, fn. 1) it will aid the reader to emphasize that the charity school was not incorporated during Wheelock's life, although it functioned continuously under his direction from 1754. In 1807 the legislature of New Hampshire granted a quasi-incorporation by authorizing the trustees of the college to act also as trustees of the school. (See L. B. Richardson, *History of Dartmouth College*, I, 233–235.)

too, has seemingly been decided upon; in fact, Colonel Phelps, Wheelock's agent, had decided on Haverhill. But now proprietors in other parts of New Hampshire spread the rumor that Phelps had acted for his own interests in making his decision. And Governor Wentworth, having learned that proprietors were speculating in land on the probability of the establishment of a college, recommended that Wheelock settle in Landaff, northeast of Haverhill, and granted to the college on January 25, 1770.

Wheelock was now clearly obliged to visit New Hampshire himself, and so in June of 1770 we find him inspecting sites in that province. How he was able to change Governor Wentworth's mind we do not know, but he did succeed in persuading him that Hanover and not Landaff should be the location, and was ratified in his choice by the trustees of the college and the Connecticut trustees of the charity school. Having settled this problem, he so informed the English trustees (July 29, 1770):

I have spent many weeks in this wilderness, or newly settling country, with the Reverend Mr. Pomeroy, and another gentleman of known ability in such affairs, whom I desired to accompany and assist in viewing the many places proposed along Connecticut River for 70 miles together and to hear the reasons and arguments offerd in favor of the same; in doing which we were abundantly satisfied of the expediency of seeing, hearing, and judging for ourselves. And in consequence of a survey of the places to which we were invited, and availing ourselves of the reasons and arguments offerd, we were able to be so particular and circumstantial in our representation as to remove every biass antecedently conceived by representations made ex parte, and unite all the trustees in giving the preference to the southwestern corner of Hanover, adjoyning upon Lebanon where is a body of choise lands conveniently situate, given for the only use of the college by the said towns of Lebanon and Hanover, and by the Honle. Benning Wentworth, Esq., late governor of said province, containing about 3300 acres on which there is, by estimation, near 200 acres of choise meadow, annually overflowed by said river, and a large brook which runs into it. This tract is pritty well watered, and well proportioned for all kinds of tillage, and for fuel. It joyns upon the falls, called White River falls, (as you may see by the map) where is the only place for a bridge across Connecticut River, it being but eight rods wide, with well elevated rocks on each side for abutments, and is upon a direct line from Portsmouth to Crown Point, to which we were informed a good road may be had, and its distance but 60 miles; and about 140 to Montreal and but 40 miles land portage to each of these places. The Indian tribes far and near have been well acquainted with this place, and have used it as a hunting ground 'till the late wars. The college will stand within a mile of the river, and of the bridge proposed to be built. The towns on each side the river are settling fast with a religious set of people.

The college will stand upon the body of lands designed for cultivation, which situation will be well accomodate to my plan of introducing labor, as the principal or only diversion and way for students health &c. by which means they may not only contribute much to their own support, under the conduct of a prudent and skillful overseer, but young Indians with English boys may be instructed and improved in the arts of agriculture without the least impediment to their studies, and I see not why I hant a good prospect of supporting a large number as soon as those lands may be brought under improvement.

A young Indian from Canada on his hunting tour came to us at Haverhill, and seemd much pleased with the design we were upon, and promised to come to school as soon as it should be settled in those parts, and capable to receive him.

The President and trustees are all qualified for their office according to charter, by taking the oath of allegiance &c.

I have employed an agent of labourers to build baracks, or small houses, that may serve my family and students the coming winter, or 'till the college can be built, as there will likely be great advantage to the whole by my being on the spot. And accordingly I am preparing to remove immediately, unless a report very lately come amongst us, viz., that an army of worms, which have this year invaded several parts of the land, have so prevaild as to cut off great part of the crops in that country and threaten them with great scarsity, should be so confirmd as to convince me I must stay for want of subsistance.

On this occasion you will easily see that I must necessarily expend of the capital, as no resources here are to be expected equal to the expences of the building and preparing for cultivation. And I am full in the opinion that no other improvement of those monies will be equally profitable to the school with that of laying them out upon these lands, it will be better than money at 50 pr.cent.

The time had now arrived for the actual removal of Wheelock's students and family from Connecticut to New Hampshire. He himself arrived in Hanover in August, 1770, and at once prepared for the coming of the others. He writes in his (1771) *Narrative:*

I set some to digging a well, and others to build a house for myself and family, of 40 by 32 feet, and one story high, and others to build a house for my students 80 by 32, and two stories high. They had so near finished my house, that by advice of principal workmen, I sent for my family and students, but when they had dug one well of 63 feet, and another of 40, and found no prospect of water, and I had found it therefore necessary to remove the buildings, I sent to stop my family, and try'd for water in six several places, between 40 and 70 rods.

The messenger dispatched to delay the departure of the family from Lebanon was Doctor John Crane—he had a certificate from Wheelock stating that the matter was sufficiently urgent to require his traveling on the Sabbath—and with him he bore the following letter of instruction to Mrs. Wheelock:

Dartmouth College
Sept. 10, 1770

My dear Wife,

By the last of this month I expect by divine favor to have the satisfaction of seeing you, our children, and family here in these woods. I would have you let me know your motions, and what I may expect as soon, and as often as you can. I think I have found a good steward, and have a prospect of a good supply of provisions. I hope the wildness will be agreable to you; the most I regrett is, that it will not be long, nor much, that I shall be able to do for you. My absence from you and my family I find to be very burdensome to me. I hope I am in Gods way. I wait upon Him to direct my way, and perform for me and by me the thing that is right in His sight.

I have many things to say, can only throw out hints. I beleive it will be best that Jabez and the team should stay some time when he comes in order to do some work with them before he returns. I shall endeavour to make provision for them. It will not be best for Exeter to bring his cow unless she gives milk, it will cost 40s. at least to winter her here. Let some factor buy 100lb. or more of tobacco and bring. I can't determine how many teams must be had to come with the family. You are better able to judge of that than I am. I beleive it will be best that Brister should stay and make the hoggs very fat, before Jabez returns. If you have a barrel of old pork, bring it with you. I want £100 money as soon as may be. I meet with difficulty about a good well, but hope it will not retard the business long; they expect to get water to-morrow. I hire upward of 20 men to work for me; they appear in good spirits. You would do well to bring a gross of pipes. I purpose to meet you if I can hear when at Number 4. People are kind, and very civil and courteous. Mr. English was here this day but had forgot the letters he brought, so that I can't answer them. Accept love in abundance to you and all ours.

I am your constant loving husband,

Eleazar Wheelock

I leave it with you to determine who had best stay with Brister. I don't know but Exeter and Cloe till Jabez returns; if Molley inclines to stay and come in the winter in a sleigh she may tho' I don't think any of you will feel very well while the place is in its present temper. I am crowded with business. I pray God direct you and all of you in this important affair.

I am yours &c.

E. Wheelock

The family had already departed from Lebanon, however; Mrs. Wheelock in a coach which John Thornton had sent to Wheelock from England, and thirty charity students on foot. Abraham and Daniel Simon, Narragansets, the only Indians to come from the school to the new location, were to drive the cows, but objected. Jabez Bingham, Wheelock's nephew, drove the baggage wagon, in which among household and other articles were boxes of glass, six by eight inches, a barrel of rum and a barrel of molasses, a keg of wine, and half a barrel of sugar. The slave Exeter was reported as "very high in the instep, and says he won't go without Peggy goes and all his things." The group reached Hanover safely, and as Wheelock writes,

I housed my stuff, with my wife, and the females of my family, in my hutt—my sons and students made booths and beds of hemlock boughs, and in this situation we continued about a month, till the 29th day of October, when I removed with my family into my house. And though the season had been cold, with storms of rain and snow—two saw-mills failed, on which I had chief dependance for boards, etc., and a series of other trying disappointments, yet by the pure mercy of God, the scene changed for the better in every respect—the weather uncommonly favourable, new resources for the supply of boards, &c., till my house was made warm, and comfortable—a school-house built, and so many rooms in the college made quite comfortable, as were sufficient for the students which were with me; in which they find the pleasure, and profit of such a solitude; and since the settlement of the affair all, without exception, are sufficiently ingaged in their studies.

From Lebanon came two messages, the one, already quoted, from Bezaleel Woodward: "Parish people continue in statu quo—revilings dont yet cease"; and a more sympathetic one from a parishioner informing Wheelock that the removal "was not a little lemmented, it seems very maloncly to see the greean so clear of such a number of sprightly youth as was wont to be their."

CHAPTER XII

THE LAST DECADE

AT the age of fifty-nine Wheelock might reasonably have
looked forward to restful days. Behind him were
thirty-five years of pastoral service burdened at their
beginning with the additional labors of his itinerancy during
the Great Awakening and at their close by his administration
for fifteen years of Moor's Charity School. His health was poor:
asthma, eczema, pains so wracking that he had to employ an
amanuensis at times, and "hypochondriac flatulency" afflicted
him; as he wrote, "one foot was in the grave, the other this side
eternity." With the nine thousand pounds in England to fi-
nance a charity school he could have spent the rest of his days
in Lebanon free from financial cares, had he wished to limit
his educational plan to the school alone. Thirty thousand inhabitants of Connecticut are reported to have left it during this
period for other parts, but none of that large number could
have had so much impedimenta to remove—family, scholars,
slaves, cattle, equipment—or was undertaking the multiple
task of hewing a clearing in the wilderness, providing food and
shelter for those dependent on him (his "family" within a year
after his removal to Hanover numbered seventy, including
thirty laborers), governing a town, recruiting Indians from
Canada, founding and administering a college. If the account
of Wheelock's activities in this the decade of the Revolution
and the last of his life tells us little of Wheelock the pastor and
teacher, the reason is to be found in the new circumstances.
Henceforth he was a harassed administrator, a harassed farmer,
a harassed provider. "I have had no other place for study, re-
tirement, lodging, and to receive all my company on private
business but a little smoky room of about 12 or 14 feet square

which I made in the garret of the one storey house (of which I
have already informed you) which I originally intended for a
storehouse for the school, and which is now used for that purpose." Considering his many labors and the worry which accompanied them, we may excuse, at least in large part, the
querulousness which he frequently voiced in his closing years.

The opportunities for employment in Hanover naturally
attracted men of various trades and abilities, whose recommendations Wheelock scrutinized as closely as he had the sites
offered for the college. Benjamin Pomeroy nominated a certain
barber as a handy man at household chores and skillful in tending the sick. Another man was versed in "potash, sope byling,
brooing and the like." To the latter Wheelock wrote,

I don't know but you are the very man, if you are sufficiently
skillful, prudent, careful, humble minded, diligent, &c. And if you
have a mind to make the tryal you may come as soon as you please,
and the sooner the better, but you must bring a bed with you if you
can conveniently, and you must note that you are to rise here according to the fashion and custom of the country, viz. your first degree must be in a logg house but not as others have done altogether,
for it will be dry and warm, and has a chimney, some bords and
glass and a door conveniently hung, which are circumstances your
predicessors had not the honor and previlege of enjoying, and after
a while to advance as ability and merit shall dictate. And above all
you must come not as your own man to set up self as your first and
cheif object, but as esteeming it a previlege that you may be a servant of God whom you will find to be a bountiful and liberal master if he sees in you the heart of a servant to him. I love you, and
wish you well.

A bricklayer recommends himself, and one Oaks is ready to
supply feathers. Is there work in Hanover for a goldsmith? The
trustees of Dartmouth vote plots of land to encourage a steward, a physician, an innholder, a tailor, a shoemaker, "and

other suitable settlers." Wheelock looks for a millwright, and, most important of all if he himself were to be relieved of some of his labors, for an overseer to take charge of the farms and merchandising. During the decade this one and that served as overseer for Wheelock's interests in New Hampshire and Connecticut, although Wheelock was always the custodian of these custodians. A "plague of deceitful cooks" in the college kitchen increased his vexation, and in despair he urged a friend to find him a German baker (German and, therefore, presumably honest), if such could be found, in Philadelphia.

And always the sale of strong drink to be regulated. Against John Payne, tavern-keeper in Hanover, Wheelock wrote vigorous letters to Governor Wentworth, and had his own nominee, Aaron Storrs, licensed by the Court of Quarter Sessions. Half a dozen miles away in Lebanon, New Hampshire, two students showed in 1775 how that town could be a means of self-expression for the youth of Dartmouth by tearing up their bed-sheet and putting a "stone and headboard" from the cemetery in their bed. And, as the incensed innholder complained, they did foully profane a three pint basin and a cup. Yet in this year Wheelock found that love and joy were prevailing, as he informed his friends by letter, and that all vice "was drove into corners."

All things converged on Wheelock. The *dedimus potestatem* which Governor Wentworth had sent in appointing him justice of the peace could readily be construed as a warrant to handle all problems arising in the school and college and church and town. To Wheelock were sent complaints of all sorts, and from him emanated the orders for the community. What shall be done with the body of Joshua Tilden found frozen on the road one day in January? Certify to the coroner that you have removed the body and he will probably be satisfied. Directions for rafting logs down the Connecticut. Orders for grass, rum, beef. Wheelock is accused of inhospitality at the college commencement of 1773: he denies the charge, adds that his wife has been ill, the cook drunk, and besides the college has only one tablecloth. A young laborer, an Englishman, wishes to recover an estate in London, but cannot recall the location of the house or the names of his brothers. Whereupon Wheelock writes to Robert Keen, asking him to help. Abigail, the Englishman's wife, wishes that Wheelock would make them comfortable, since it was he who invited them to Hanover. From Hugh Wallace in New York City come a present and a pleasant tribute: "I send you Dr. Goldsmith's poem, *Deserted Village,* perhaps you may not have seen it. I think it pretty, and were the Dr. in England and Dr. Wheelock in America acquainted I should imagine he drew his parson from you, and I hope you have just such a schoolmaster."

A transient, convicted of stealing, is sentenced by Wheelock to pay treble damages, and is indentured to one John Deveraux, whom he will serve faithfully for two months, keeping his master's secrets and avoiding taverns and playhouses. John Crane, in his capacity of informing officer, reports to Wheelock, justice of the peace, that Amos Thompson "on the frame of John House, Esqr. (which was then raising) was guilty of uttering a prophane oath or oaths." John Crane, in his capacity of physician, has to defend himself before Wheelock: "Reverend and Honored Sir: Since I have lately been accused of malpractice in the obstetricate art by a number of good old mischief making matrons at the bar of whose shallow understanding contrary to scripture truth and humanity my character has been arraigned tried judged and condemned without my cognizance who taking the advantage of your easiness of access have presumed on your superior character and filled your ears with false reports—." Some misdemeanor, perhaps that of the students in Lebanon, causes Wheelock to write that "the Old Serpent has waked up lately and acts like himself yet. I hope he will bite his tongue and become speechless by and by." Elijah Kent wishes Wheelock to go bond for his appearance at court; he had refused to pay for a mare the age of which had been falsely stated. Another would like credit at the college store for Sabbath clothes. More trouble with the cooks: "Discoursed with black Eliza the cook of some imprudence in the kitchin." Members of the freshman and sophomore classes wish to be allowed "to spend certain leisure hours allotted to us for the relaxation of our minds, in such sort as steping the minuet and learning to use the sword—."

Wheelock has to inform the Governor that a man plans to set up a pearl-ash industry in Thetford, Vermont, a dozen miles away, and that trade will likely be diverted thereby out of the province of New Hampshire. Ferry rights on the Connecticut must be adjusted. "I feal as tho' my day was closed and I long to be at rest." Let the motto on the college seal be *Vox Clamantis in Deserto*. Will Mr. Payne please pay for the cart he borrowed from Wheelock and broke? Trips to Portsmouth, New Hampshire, to Cambridge, to towns in Connecticut. "Concerted prayer" for the missionaries, the appointed evening hour being variously given as six o'clock, six-thirty, between six and seven. In Connecticut the inhabitants of a town wish to turn part of one of Wheelock's farms into a common. A letter of congratulation to Mrs. Barbara Watts, a member of the new sect of Methodists and living in Quebec; she had induced several army men to meet with her in devotions: "I indeed much rejoice that God has graciously put the leaven into the lump at Quebec." Recruiting parties have to be organized and sent to Canada. A permit is issued for transporting supplies on the Sabbath. Some one, facetiously or fanatically, recommends for admission to Dartmouth a student proficient in music and able to drive away evil spirits from the college, as David did from

Saul. A scholar confesses to a lack of zeal in hindering residents from chopping down a tree on Sunday.

Seven inhabitants of Hanover thank Wheelock for bringing Dartmouth College to the town, congratulate him on her prosperity, and assure him that his conduct is beyond criticism. A warrant is sought against Joseph Skinner for posting notice on the door of a college building that Wheelock is a "liar and hypocrite, with many other menacing words and speeches." Twenty-eight inhabitants sign a statement of confidence in Wheelock, and believe that Dartmouth is a barrier against ungodliness. Joseph Verrieul, student, while reading his declamation before the college, is seriously discomfited when Eleazar Wheelock, junior, roguishly advances a candle "near to his face," and young Eleazar (he was sixteen) confesses that his conduct has been "very unhandsome, unchristian, and ungentleman."

From below-stairs certain gossip among the help which had to be attended to:

To the Shereif: In His Majesty's name you are commanded forthwith to arrest the body of Caesar a negro man now for some time past residing in the kitchen appertaining to Dartmouth College and him forthwith have before me the subscriber, to answer to a complaint alledged against him by Mary Sleeper, now residing at my dwelling house, for defamatory words uttered by the said Caesar tending to the injury of the character of the said Mary, particularly that he has said of late that he has no doubt but that Bristo and Archelaus (negro servants to the subscriber) have had carnal knowledge of her the said Mary, and that she was fond of it, and that the said Caesar said that he knew something which if known to the world would ruin the character of the said Mary to her dying day, and that he has uttered words of the same import and meaning with those above-mentioned at other times, contrary to the peace of our Sovereign Lord the King his crown and dignity, and in violation of the good and wholesome laws of this province, and to the damage of the said Mary, as she says, the sum of fifty pounds.

Caesar is found guilty, fined ten shillings, lawful money, and ordered to produce sureties in the sum of ten pounds "before sunsetting; and in failing thereof that he receive seven stripes on the naked body in some public place." The slave must have been popular in the community because a number of students and a shopkeeper bound themselves, their heirs and assigns, forever, for the sum required.

The Committee of Safety for Hanover has dared to appropriate the college mill, a mile and a half from town, to house students and townspeople inoculated against smallpox. It is doubtful if anything ever aroused Wheelock to greater anger, unless it were the matter of his salary in Connecticut, or Sin, itself. He accused the Committee and the selectmen of breaking the fifth, sixth, and eighth commandments (his usual type of ready-reckoning), suggested to influential leaders in New York that Dartmouth be moved to that province on the forfeited estate of Sir William Johnson, and vainly tried to arouse the trustees to take definite action upholding his supreme authority. Worry, age (he was sixty-six), poor health, the state of the country, and his exaggerated sense of personal dignity and authority combined to rob him for the time being of a reasonable perspective.

In the winter of 1770 Wheelock had about thirty students in school and college, "who seem all to rejoice in a solitude so favourable for their studies." Some of them may have rejoiced but some were clearly rebellious. William Crosby, for example, setting forth that he was ill and discouraged and had been so ever since coming to Hanover, asked to be dismissed, and thereby involved himself in a bitter quarrel with Wheelock. According to the President, Crosby objected to spending his summer vacation on the farm, and more important, wanted to join Wheelock's old rival, the Boston Board of the Society in Scotland. Crosby was therefore "scandalously guilty of the breach of the 5th and 9th Commands.," in that he had failed to honor Wheelock, his "father," and had borne false witness, presumably against the circumstances. As late as 1775 (Crosby by that time had entered Harvard with the financial aid of the Boston Board) Wheelock was still pursuing him with invective and accusing him of another breach, this time of the eighth commandment, in that he had profited at Wheelock's cost without making recompense. In defense of the President it must be added that Crosby was only one of many charity scholars whom Wheelock had carried along only to see them give up the missionary work to which they had pledged themselves in return for an education.

Others had their reasons for desiring to leave Dartmouth. Joel Loomis objected to the remoteness of the college. Noble Everett found that it was "too inconvenient to study here," and would rather by fifty pounds that he had stayed in Connecticut; he was tired of hearing members of the Wheelock family say that they had come north for the good of the students and had more to complain of than they. Augustine Hubbard in 1771 found that at Hanover he had no chance to acquaint himself with mankind: "I beleive it will be of great service to me, to withdraw from this tumult for a little while, for by that means I shall git my head clear'd of that fountain of confution it tis now filled with." Francis Quarles threatened to sue Wheelock for defamation of character; in Wheelock's letter recommending that Yale accept Quarles as a transfer student "you could not (everyone said that saw it) wrote any thing more prejudicial to my caracter unless you had accused me of murder." And Quarles added that in court he would tell how "you treat your men that are sent to your college. Sometimes to blow stinky horns eat stinking provisions kill dogs &c &c and many other things scandelous to relate." John Ledyard improved the occasion of Wheelock's absence in the spring of 1773 to fashion a canoe from a pine tree and slip away on the flood waters of the Connecticut. David Goodall preferred English authors to Homer. One Osbourne would like to give up the study of languages because time is short and souls must be saved. In spite of these complaints and many others, Wheelock believed that the scholars were "well pleased with my plan of improving the vacancies (*vacations*) in cultivation of their lands," and that "all the students are most cordially agreed in it (*the constitution of the college*) and chearfully practise it, according to the example not of Yale or Harvard but of the colleges of Elijah of old."

Such were some of the many concerns of this educator as we glimpse them in the correspondence of his last nine years. Circumstances were pelting him, irritating him, but not defeating him. In the new environment of a pioneering country he had at first literally renewed his vigor, as Antaeus in touching the earth: "the salutary roots &c which this country abounds with, and which I have found to be under God the greatest restorative and preservative of my health of any thing I have ever tryed," although as the decade wore on even the herbs of New Hampshire could not make him whole. Is it not an indication of great faith in his institution that this bombardment of complaints, this barrage of worries, failed to shake Wheelock? He was too often petty in his reproaches, he imagined insults to his dignity and authority. Whether or not Dartmouth was modelled after the so-called colleges of Elijah, that vigorous man of God, Wheelock believed that she was. Therefore, she was. To him, because he believed something to be true, it was true. Belief and fact were identical. And however wrong this reasoning may be from a logician's point of view, it had the merit of stimulating Wheelock to unceasing action. Reasoning in a circle produced a straight line of accomplishment!

August 28, 1771. The first commencement at Dartmouth. Four (white) students were graduated: Levi Frisbie, Sylvanus Ripley, Samuel Gray, and John Wheelock, the former two being intended as missionaries, the latter, not having been charity students, being relieved of that obligation. Since the trustees lacked a quorum the degrees were not voted to the graduates until 1773.

There was one very definite result from this commencement: a renewal of the charge that Wheelock was diverting the "grand design" into an educational program for whites to the neglect of the Indians. In answer to Samson Occom's question, "Whether Dartmouth College is for the Indians or whites or both equally alike?" Wheelock replied (February 24, 1772):

I thought my dear sir you had fully known my object to be the Indians which has been invariably the same from the first. They are also the first object in the charter. These lands are all given for that purpose, and will be so used for them so long as there shall be Indians upon the continent to partake of the benefit. I have not taken a step nor struck a stroke since I have been here but with that view. In that course I am worn out, and have now risqued all my estate. The plan is such that all the benefit done or proposed to be done to the English is subserviant to the best manner to the Indians cause; and greatly adds to and increases my ability to help the Indians and that many ways, insomuch that I hope in God to be able to support an hundred Indians and youths designed for Indian service on charity in a little time—hant you seen my late Narrative—you may have one at Hartford if you will send, and in that be informed what I have been and now am about. My heart is broken and spirits sometimes almost overwhelmed with the behavior of some I have taken unweired pains for—perhaps God intends to wrast them away from this land—but however that may be my resolution yet continues to follow them with my endeavors for them as long as I live, and I beleive in so doing I am unto God a sweet savor of Christ, though they all perish after all that can be done to save them.

Just how much was Wheelock doing for the Indians? As we have seen, he did try to recruit from the Six Nations at the beginning of this decade. David Avery and the two Narragansets, Abraham Simons and John Matthews, had tried in vain to bring back children from the province of New York; James Dean also had been unsuccessful among the Oneidas but had returned with two Stockbridge (Massachusetts) Indians from the Reverend John Sargent.

At Hanover there were only five Indians in the spring of 1772, and they all were from New England. To "stop the clamor against the cause" Wheelock arranged, also in 1772, to send Sylvanus Ripley and Lieutenant Thomas Taylor of Claremont, New Hampshire, later a spy in the American army, to Canada. They were to proceed to Montreal and thence to Quebec,

if you shall be advised of an incouraging prospect of success, in the business of your mission thereby, which is to open and prepare a way for communication, commerce, and intercourse between Canada and Dartmouth College. And you are by proper endeavours, by the advice of Governor Cramake, Capt. Depeyster, Mr. Austin, and other gentlemen of character for prudence, integrity, and influence to get an understanding of the state, and temper of the Indian tribes in those parts, and whether there be a door open to find missionaries and schoolmasters among them, and the best way for affecting the same—to obtain a number of likely Indian boys to receive an education here upon charity; or which I rather chuse if it may be the children of English captives, who were taken and naturalized by Indians and married among them. You are also to let gentlemen of any denomination know the state of the infant college, and upon what condition independent children may be educated here, and in what produce of their country their remittances may be made instead of money, if a scarcity of money should be an objection against their sending their children.

In spite of opposition from Canadian priests, this mission was successful; two Hurons from Lorette and eight Caughnawagas, two of whom were half-breeds, returned with Ripley and Taylor, and all arrived safely in Hanover. Thus the total number of Indians was suddenly increased to eighteen: to the five New England Indians James Dean had added two, John Sargent had brought still another from Stockbridge, and now ten from Canada were enrolled. Four of the Canadian Indians soon proved intractable and were sent back, four others were recruited, again from Stockbridge, and the total remained at eighteen. Without giving the details of other recruiting parties, we may state that Wheelock had under his supervision at Hanover during this decade about forty Indians, of whom fifteen were from Canada. The white students enrolled in Dartmouth College in this decade were a little in excess of one hundred and twenty; it is impossible to discover how many others attended the charity school.

From England and Scotland came the charge, frequently reiterated, that Dartmouth College would soon be given over to the Church of England. John Erskine of the Society in Scotland was quoted by Thornton as having said that the charter of the college was artfully drawn to conceal the fact that Dartmouth would soon be controlled by the Church. Thornton, himself, pointed out that five of the trustees of the college were men of high position in New Hampshire and therefore open to the Court influence which favored Episcopacy. Wheelock replied that but three of the trustees were Churchmen, and only one was thought "to be so in heart and he is a very honest man and far from party spirit and bigotry." Still Wheelock must have been troubled by the criticisms because he sent a copy of the charter to William Smith and William Livingstone in New York, asking them to study it to see whether there was anything "dangerous or unsafe in it." Governor Wentworth wrote to Wheelock that "the conduct of our maligners is intirely disingenuous, and utterly false. To Dissenters we are represented as the child of Episcopacy, to Episcopalians as a seminary of devoted sectaries, combining for the extermination of the Church of England."

For some time Wheelock had been trembling at the drafts made on the English fund, and on one occasion reported himself as "outrunning the constable." He had cause to tremble and to run. Even nine thousand pounds cannot be drawn on indefinitely, and in 1774, to Wheelock's amazement the fund was not only exhausted but overdrawn by five hundred pounds.

The blame he placed not on himself but on the English trustees, who had allowed him to exceed the total. They, on their part, had insisted on a strict accounting, and, as stated earlier, had cautioned him against confusing the expenses of the charity school with those of Dartmouth College. Thornton, always scrupulous and generous, had emphasized that the fund raised for educating the Indians should not be used for college purposes, and allowed Wheelock to draw on him personally for five or six hundred pounds.

But it was apparently impossible for Wheelock to keep separate his various expenses, personal and academic, because they were closely identified. If he used part of the fund to build a lumber mill, should the output of the mill be used only for charity school needs or for the college and family as well? Should the grain raised by means of the fund and ground at the gristmill, erected also from the fund, be weighed out carefully, so much for the Indians and white charity students, so much for paying students, family and laborers, to be paid for from some other donation? At what point did the charity school cease and Dartmouth College begin? The identification becomes all the more blurred when we find Wheelock in 1773, instead of using five hundred pounds received from the New

193

Hampshire Assembly for a college building, as the Assembly intended, appropriating the money to defray part of the building expenses of his own dwelling-house. With surprising naïveté he explained to Thornton that this borrowed money would have to be repaid as soon as it was needed for its original purpose!

In spite of Wheelock's disclaimer, he knew that he was overdrawing and he relied on the generosity of the English trustees to make up the deficit. Thus, in a draft of a letter to Thornton is found a deletion which shows that he fully understood the true condition of the fund: he regrets that he has overdrawn, "as my bookkeeper as well as your own account informs me." In the draft of this letter the words "my bookkeeper as well as" have been crossed out, thus placing the onus on the English trustees alone. Wheelock would have departed from his lifelong practice if in this instance he had admitted guilt.

At the opening of the Revolution he found himself, consequently, once more deeply in debt, with twenty Indians and ten white students on charity, "without a penny" for the support of them, himself, his four tutors in the college, and a schoolmaster. If he had been able to collect his debts, affairs would have worn a "pleasing aspect," to use one of his favorite phrases. These debts totaled one thousand pounds, but "all seem to think I act out of character and contrary to my nature if I so much as ask them to pay what they have promised." It is pleasant to record a gentle caution which Wheelock in the midst of his troubles sent at this time to his agent: "But if any of the subscribers are by the Providence of God reduced to needy circumstances, I cant desire you to add to their distresses by crowding upon them, nor to take any thing but what Christ himself would receive at their hands."

The English trust now ceased, of course. As individuals they, or at least some of them, continued to show interest in Wheelock. Samuel Savage told Wheelock to draw on him for one hundred pounds, and was rewarded with the encomium, "he is an Israelite indeed." Robert Keen advised Wheelock to continue his *Narratives* and offered to distribute copies in England with the hope of raising money. John Thornton continued his aid; in earlier days he had given one hundred pounds to the school, a chaise to Wheelock, and had contributed to Occom's support. Later he had offered to pay for Wheelock's house, and on several occasions told Wheelock to draw on him freely; his benefactions to Wheelock personally and to the school probably totaled a thousand pounds. Well did he merit the praise in William Cowper's *Charity,* and the lines in *In Memory of Thornton*

> Surpassing all that mine or mint have given.
> And if the genuine worth of gold depend
> On application to its noblest end,
> Thine had a value in the scales of Heaven,

From the American side there were also benefactions, notably from John Phillips of Exeter, New Hampshire; these (including a donation of one hundred pounds to the charity school in 1764) amounted to a thousand pounds. Wheelock, himself, gave generously: in 1778 an auditor's report showed that his disbursements from his private fortune since 1770 now amounted to £1,747.19.7 1/2, lawful money, which sum was to be considered as owing to him. The contributions from the Continental Congress will be mentioned later.

Wheelock's resilience was remarkable. Just when we are about to assume from the tone of his begging letters that he is completely discouraged, we are surprised by a cheerful note. The lack of funds is compensated by a religious revival: "Love, peace, and joy in God reign triumphant—the only discourse now in fashion when students visit one anothers rooms is of the things of the Kingdom of Heaven, and it would be a reproach to any one if he should introduce any thing frothy, vain, trifling or unprofitable into conversation." Nevertheless spiritual income does differ from financial. "Where should I get a thousand pounds? Can I make money?" He begged George Washington for "shirting" taken by privateers, from which he might have clothing made for the Indians. And unwilling that his Indians should be sent home, he not only planned to mortgage his personal property, but sold most of his holdings in Connecticut for £1,250. It was difficult, he wrote, to raise money on real estate, "until we know whether we shall be free men or slaves."

Wheelock and the Revolution

It is said that Wheelock once tried to induce Joseph Brant, the brother of Sir William Johnson's Molly, and at one time a student in Moor's Charity School, to side with the Colonists during the Revolution. Brant, in reply, stated that he could never forget the many happy hours spent with Wheelock, or the prayers which he had heard while at the school. One passage in particular, he said, had impressed him: "that they might be able to live as good subjects, to fear God, and honor the King." With that answer Brant dismissed the subject.

As early as 1770 Wheelock had declared his stand with the Colonies, having agreed not to import goods from the British Isles. One exception he requested would be granted him by the merchants who had covenanted to boycott British products, namely, that some friends in Scotland be permitted to transmit to him one hundred pounds worth of clothing and books as a donation. The boycott irked him, however, and he tried to circumvent it. In 1774 he directed John Thornton to send clothing from England to a friend in Boston, who would take care of it for the school. If this were done, Wheelock would not incur, he wrote, the displeasure of the Colonies. Wheelock's self-justification was that he needed the clothing for his charity scholars, and that he was not importing goods for the purpose of trading.

In the same year Wheelock wrote a letter to Governor Wentworth which would have seriously damaged Wheelock's reputation as a patriot if it had been made public at the time. The situation was this: the carpenters in Boston, partly because of their own aversion to the task, partly because of public hostility, had refused to assist in building barracks in Boston for British troops. General Gage thereupon asked Wentworth to supply him, if possible, with carpenters from New Hampshire. Without letting the workmen know the nature of the proposed employment, Wentworth secretly hired fifteen New Hampshire men, keeping secret even from the agent who hired them (as he wrote to the Marquis of Rockingham on November 9) the details of the work.

Three days before Wentworth wrote to the Marquis, Wheelock had his amanuensis write the following paragraphs to Wentworth:

I have had such important affairs of my own to demand my attention, while the dispute between the mother country and the colonies has run so high as to kindle a fire which I fear will not be soon, or easily extinguished in either party that I have not understanding in the matter, nor penetration enough to see what injury the building of those barracks will be to Boston, or to the cause of liberty which is so justly dear to them; and if no injury at all, and if it be so esteemed by the most judicious and warmest friends to liberty there and they themselves are therefore willing that 87 carpenters from New York should be employed in that service, I can't conceive what crime you are chargeable with in being willing that a number of your poor people should share some advantage with others by joining them in that service.

But supposing you have been a little out of the way in it, which I don't see that you have, I must think that in our situation, there is just doubt of good policy, in their making a public bustle and clamor about it, as they are not likely thereby to strengthen that cause, or add one friend to their number, but on the other hand will expose us, the infant settlers on your frontiers, to the fury of a merciless northern army, if such should be sent, as we fear to crush what is (I hope) unjustly called a general rebellion in other provinces; and greatly weaken your influence to save us from the terrible consequences of it.

This part of your province is as unanimous and warm (according to their ability) for the defense of that liberty which is threat'ned, as any part of the continent, and when duty calls, will be as active to do their part; but at the same time are firmly attached to your person, and esteem the past silence of this province, in the controversy, and your Excellency's friendship for your people, and your influence with the Governor of Quebec to be our strongest and surest bulwark against a herd of savages, who, we hear, are already in high spirits for plunder here.

Wentworth's manoeuvring was clearly unpatriotic and was considered to be so by the committee at Portsmouth, New Hampshire, which passed judgment on it. According to the committee's findings, Wentworth was "an enemy to the community," the carpenters were ordered to "leave such scandalous employment and return to their respective habitations," and the agent who had hired them was obliged to beg forgiveness on his knees.[1] Since the disapproval of the public had been clearly expressed by the verdict of the committee, Wentworth must have found but little to console him in Wheelock's doctrine of expediency and his avowal of personal loyalty in the western part of the province. Fortunately he did not attempt to justify his employment of New Hampshire carpenters by citing the opinion of the president of Dartmouth.

The greatest fear of the inhabitants of Hanover just before and during the war was not of the redcoats but of the redskins. Hence Wheelock's requests that firearms be furnished the students; hence, too, his sending of James Dean to Canada "to

[1] Mayo, 137–139.

keep the fires of friendship burning between the Indians and this seminary." Frequently he expressed his opinion that Dartmouth College was a bulwark against the Indians, not only because Indians from Lorette and Caughnawaga, Canada, were resident at the charity school, but because his agents had established friendly relations with Canadian tribes.

The first lengthy statement we have from Wheelock on his attitude toward the Crown dates from May 5, 1775. It attempts to answer the question, "Whether persons holding royal commissions should resign them because of His Majesty's oppressive acts?" Wheelock's answer is ponderous and pretentiously analytical. According to the analysis, kings are set up by God, and any who resist kings in the proper exercise of authority expose themselves to damnation. A king has a claim to obedience, but only in the Lord and in that which is lawful, and the king's authority is lawful until he is "put out." Commissions ought to be used for the good ends for which they were given, although the use of the commissions may militate against the evil conduct of the king. A king is not to be removed by a little party unable to establish and defend a constitution agreeable to the members of it. Commissions must not be thrown away contemptuously because the king is "doing that which is very bad." We must be guided by the Continental Congress. By retaining commissions we show the king that we are liege subjects.

The document is of little value either as an expression of patriotism or an exercise in composition. More definite is his subscription to a plan to send Lieutenant Taylor to Canada as a spy. It will be recalled that once before Wheelock had sent Taylor to Canada to recruit students for the school. On this second occasion he offered to send an Indian boy along with the spy to allay suspicion, "and I can make business for Lieut. Taylor that will appear to justify his journey." As additional evidence of his interest in the American cause, he successfully proposed Sylvanus Ripley to George Washington as chaplain at Montreal, stressing that Ripley might thus help the cause of liberty by uniting the Canadian Indians to the colonies; and to Governor Trumbull of Connecticut he offered Caleb Watts, a mulatto student, for service either in the West Indies or in the South, believing that Watts could help to pacify the negroes. And yet Wheelock complained that his son Eleazar had allowed a student to enlist under him, thus spoiling, he wrote in his diary, a scholar in addition to taking away a laborer and showing a want of tenderness "towards an aged and distressed father, on the verge of the grave, and oppressed with a weight of cares of many kinds enough for an angel." To the military officers assembled at Windsor, Vermont, Wheelock proposed a plan to stop the invasion of the Indians as threatened by Burgoyne, namely, that the officers "forthwith take a course to interest the Great Name of our God in our cause, and when this is done we are safe enough," that the oath of allegiance to Jesus Christ be renewed, that a time for common prayer and supplication be set aside, that a stand be taken against all vice and profaneness, and that the officers draw up regulations for the use of arms and ammunition. Meanwhile in England an old friend of Moor's Charity School was helping Wheelock: John Thornton asked the Earl of Dartmouth to recommend to Lord Howe and his brother that if "those in Hanover" give no just occasion of offense "they may not be wantonly hurt."

The most severe criticism of Wheelock during the Revolution was caused by, of all things, his observance of Thanksgiving Day. Wheelock had read "in a Connecticut paper" that November 16 (1775) had been appointed in Connecticut, and in the belief that the authorities of that colony understood the doings of the Continental Congress, he had accordingly celebrated Thanksgiving in Hanover, with the full consent of his parishioners. During the following week, however, a delegate from the New Hampshire Congress at Exeter gave Wheelock a proclamation appointing November 30 as the proper date. But the day had already been observed in Hanover, and Wheelock, not knowing at the time that the Continental Congress had permitted each colony to set its own date, refused to read the proclamation to his church. But hearing that he "would be sent 150 miles to Exeter as a Tory," he called the church together, urged them to remember that he had always been loyal, demurred at preaching to them again in observance of the day, consented to allow one of the young preachers to officiate, and finally agreed to serve, himself.

The title of the sermon which he preached on this second occasion is "Liberty of Conscience or No King but Christ in His Church." It is a mélange of wilfulness, stubbornness, and assertions of his loyalty. The text is, "Jesus answered, My Kingdom is not of this world," and the "doctrine" is divided into two parts: (1) there are differences between Christ's Kingdom and a kingdom of this world (2) it is not lawful and it is an open affront to Jesus to repeat what we did a fortnight ago, merely out of obedience to and respect for civil authority. In developing the second point, Wheelock insisted that he had always been loyal to Congress and always would be, consistent with his duty to Christ. To repeat the service would be an affront to Christ because the repetition would be an admission that the first service was null and void, and the "very essence of popery." When civil power encroaches on Christ's prerogative, a sanctified conscience can never be forced to comply. And finally, in the "improvement," or application of the text, Wheelock urged all his listeners, and "especially the members of this seminary," to look thoroughly into the subject and to form their conclusions by the Word of Truth, and not by the "floating, undigested opinion of an ignorant, giddy, stupid, unprin-

cipled multitude." The sermon shows a narrowness of mind
and an unwarranted sense of dignity which may be excused
only in part by referring to the "spirit of the times."

Immediately rumors that Wheelock was not a patriot were
spread, and official notice had to be taken of them. Consequently the Committees of Safety of Hanover, Lebanon, Plainfield, and Cornish met in January, 1776. They fully exoner-
ated Wheelock, praised his public character, and traced the
slanders to John Payne, the tavern-keeper of Hanover.

Fortunately, the Continental Congress at Philadelphia was
not alarmed about Wheelock. On the contrary. In 1775 Nathaniel Whitaker addressed the Congress on Wheelock's work
with the result that the Congress, through Patrick Henry,
chairman of the Committee on Indian Affairs, appropriated
$500 to defray the expenses of a trip to Canada taken by James
Dean, Wheelock's agent. In 1778 Wheelock sent a memorial
to the Congress stating that he had about thirty charity students, that his Canadian Indians now numbered four, of whom
two were in Dartmouth College, and urged the Congress to
assist him. His petition succeeded, and in December of that
year he was granted $925.

A final estimate cannot be given of the influence of Wheelock and his associates during the Revolution, although certain statements are in order. It is known, for example, that
Samuel Kirkland, who had been trained at Moor's Charity
School when it was located in Lebanon, Connecticut, helped
the American cause by reducing the hostility of the Six Nations. James Dean, adopted in his youth by the Oneidas, accepted by Wheelock into the charity school in 1762, and a
graduate of Dartmouth College in 1773, was Indian agent of
the Continental Congress, serving with the rank of major. Two
of Wheelock's sons, John and Eleazar, served as officers in the
American army. And George Washington, as the following let-

ter shows, recognized the value of the Mohegan Joseph Johnson, who had been associated with Wheelock intermittently from 1758 as scholar and teacher:

Sir,

I am very much pleased to find by the strong recommendations you produce, that we have amongst our brothers of the Six Nations a person who can explain to them, the sense of their brothers on the dispute between us and the ministers of Great Britain; you have seen a part of our strength, and can inform our brothers, that we can withstand all the force, which those who want to rob us of our lands and our houses, can send against us.

You can tell our friends, that they may always look upon me, whom the whole United Colonies have chosen to be their chief warrior, as their brother, whilst they continue in friendship with us, they may depend upon mine and the protection of those under my command.

Tell them that we don't want them to take up the hatchett for us, except they chuse it, we only desire that they will not fight against us, we want that the chain of friendship should always remain bright between our friends of the Six Nations and us. Their attention to you, will be a proof to us that they wish the same, we recommend you to them, and hope by your spreading the truths of the Holy Gospel amongst them, it will contribute to keep the chain so bright, that, the malicious insinuations, or practices of our enemies will never be able to break this Union, so much for the benefit of our brothers of the Six Nations and of us.

And to prove to them that this is my desire, and of the warriors under me, I hereto subscribe my name at Cambridge this 20th day of February 1776.

G. Washington

Mr. Joseph Johnson

Before the actual assumption of hostilities Wheelock showed that he was primarily interested in the rights of the colonies, but that he was by no means willing to agree entirely with the jingoists. Such an attitude was to be expected. He was in his sixties; he had been granted a royal charter by a governor who was consistently a Tory; some of his main benefactors were English. But after 1775 he worked as assiduously for the American cause as his administrative duties and health permitted. Whether the converted Indians, as he had believed in 1763, were a "far better defense than all our expensive fortresses" is a problem too complicated to solve. The fact remains that the good-will which his agents had established with the Canadian tribes, and the influence of former students turned missionaries were not entirely dissipated during the course of the Revolution.

An old man, distressed in body, harassed by debts and duties, and sharing the public worries of the times. One would like to think of him seated in repose before his fireplace, the patriarch surrounded by his family and attended by his slaves. The picture of a fireside scene would be pleasing, but false to the actuality. It was not in Wheelock's nature to rest. Nowhere do we find evidence that he at any time took to a sickbed, and only once, in the spring of 1770, did he take what we might call today a vacation: a visit to Lebanon Springs, New York, to try the effect of the waters on his "cuticular eruptions." The springs, however, were no Bethsaida for him. The doctor might advise, "You are of a plethoric habit of body, have a great fullness of blood and humors, a very weak, broken, relaxed and unelastic system of nerves," and might recommend that he avoid salt meat and wear a root at the pit of his stomach. This advice was unavailing, also. But bodily ailments had been long-standing enemies of his, and had not been permitted to interrupt his work.

When at last he did take to his chair it was from utter weariness. He wrote to Nathaniel Whitaker,

My dear sir,
 I believe there is no man on earth now I have a greater desire to

see than you and converse freely on a variety of very important subjects; but likely I shall never have the opportunity unless you can
find it in your way to make us a visit. I have been a long time in a
very low state and my case of late has been esteem'd desperate by
my physicians; but, by the pure mercy of God, I am so far reviv'd
as to be able unassisted more than by my staff, to walk from my bed
to the fire, and back again, and to sit in my chair near half my
time. My outward circumstances are not favorable to such a state
of weakness in that they don't nor can't afford me such a diet as experience teaches and my physicians assure me to be quite necessary
for me. I have near or quite run through the little estate I left in
Connecticut in supporting this school in its deserted state and have
yet but small means of subsistence more than the little remains of
my principal, and now feel more than ever the want of a pension,
which I think the world owes me with which I might buy a cask of
wine and other suitable spirits which my physicians all advise to be
necessary for me also coffee, chocolate, tea, &c., &c., which I am
oblidged to live wholly without for want of money to purchase the
same. I wait upon God to provide for me in these respects and assure myself as long as He has work for me to do for Him He will
feed me.

A month later, on April 24, 1779, the founder of Dartmouth
College died.

APPENDIX

In the Name of God Amen I, Ralph Wheelock of Windham in the County of Windham in the Colony of Connecticut in New England, yeoman, being healthy of body and of sound mind and memory (thanks be unto God) and calling to mind the mortality of my body, knowing that it is appointed for all men once to dye, do make and ordain this my last will and testament.

And first of all I recommend my soul into the hands of God that gave it and my body to the earth to be buried with a decent Christian burial, at the descretion of my executors hereafter named, nothing doubting, but I shall receive the same again at the general resurrection by the mighty power of God. And as touching such wordly goods or estate as God hath bestowed upon me I give demise and dispose of the same as followeth.

Imprimis I give unto my well beloved wife Mercy Wheelock all my goods chattels and moveables whatsoever after my debts and funeral charges are paid. And do appoint her and my son Eleazer Wheelock to be the executors of this my will.

Item I give unto my well beloved son Eleazer Wheelock all my farm lying on the west side of Shatucket River in Windham to belong to him his heirs and assigns forever excepting a small parcel thereof hereafter mentioned to be given to my daughter Mary. Provided that my said son his heirs &c shall pay unto my said wife or the guardian of my children Sarah Wheelock and Mary Wheelock the sum of seventy pounds in money annually untill they shall arrive to the age of eighteen years, for and towards their bringing up and portion. And it shall be understood that after the eldest is arrived to the age of eighteen years or in case either of them should die before that age that then he should afterward pay but ten pounds per annum.

Item whereas I have given unto my well beloved daughters Elizabeth Hendy and Ruth Hebard their full portion already in lands I give them nothing in this will.

Item I give unto my said wife Mercy Wheelock the use and improvement of the housing and all the land which I purchased of Lewis Serril during her natural life and my will is that after her decease the said housing and land shall be equally divided between my daughters Abigail Pomroy, Sarah Wheelock and Mary Whee-lock and the survivors of them in case either of them dye without issue, and the said shares to belong to each of them, their heirs and assigns forever.

Item I give unto my well beloved daughter Mary Wheelock a parcel of land lying in Windham abutting eastewardly on Sha-tucket River southerly on the land of Stephen Tracy westwardly on land which I gave to Robert Hebard jnr and northwardly by a line which runs from the northeast corner of the said Hebards land the same point of compass with his north line untill it comes to the river. Excepting what has been heretofore granted for highways the said parcel of land to belong to her her heirs and assigns forever and if she shall die without alienation or issue I give it to my son Elea-zer Wheelock.

In witness whereof I have hereunto set my hand and seal this thirty-first day of May in the year of our Lord one thousand seven hundred and thirty nine.

Ralph Wheelock

Signed sealed pronounced and declared by the said Ralph Whee-lock to be his last will and testament in the presence of the sub-scribers who in the presence of the testator have hereunto set our hands as witnesses.

Thomas Clap
Joseph Whiting
Mehetabel Bingham

ELEAZAR WHEELOCK'S WILL

In the Name of God Amen

This second day of April A.D. 1779 I Eleazar Wheelock D.D. President of Dartmouth College on the east side of Connecticut River in the county of Grafton formerly supposed to be in, and now claimed by the state of New Hampshire, being infirm of body and apprehensive that the time of my departure draws nigh, and that I am thereby admonished and called of God to set my house in or-der and dispose of my interest suitably thereto now while I enjoy health of body sufficient for it, and God is also graciously continuing to me a sound and disposing mind and memory, for which favours I desire to bless his Holy name and after supplication and prayer to the Father of Light and source of all divine influence that I may be directed and disposed to exercize impartial justice towards all concerned, I do make and ordain this to be my last Will and Testament in the manner following that is to say

In the first place and above all I do cheerfully and solemnly commit my soul to the disposal of God who gave it trusting in the merits of my Redeemer alone for that pardon and life eternal, which he has purchased for perishing sinners by his ever precious blood and my body I commit to the earth to be buried in a decent manner at the discretion of my Executors, hereafter named, in confidence I shall receive the same by the power of God at the last day.

And as to that worldly estate, with which God has blessed me in this world, I do give and dispose of the same in the manner following—Imprs. To Mrs. Mary my loving wife I give the use and improvement of such a part of my dwelling house and barn and other buildings as she shall find occasion for, for her use and comfort in life and as much of my household stuff, excepting what shall be hereafter named in this will, and as many cows and swine as she shall judge she shall have occasion to use for her own comfort and if she shall chuse it that they be set off to her and be under her controul, direction, and disposal as her own. I also give unto her a decent and comfortable maintenance with provision of all kinds needful for her in health and sickness and to be provided at the expence of my son John, a compensation for which to be hereafter mentioned in this will.

Item—To my loving and afflicted son Ralph or Radulphus Wheelock (who has been by the holy hand of God upon him rendered useless a great part of his life and is reduced to such a state that there is little or no prospect he will ever be able to get into any business, which he may depend upon for his support) I give fifty pounds lawful money per annum for his support so long as he shall live and be incapable of performing business for his own subsistence, and this to be paid him in boarding or in whatsoever shall be necessary for his support and comfort by either of my heirs, which he shall chuse to take the care of him and who shall consent to perform this service for him and this to be paid by means hereafter named.

And whereas the public calamities of the present day by which all sources for the support of this school have been cut off and suspended, have rendered it necessary and no other way appearing to pay the debts of said school and support such a number as I then had and till now on charity and preserve the reputation of this school and save it from sinking, but by the disposal of my patrimony and other private property which I left in Connecticut, and which I have disposed of for that purpose to the amount of upwards of a thousand pounds lawful money, fifty pounds of the interest of which I devote as above said to the support of my said son Ralph as above said, the rest of said interest whatever it may be, I give to be improved towards the support of his mother during her life as long as she shall have occasion for it for her own support, and when they, my said wife and my said son Ralph shall be by any means either by death or any favourable circumstances in life in no necessity thereof for their support, I give and bequeath the whole debt, that now is or shall be due me from the school both principal and interest at my decease to the only use and benefit of said school forever to be improved at the discretion and by the direction of the honourable corporation towards the support of the President or a professor as they shall judge most necessary or convenient, and this I the rather do to compensate the injury done to the school by several, who at the expense of the charity received an education with a view to their serving in the Indian cause, but have failed of it and are either unable or unwilling to refund the expense of their education. I also give and bequeath to him my said son Ralph a piece of land meadow and upland belonging to me west of the road across Mink Brook to Lebanon, bounded easterly on said road westerly on college lands and southerly on Tilden's lands.

I also give him twenty acres of land bounded westerly on the college land, northerly on lands I gave to Field and John Russell and Capt. Hendy to be laid out as conveniently as may be in that corner of this farm, and this I do in confidence that the Trustees will be willing to exchange the land belonging to the College, which separate this land from Lebanon road, for the aforesaid piece of land adjoining upon College lands at Mink Brook, by which means my said son may have communication with or from the road to enter upon his own land; and I also give him timber of all sorts for building house, barn, and any buildings which he shall have occasion for. I also give and bequeath to him Henry's Annotations upon the whole Bible and also my riding horse.

Item—I give and bequeath to my loving daughters Theodora Young and Ruth Patten the house and lot of land lying in Lebanon-Crank near the meeting house where I once dwelt and also all my rights of land in Bridgewater, the whole to be equally divided among them.

Item—I give and bequeath to my loving son-in-law the Revd. Sylvanus Ripley fifteen acres being equal to that which I gave of the same lot to my son-in-law Bezal. Woodward Esqr. of the lot which was given me by Mr. John House bounded southerly on the college farm, westerly on Connecticut River, northerly on lands which my wife bought of said House &c. and this I do in consideration of his settling as tutor of Dartmouth College. And to my loving daughters Mary Woodward and Abigail Ripley I give the rest of said lot to be equally divided between them.

Item—To my loving son John Wheelock unto whom I commit the special and immediate care and charge of my loving wife in her declining life. I give and bequeath my dwelling house in which I now live my horse, chaise-house, and log house, and two hundred acres of land adjoining and running easterly and as shall be most convenient for him and not incomode any purposes designed by the disposal of other parts of this farm. I also give him further to requite him for taking charge of his mother, all my interest in and rights to my servants not to interfere or be inconsistent with any disposal I shall make of them hereafter in this will, viz. Brister, Archelaus, Anna and the infant child. I also give him all my working oxen, and all my husbandry tools that he shall have occasion for, and also my horses and as many swine as he shall have occasion for. And whereas I have founded on my own tenemants and at my own expence an Indian Charity School, now called Moor's Charity School which from small beginnings has thro' much labor application and care for more than twenty years last past, under a series of most signal and evident smiles of Divine Providence arisen to its present state of importance, and appears to exhibit a fair prospect of great usefulness towards the Christianising and civilizing of the

nations of our American wilderness, which is the first object and
of conciliating, establishing and perpetuating a firm and lasting
friendship and peace between all those numerous tribes and the
American colonies as well as of great edification to the Church of
God among the English and is now incorporated by royal charter
into and with Dartmouth College, which seminary is by said charter endowed with all the powers, privileges and immunities of a
university as by said charter may fully appear: And where as it ap-
pertains unto me as founder and proprietor thereof as well as by
grant in said charter to dispose of said school and all donations and
grants of lands and other interests any way given or granted for the
benefit and use of the same and appoint any successor in the office
of President of said seminary

I do therefore hereby nominate constitute and appoint my said
son John Wheelock to be my successor in said office of President of
my Indian Charity School and Dartmouth College with and into
which said school is now incorporated and to him I give and grant
all my right, title, and claim to said seminary and all the appurtenances, interest, jurisdiction, power and authority to, in and over
the same belonging to me as the founder of it or by grant in the
charter to me by any other ways or means whatever. And in case my
said son John shall refuse or by any means fail to accept of or enter
into said office, I do hereby constitute and appoint my trusty and
faithful brother the Revd Joseph Huntington pastor of a church
in Coventry in Connecticut thereto in his stead. And in case he
should fail I nominate and appoint my son-in-law the Revd. Sylvanus Ripley in his room and to either of them the said Huntington or Ripley, who shall accept the place and office of my said son
John, I do give all my rights, titles, claim, power jurisdiction, and
so forth as aforesaid into and over said seminary. And moreover to
this said charity school I do give and bequeath the stream called
Mink Brook, that is the part and place where the saw and grist mills
belonging to this school now stand, so long as the trustees of the
college shall think fit to maintain said mills by repairing the present buildings in that place: and also the log-way and necessary mill-
houses and only to the use and benefit of the same; and after that I
give and bequeath the same with all the privileges belonging to it
to my said son John repaying to the school the irons and tools be-

longing to the mills and the labour bestowed upon them what they shall be apprised at by indifferent and judicious men.

I also give two acres of land where the trustees have or shall chuse to erect a larger and more convenient building for the college: also the ground on which the storehouse and hall, and the ground on which the potash-house and malt-house stand, which said houses I give to the only use and benefit of this school forever, with all the appurtenances thereunto belonging.

I also give and bequeath to John Russell of this vicinity and to Mary his wife the sole use and improvement of the house in which they now live, and the acre of land on which it stands with the appurtenances thereof, during their natural life and the life of the survivor of either of them and to the heirs of either of their bodies lawfully begotten forever. But in case they should have no such heir, I give it to my successors for the time being in the care and oversight of the Indian Charity School in this place to be improved as a washing place for their benefit and for the use and benefit of Indian and other charity scholars; educated in said school forever.

I also bequeath to said Mary the wife of said John Russell a cow.

And whereas I have given to Exeter my negro man his freedom I hereby ratify the same and also give to him the use of Chloe his wife so long and so far as he shall have occasion for her service, she behaving herself well after which she to be disposed of by my heirs.

I also give my servant man Brister his freedom as soon as he can get him a wife, and be in a capacity to support himself and family and a hundred acres of land at Landaff provided he shall see fit to settle upon it. and recommend him to the guidance and kindness of my executors hereafter to be named; or if he should not be inclined to settle at Landaff I give him fifty acres of my out lands where it shall be more agreeable to him.

Item—To each of my two loving sons Eleazar and James Wheelock, I give and bequeath two hundred acres apiece of the farm I live upon, that is four hundred acres to be estimated and equally divided for quantity and quality between them, the remaining part of this farm I give to my three sons, viz. John, Eleazar, and James to be equally divided between them.

Item—I give and bequeath to my loving grandson William Patten the whole expence of his education here till he shall have completed his course of collegiate studies together with the expence of the honors of this college at the close if he shall be judged worthy thereof excepting such assistance as to his clothing as he has or shall receive from his mother and others.

Item—To my servant boy Archelaus. I give his freedom from slavery when he shall arrive at the age of twenty five years, provided his moral character his abilities to conduct himself among men and provide for his own subsistence shall be judged by the Revd. Grafton Presbytery to be such as that he may safely be trusted with his freedom. And I also give him fifty acres of land in Landaff or some other of my out-lands convenient.

Item—To my successors in the Presidency of this college and school I give and bequeath my chariot. which was given me by my much honored friend and patron John Thornton Esqr. of London by whose liberality my family has been cheifly supported for a number of years before the present war. I also give to my successors my house-clock which was also a donation made me by my much honored patrons the Honorable Trust in London.

And to my loving daughter in law Mrs. Elizabeth the wife of Doctr. Thaddeus Betts of Norwalk I give Doctor Manton on the 119th Psalm, and to my daughters Theodora Young and Ruth Patten I give Mr. Leighs Body of Divinity and Doctor Bates Works. The rest of my library I give to be equally divided between my sons John, Eleazar and James.

It is my will that my debts and funeral charges be paid out of my moveable estate, and after my wife and son John have taken to themselves as aforesaid. I give the rest of my stock, viz. cattle, horses, sheep and swine and all my husbandry tools and wearing apparel to be equally divided between my sons Eleazar and James; and all my household goods, only reserving for the use of my sons what shall be necessary for them while they shall have occasion to pursue their studies at home, I give to be equally divided among my daughters, excepting that to my son Ralph, I give my silver tankard, which was his mothers. And all my lands lying west of Connecticut River I give equally to my daughters Mary and Abigail. And all my lands not mentioned on the east side of said river, I give to be equally divided, including what I have already given by deed between my three sons, John, Eleazar and James. It is also my will

APPENDIX

that the produce of cultivated lands, that is, crops of all kinds of grain and hay that shall be upon the grounds, if any such there shall be at my decease, shall be for the use of my son John, his mother and the family, which he may have without any division of them.

And lastly I do appoint and ordain my three sons, John, Eleazar, and James Wheelock to be sole executors of this my last will and testament—hereby ratifying and confirming this and no other to be my last will and testament.

BIBLIOGRAPHY

CITED WORKS

Blodgett, Harold, *Samson Occom,* Hanover, N.H., 1935.

Caulkins, F. M., *History of Norwich, Conn.,* Norwich, 1845.

Chase, Frederick, *History of Dartmouth College and the Town of Hanover, New Hampshire (to 1815),* Brattleboro, 1928.

Chauncy, Charles, *Seasonable Thoughts on the State of Religion in New-England,* Boston, 1743.

Connecticut, Colonial Records of (VIII), Hartford, 1874.

Connecticut Valley Historical Society Papers and Proceedings, Springfield, Mass., 1876–1881.

Dartmouth Alumni Magazine (June, 1930, L. B. Richardson, *The Dartmouth Indians*), Hanover, N.H., 1930.

Dedham Records, Church and Cemetery, 1638–1845, Dedham, Mass., 1888.

Dexter, H. M., *The Congregationalism of the Last Three Hundred Years, As Seen in Its Literature,* New York, 1880.

Dictionary of American Biography, article *Thomas Clap.*

Dictionary of National Biography, articles *William Legge, Abraham Wheelocke.*

Johnson, F. C., *Rev. Jacob Johnson,* Wilkes-Barre, Pa., 1911.

Johnson, Sir William, Papers of (IV, V), Albany, 1921, ff.

Larned, E. D., *History of Windham County, Connecticut* (2 vols.), Worcester, Mass., 1874–80.

Massachusetts Bay, Acts and Resolves of the Province of (IV), Boston, 1869, ff.

Massachusetts Historical Society Collections (I), Boston, 1792.

Massachusetts, Publications of the Colonial Society of (XV), Boston, 1925.

McCallum, J. D., *The Letters of Eleazar Wheelock's Indians,* Hanover, N.H., 1932.

M'Clure, David, and Parish, Elijah, *Memoirs of the Rev. Eleazar Wheelock,* Newburyport, 1811.

Mayo, L. S., *John Wentworth,* Cambridge, 1921.

Mendon, Massachusetts Proprietors' Records, Boston, 1899.

Metcalf, John G., *Annals of the Town of Mendon,* Providence, R.I., 1880.

217

New Plymouth, Records of the Colony of, in New England, Boston, 1859.

New York, Documentary History of (IV), Albany, 1851.

Ormerod, George, *The History of the County, Palatine, and City of Chester* (3 vols.), London, 1882.

Pascoe, C. F., *Two Hundred Years of the S.P.G.* (2 vols.), London, 1901.

Quincy, Josiah, *History of Harvard College* (2 vols.), Cambridge, 1840.

Richardson, L. B., *History of Dartmouth College* (2 vols.), Hanover, N.H., 1932.

Richardson, L. B., *An Indian Preacher in England,* Hanover, N.H., 1933.

Sclater, William, *The Crowne of Righteousness,* etc. (Funeral oration for Abraham Wheelock, Sept. 25, 1653), London, 1654.

Small, W. H., *Early New England Schools,* Boston, 1914.

Sprague, W. B., *Annals of the American Pulpit* (vols. I, II), New York, 1857, ff.

Steward, George, *A History of Religious Education in Connecticut to the Middle of the Nineteenth Century,* New Haven, 1924.

Stiles, Ezra, *The Literary Diary of* (II), New York, 1901.

Trumbull, Benjamin, *A Complete History of Connecticut* (II), New Haven, 1818.

PUBLISHED WRITINGS OF ELEAZAR WHEELOCK

1. *A Plain and Faithful Narrative of the Original Design, Rise, Progress and Present State of the Indian Charity-School at Lebanon, in Connecticut,* Boston, 1763.

2. *A Continuation of the Narrative of the State, &c. of the Indian Charity-School, at Lebanon, in Connecticut; From Nov. 27th, 1762, to Sept. 3d, 1765,* Boston, 1765.

3. *A Brief Narrative of the Indian Charity-School, in Lebanon in Connecticut, New England,* London, 1766.

4. *A Brief Narrative of the Indian Charity-School in Lebanon in Connecticut, New England,* London, 1767.

5. *A Continuation of the Narrative of the Indian Charity-School in Lebanon in Connecticut, New England,* London, 1769.

BIBLIOGRAPHY

6. *A Continuation of the Narrative of the Indian Charity-School in Lebanon, in Connecticut,* Hartford, 1771.
7. *A Continuation of the Narrative of the Indian Charity-School,* Portsmouth, N.H., 1772.
8. *A Continuation of the Narrative of the Indian Charity-School,* Hartford, 1773.
9. *A Continuation of the Narrative of the Indian Charity-School,* Hartford, 1775.

The Preaching of Christ an Expression of God's great Love to Sinners, and therefore a sweet Savour to him, though a Savour of Death unto Death to them. Illustrated in a Sermon Preach'd at North Haven, Dec. 25, 1760, at the Ordination of the Reverend Mr. Benjamin Trumble, Boston, 1761.

A Sermon Preached Before the Second Society in Lebanon, June 30, 1763, at the Ordination of the Rev. Mr. Charles-Jeffry Smith, Edinburgh, 1767.

Liberty of Conscience or No King But Christ in His Church, A Sermon Preached At Dartmouth Hall, November 30, 1775, Hartford, no date.

INDEX

PREPARED BY MARGARET BECK MCCALLUM

INDEX

mother, 4 (see Eleazar Wheelock of Mendon, Massachusetts)

Cherry Valley, New York, 110

Chester, England, 1

Chloe, slave, bill of sale for, 65; for sale by Wheelock, 66; 67, 179, 213

Church of England, 120, 121 note 2, 151, 156, 157, 159, 166, 172, 192

Clap, Nathan, Cape Cod Indian, 99, 137

Clap, Thomas, President of Yale College, 16 note 2, 59; letter from Wheelock to, 59–60 note 2; 208

Claremont, New Hampshire, 191

Clark, Abigail, 45

Clark, Joseph, 50

Clark, Mary, 45

Clark, William, bill of sale for slave Ishmael, 63

Cleaveland, Ebenezer, 119, 125; with John Wright investigates New Hampshire sites for Dartmouth College, 168–169

Closs, Enoch, Delaware, 135

Colden, Lieutenant-Governor of New York, 156, 170

College of New Jersey, 118, 126, 134, 170

Colonies, Colonists, Wheelock sides with in Revolution, 196

Columbia, Connecticut, modern name of "Second or North Society, and Lebanon Crank," Lebanon, Connecticut, 8

Committee on Indian Affairs, of Continental Congress, appropriates funds to Wheelock, 202

Company for Propagation of the Gospel in New England and the Parts Adjacent in America (see also Boston Board of), contributes to School, 141; discontinues grants, 143; 153, 156, 158–159

Congregationalism, Congregationalists, 121, 122

Connecticut, Wheelock born in, 4–5;

scourges on, 10; Wheelock's preaching tour through, 15–18; harsh towards Separatism, 32; Wheelock's property in, 68, 196, 210; contributes to School, 149; Wheelock leaves, 178; emigration from, 181; 39, 40, 63–66 *passim*, 75, 85, 87, 90, 114, 117, 120, 122, 152, 183, 185, 188, 200, 207

Connecticut Board of Correspondents, see Society in Scotland for Propagating Christian Knowledge, trustees of Moor's Charity School, 97, 98 note 1, 103, 151, 153, 154, 155, 176

Connecticut General Assembly, refuses charter to Moor's Charity School, 112

Connecticut, General Court of, approves Half-Way Covenant, 10; 25–26

Connecticut River, 167, 168, 176, 183, 185, 189, 208, 214

Constitution, the British, Sir William Johnson considers members of Church of England surest supporters of, 122

Continental Congress, 195, 199, 200, 202

Cornish, New Hampshire, Committee of Safety of, 202

Coventry, Connecticut, 29, 64, 212

Cowas, New Hampshire, 170

Cowper, William, 157, 195

Cramake, Governor, 191

Crane, Doctor John, 178, 184

Crosby, William, student at Dartmouth, quarrels with Wheelock, 187–188

Crown Point, New York, 177

Daniel, Charles, Narraganset, 86, 137

Daniel, John, Narraganset, complains to Wheelock, 86

Dartmouth College, Hanover, New Hampshire site of, 176; charter ap-

INDEX

tors to, 165–166, 170; exhausted and overdrawn, 193

English, John, testifies against Timothy Hutchinson, 44

English language, Indians instructed in, 80, 85, 145

English trust, board of trustees managing English fund raised by Occom and Whitaker, 159 note 1; questions Wheelock on his handling of fund, 159–160; accepts Wheelock's explanation, 164; Wheelock refuses to have Bishop of London as trustee, 170–173; objects to charter of Dartmouth College, 173–175; cautions Wheelock to keep expenses of school and college separate, 175, 193; ceases to exist, upon exhaustion of fund, 194, 214; Wheelock reports to, on Hanover site, 176–178

enthusiasm, enthusiastic, enthusiastical, Wheelock condemned for, 19, 27, 31; Wheelock denies being "enthusiastical," 22

Episcopalians, Episcopacy, 121, 153; fear that Dartmouth College might be controlled by, 192–193

Erskine, John, 193

Estabrook, Hobart, 65

Estabrook, Jerusha, 65

Everett, Noble, 188

Exeter, New Hampshire, 195, 201

Exeter, slave, bill of sale for, 65; Wheelock puts on market, 66–67; 179, 180; freedom ratified in Wheelock's will, 213

Farmington Indians, see Mossoch, Daniel

Ferris, David, Quaker, 19–20

Finley, President, of College of New Jersey, 126

Finney, Molle, 73

Fitch, Governor, of Connecticut, 156

Fitch, James, missionary at Norwich, Connecticut, 78

"Five hundred gallons of New England rum," 91, 180

Fort Hunter, New York, Hezekiah Calvin at, 99; 110, 134

Fort Stanwix Congress, 123–125, 139

Fortune, slave, 63

Fowler, David, Montauk, missionary to Six Nations, 95; teaches at Canajoharie, 98, 99; career, 103–109; complaints of, 107; matrimonial aspirations, 104, 106; marries Hannah Garret, 107; 135, 136, 148, 150, 163; letters to Wheelock, 104, 105, 106; letter from Wheelock, 108–109

Fowler, Jacob, Montauk, missionary to Six Nations, 99, 136

France, competing for Indian allegiance, 76

Franklin, Benjamin, 147

Franklin, Governor, of New Jersey, 156

Frisbie, Levi, missionary, member of first class to graduate from Dartmouth College, 190

Frost, Dr. Gilman D., tabulation of Wheelock's children, 63 note 1

Fullsom, Goody, "a w--ch," 53

Gage, General, Commander-in-Chief of the British Forces in America, 125, 156; asks for New Hampshire carpenters, 197

Gager, William, tried by Wheelock for drunkenness, 50

Garret, Hannah, Pequot, David Fowler marries, 107; 136

Gaylord, William, 61

General Assemblies, 77; see General Assemblies of Connecticut, Massachusetts, New Hampshire

Georgia, 117, 147

German, baker desired by Wheelock, 183

Gibbs, John, 73

INDEX

INDEX

INDEX

considered as site for Dartmouth College, 168–169

Otis, James, 144

Parish, Elijah, co-author of first published biography of Wheelock, 14

Parliament House, London, Occom and Whitaker visit, 157

Partridge, Colonel Oliver, offers land in Pittsfield, Massachusetts, 118

Patten, Mrs. Ruth, see Wheelock, Ruth

Patten, William, Wheelock's grandson, 213–214

Paulus, Mohawk, 137

Payne, Benjamin, 65, 66

Payne, John, tavern-keeper in Hanover, 183, 185, 202

Peck, Moses, 160, 161, 163

Peggy, slave, 67, 180

Pemberton, Reverend Ebenezer, letter from Wheelock to, on Charles Chauncy, 20–24; Wheelock apologizes to for letter on Chauncy, 24

Penn, Lieutenant-Governor of Pennsylvania, 156

Pennamite-Yankee Wars, 117

Pennsylvania, 113, 114, 117

Pequots, see Hannah Garret, Samson Wayboy

Phelps, Colonel Alexander, Wheelock's son-in-law, 172, 176

Philadelphia, 183, 202

Phillips Exeter Academy, 147

Phillips, John, benefactions to Wheelock, 147, 195

Phyllis, slave, 51

Pierson, Abraham, missionary, 77

Pinno, Joseph, 47

Pittsfield, Massachusetts, offers land for Dartmouth College, 118

Plainfield, New Hampshire, Committee of Safety of, 202

Plumb Island, "case of the golden candlestick," 52

Plymouth, Massachusetts, 63

Plymouth, New Hampshire, offers site for Dartmouth College, 168

Poems on Divers Occasions, Martha (Wadsworth) Brewster, 62

Pomeroy, Mrs. Abigail, see Wheelock, Abigail

Pomeroy, Benjamin, missionary and itinerant, Wheelock's brother-in-law, 20, 23, 24 note 1, 26–27, 42, 58 note 1; letter to, from Wheelock, on the starving oxen, 70–73; 80, 119, 120, 126, 162; with Wheelock visiting New Hampshire sites for Dartmouth College, 176; 182

Pomfret, Connecticut, 27

Pontiac's War, 95

Poquinatup, Hannah, Niantic, 136

Portsmouth, New Hampshire, 177, 185, 198

Pratt, Peter, missionary, 78

Presbyterian, 35, 120; Presbytery, Revd. Grafton, 214

President and Society for the Propagation of the Gospel in New England, 77

priests, Canadian, 191; see Jesuits

Princeton, New Jersey, 134, 155

proclamation money, 42, 140

Proposal for Introducing Religion, Learning, Agriculture, and Manufacture among the Pagans in America, Wheelock's plan for Indian reservation, 115–116

Protestantism, Protestant ministers, 76

Providence, Rhode Island, 15

Provincials, 114

Pumshire, John, Delaware, 80, 82, 134

Puritans, 120

Pyamphcouch, Hannah, Indian, 106

Quaker, Wheelock led astray by, 19–20

Quakerism, 24 note 1

Quarles, Francis, threatens Wheelock

INDEX

Trumbull, Benjamin, 24 note 1, 25, 27, 36, 55
Trumbull, Jonathan, Governor of Connecticut, 43, 200
Truth, William Cowper refers to Lord Dartmouth in, 157
"Tulley," Indian scholars read, 85, 142

Uncas, Ben, Mohegan, 150
Uncas, Isaiah, son of Ben, Mohegan, in school brawl, 91; 135, 150
Uncas "the great," 152
United Colonies, 203; Commissioners of, 77

Verrieul, Joseph, 186
Virgil, Indians instructed in, 85, 142
Virginia, 118
Voluntown, Connecticut, 15
Vox Clamantis in Deserto, Wheelock chooses for college motto, 185

Wales, Elisha, bill of sale for slave Sippy, 64
Wales, Nathaniel, Jr., 64
Wallace, Hugh, 125, 170, 184
Warmincham, Cheshire, England, 1
Warner, Oliver, 59
Warren, Benjamin, 24
Warren, Sir Peter, uncle of Sir William Johnson, donor of Sir Peter Warren Fund, 143, 144
Washington, George, Wheelock begs for shirting for his Indians, 196, 200; letter to Joseph Johnson, Mohegan, 202–203
Watertown, Massachusetts, first Wheelock in America arrives in, 1637, 1, 2
Watts, Mrs. Barbara, Wheelock writes to, 185
Watts, Caleb, mulatto student, 200
Wealch, Selinda, slave, letter to slave Brister, 66
Webster, Noah, summons for, 44
Wentworth, Benning, Governor of New Hampshire, 155; offers land in New Hampshire, 167; 176
Wentworth, John, Governor of New Hampshire, 168; Wheelock applies to for royal charter for Dartmouth College, 169–170; 172 note 1, 176, 183, 185, 192; sends New Hampshire carpenters to Boston to build barracks for British troops, cited as "enemy to the community," 197–198; Wheelock writes to, encouraging, 197–198
Weogs, Sarah, Mohegan, 89, 135
West, Daniel, member of English trust, 159 note 1
West Indies, 200
Wethersfield, Connecticut, 17
Wheelock, Abigail, Wheelock's daughter by second marriage, wife of Sylvanus Ripley, 63 note 1, 211, 214
Wheelock, Abraham, 2
Wheelock, Eleazar, Wheelock's grandfather, settled in Mendon, Massachusetts, 3; second wife, Mary Chenery, Wheelock's grandmother, 4
WHEELOCK, ELEAZAR (Founder of Dartmouth College), birth, 4–5; education, 5, 7; receives Dean Berkeley Award, 5; first marriage, 8, stepchildren by, 57, children by, 63 note 1; second marriage, 61–62, children by, 63 note 1; household, 63–67; health, 59, 181, 189, 204, 205; begins pastoral career, 8; farmer, 68–73; judge, 43–54; account books of, 73; medical lore, 73–74; given horse, 55; difficulties with parish over salary, 39–43, 112; active in Great Awakening, 12, 14–19; upholds Saybrook Platform, 31–36; number of sermons preached by during Great Awakening, 14, 36 note 1, 37; criticism of, 19, 27–31, 33–35, 53, 54, 86, 184, 190, 200–202; attitude toward Indians, 75, 82; establishes Moor's Charity School,

234

DATE DUE
REMINDER

MAR 20 '97

Please do not remove
this date due slip.